Advancing Maths for AQA
STATISTICS 8

Roger Williamson and John White

Series editors
Roger Williamson   Sam Boardman
Ted Graham   Keith Parramore

Heinemann

Heinemann Educational Publishers
a division of Heinemann Publishers (Oxford) Ltd,
Halley Court, Jordan Hill, Oxford OX2 8EJ

OXFORD JOHANNESBURG BLANTYRE MELBOURNE
AUCKLAND IBADAN GABORONE PORTSMOUTH NH (USA)
CHICAGO

New material © Roger Williamson and John White 2002
Existing material © CIMT 1994

First published in 2002

06   05   04   03   02
10   9   8   7   6   5   4   3   2   1

ISBN 0 435 51323 0

Cover design by Miller, Craig and Cocking

Typeset and illustrated by Tech-Set Limited, Gateshead, Tyne & Wear

Printed and bound by Scotprint in the UK

Acknowledgements
The publishers and authors acknowledge the work of the writers
David Burghes and Nigel Price of the *AEB Mathematics for AS A-Level Series* from
which some text, exercises and examples have been taken.

The publishers' and authors' thanks are due to the AQA for the permission to
reproduce questions from past examination papers.

The answers have been provided by the authors and are not the responsibility
of the examining board.

About this book

This book is one in a series of textbooks designed to provide you with exceptional preparation for AQA's new Advanced GCE Specification B. The series authors are all senior members of the examining team and have prepared the textbooks specifically to support you in studying this course.

Finding your way around

The following are there to help you find your way around when you are studying and revising:

- **edge marks** (shown on the front page) – these help you to get to the right chapter quickly;
- **contents list** – this identifies the individual sections dealing with key syllabus concepts so that you can go straight to the areas that you are looking for;
- **index** – a number in bold type indicates where to find the main entry for that topic.

Key points

Key points are not only summarised at the end of each chapter but are also boxed and highlighted within the text like this:

> Experimental error is the effect of factors other than those controlled by the experimenter.

Exercises and exam questions

Worked examples and carefully graded questions familiarise you with the specification and bring you up to exam standard. Each book contains:

- Worked examples and Worked exam questions to show you how to tackle typical questions; Examiner's tips will also provide guidance;
- Graded exercises, gradually increasing in difficulty up to exam-level questions, which are marked by an [A];
- Test-yourself sections for each chapter so that you can check your understanding of the key aspects of that chapter and identify any sections that you should review;
- Answers to the questions are included at the end of the book.

Contents

4 Statistical process control

5 Acceptance sampling

Exam style practice paper

Appendix

Answers

Index

CHAPTER 1

Experimental design

Learning objectives

After studying this chapter you should be able to:

- understand what is meant by experimental error
- understand how paired comparisons or blocking may be used to reduce experimental error
- appreciate the need for randomisation and the practical difficulties of achieving it
- appreciate why experimental and control groups are used
- understand the concepts of blind and double blind trials.

1.1 Introduction

You have already met some of the main ideas of experimental design spread throughout the earlier units and more specifically in S3/6 chapter 5. In this book the main principles are brought together in chapter 1. In chapters 2 and 3 particular designs are further discussed and analysed. Examination questions on this topic are likely to be short introductory questions such as questions 1 and 2 in exercise 1A or parts of longer questions which will also contain some calculations.

> You may prefer to study the calculations in chapters 2 and 3 first and then return to this chapter.

The main purpose of experimental design is to ensure that relevant and valid conclusions can be drawn from experiments, and to do this as efficiently as possible; that is, to try to extract a lot of information from a relatively small amount of experimentation. Frequently statisticians are asked to summarise and look for patterns in large (often very large) amounts of data which may have been collected haphazardly with no very clear purpose in mind. Work on this sort of data is called exploratory data analysis. More recently the term data mining has been applied to exploring huge data sets. By contrast, in a designed experiment the data to be collected is specified exactly and the purpose and method of analysis is known before the experiment is undertaken. In practice, it is not always possible to achieve this ideal situation.

1.2 Experimental error

A greengrocer normally obtained her fruit and vegetables from a market in Manchester. She wished to find out whether obtaining her supplies from a different market in Preston would increase her daily takings. As an experiment she used the Preston market on eight days and recorded her daily takings. The results, together with her takings on ten days when she used the Manchester market, are shown below.

Takings, £	
Preston	**Manchester**
323	286
274	517
269	492
552	264
435	367
391	399
208	198
529	581
	362
	303

The first point to note is that the takings for both markets vary. If every time she bought from Preston her takings were £323 and every time she bought from Manchester her takings were £286 it would be obvious that buying from Preston increased her takings and there would be no need for any statistical analysis.

However, the takings when she buys from Preston are not always the same and this is said to be due to **experimental error**. This does not mean that a mistake has been made. It simply means that factors other than the market she is buying from will affect the takings. In this case, it is probable that the weather, the traffic conditions in the area, and the types of fruit and vegetables available will affect the takings. Almost certainly the shop will be busier at the weekend than in the middle of the week and this will have a substantial effect on the takings.

> Experimental error is the effect of factors other than those controlled by the experimenter.

If there is a difference in the average takings from the two markets, it may be difficult or impossible to tell whether this is due to the effect of the factor(s) being investigated – in this case the market – or due to experimental error alone.

The only factor being controlled in this experiment is the market. As far as this experiment is concerned all the observations on days when she bought from Preston are taken under identical conditions. The difference between the takings on these days is due to experimental error. These repeated observations are known as **replicates**. The standard deviation of the sample of observations from Preston is £126 and this gives a measure of the magnitude of the experimental error. The larger the standard deviation the more experimental error there is and the more difficult it is to determine whether there is any difference in the mean takings between markets.

Clearly it is desirable to minimise experimental error. One way of doing this is to keep factors which are not being investigated as constant as possible. In this case it may be impossible to standardise the weather or the traffic conditions but the opening hours of the shop and the number of assistants working there should be kept constant. In a laboratory experiment temperature, humidity and various other factors could be held constant. A second way of reducing experimental error is by experimental design and, where possible, both these approaches should be used.

1.3 Experimental design

The simplest experimental design is the use of paired comparisons. Here two treatments being compared are each applied to similar raw material. For example, if the yield of two types of wheat were to be compared, a field might be split into small plots and the two types of wheat planted in adjacent plots. This is to minimise differences in the conditions in which the wheat grows and so reduce experimental error due to the two types of wheat growing under different conditions.

> Experimental error cannot be completely eliminated, but two small plots close together will be more similar than two separate fields.

Similarly, to compare the weight loss due to two different slimming diets, an ideal design would be to secure the cooperation of several pairs of identical twins. One twin of each pair would follow one diet and the other twin the other diet. Thus experimental error due to physiological differences in the people undertaking the diets would be minimised.

> In a paired comparison, experimental error is reduced by applying both treatments to the same subjects or in the same conditions.

For the greengrocer, an obvious source of experimental error is the day of the week. Takings are likely to be much higher at weekends. Therefore if we examine the differences between the takings from each market on the same day of the week, one major source of experimental error will have been eliminated.

The experiment might be carried out as follows:

Manchester market						
Week 1	Mon	Tue	Wed	Thu	Fri	Sat
Takings, £	272	295	318	307	532	599

Preston market						
Week 2	Mon	Tue	Wed	Thu	Fri	Sat
Takings, £	268	272	324	352	511	604

The paired comparison design would be perfectly satisfactory for analysing data of weight loss by identical twins who had followed different diets. However, in this case, the design can be improved further. Suppose that Week 1 was fine and dry but Week 2 was wet and windy. Alternatively, suppose new potatoes were available from the market in Week 2 but not in Week 1. If a difference was found between the takings in the two weeks we would not know whether this was due to a difference between the markets or whether it was due to the different weather conditions (or the availability of new potatoes). The two effects are said to be **confounded**.

A better arrangement would be as follows:

Week1	Mon	Tue	Wed	Thu	Fri	Sat
Market	*A*	*B*	*A*	*B*	*A*	*B*
Takings, £	285	296	333	376	490	517

Week 2	Mon	Tue	Wed	Thu	Fri	Sat
Market	*B*	*A*	*B*	*A*	*B*	*A*
Takings £	276	308	307	400	482	512

In this arrangement the two markets, *A* and *B*, are used during the same week. This is an attempt to balance out any effect due to weather or other differences between weeks, thus overcoming the problem of effect of markets being confounded by the effect of weeks.

The final decision to be taken is whether *A* represents Manchester and *B* represents Preston or the other way round. Where there is no obvious reason for choosing one way in preference to the other the choice should be made by a random process such as tossing a coin. This is known as randomisation and helps to prevent unconscious or unsuspected bias from affecting the result. There are no obvious further improvements which can be made to this design. Suppose *A* had been chosen to be Manchester, then the data could be rearranged as follows:

	Mon	Tue	Wed	Thu	Fri	Sat
Manchester	285	308	333	400	490	512
Preston	276	296	307	376	482	517

In chapter 2, paired data will be analysed using the paired *t*-test. For now, Wilcoxon's signed-rank test will be used.

In S3/6 paired data were analysed using the sign test or Wilcoxon's signed-rank test. The latter is preferred if it is reasonable to assume that the differences come from a symmetrical distribution.

H$_0$ Population mean difference $= 0$

H$_1$ Population mean difference $\neq 0$

	Mon	Tue	Wed	Thu	Fri	Sat
Manchester	285	308	333	400	490	512
Preston	276	296	307	376	482	517
Difference	9	12	26	24	8	−5
Rank +	3	4	6	5	2	
Rank −						1

$$T_+ = 20 \quad T_- = 1$$

For a 5% two-tailed test the critical value from Table 10 is 1.

This leads us to reject **H$_0$** and conclude that the population mean difference is not equal to zero.

> The critical region includes the tabulated value and so 1 is in the critical region.

Buying vegetables from Manchester gives higher takings on average. Not only is there no advantage in buying vegetables from Preston but it appears to lead to lower average takings.

1.4 Randomisation

Throughout the earlier statistics books in this series the importance of random sampling has been emphasised. There are many examples when ignoring this can lead to completely misleading results. For example, if in an investigation of the average wage in an area the sample is drawn from the employees of one particular firm which pays unusually high wages, the average wage is likely to be greatly overestimated.

Alternatively, in an investigation of the amount of time spent in public houses by adults, the sample was drawn from people coming out of public houses on a Monday night. All the people in the sample had spent some time in a public house which is not true of the population as a whole. In addition many people only go in public houses at weekends and so the members of the sample would tend to be people who spent a lot of time in public houses. Both these factors would lead to an overestimation of the average amount of time spent in public houses.

In practice, genuinely random samples are very difficult and often impossible to obtain. For example, when applying different diets to identical twins it might be hard enough to find sufficient pairs of identical twins willing to take part in the trial, let alone trying to obtain a random sample of all identical twins in the population. Even if this could be done, it might still be argued that the results only applied to the population of identical twins and not to the population as a whole. Similarly, when investigating the takings of a grocery, ideally the takings should be observed on a random sample of days on which the shop is open. This might result in having to wait several years to complete the experiment, by which time the results would be useless.

> If you take notice of every criticism, however small, you will end up doing nothing at all.

Faced with these difficulties it is tempting to give up on the idea of randomisation. This should be resisted. Choices such as which twin follows which diet should be made by a random process and, while taking account of practical difficulties, an attempt at random sampling should be made. At the very least, thought should be given to avoiding obvious bias like the examples quoted in the first two paragraphs of this section. It is not possible to remove all possible sources of bias from an experiment. A well-designed experiment will eliminate all likely sources of bias.

The purpose of randomisation is to eliminate bias.

Worked example 1.1

The mean payment made by an insurance company on household claims in 2000 was £632. The manager now examined 180 randomly selected claims made in 2001. She found the mean payment was £768 with a standard deviation of £299.

(a) Assuming that the size of the payments may be modelled by a normal distribution, use the results from these 180 claims to investigate, at the 1% significance level, whether the mean payment has increased in 2001 compared to 2000.

(b) How would your conclusions be affected if it was later discovered that:
  (i) the size of the payments was not normally distributed,
  (ii) the sample was not random?

Solution

(a) $\mathbf{H_0}\,\mu = 632$

 $\mathbf{H_1}\,\mu > 632$

 $z = (768 - 632) / (299/\sqrt{180}) = 6.10$

The critical value for 1% one-tailed significance level is 2.3263.

Reject $\mathbf{H_0}$, since $6.10 > 2.3263$, conclude size of payments has increased.

(b) (i) Conclusions unaffected because sample is large.

(ii) Conclusions unreliable. The sample may be biased. For example, in choosing these claims, smaller claims may have been deliberately ignored.

See S4, chapter 3.

1.5 Blocking

If the greengrocer in our example wished to compare the effect on takings of several possible markets, she could visit each market and record her takings. If she allocated 22 days to the experiment she could use a random process to decide which market to go to each day, subject to using the same market no more than six times.

	Takings, £		
Kirkham	**Manchester**	**Oldham**	**Preston**
344	459	322	292
479	234	600	588
503	602	308	347
290	222	344	399
207	598	506	544
	479		406

This is known as a completely randomised design. Such designs are analysed using **one-factor analysis of variance** as explained in section 3.3.

However, the ideas of the paired comparison can be extended to this case. The experiment could be carried out as follows.

	Mon	**Tue**	**Wed**	**Thu**	**Fri**	**Sat**
Kirkham	294	306	343	386	494	527
Manchester	277	318	399	360	524	566
Oldham	299	265	302	410	488	530
Preston	260	289	299	391	460	488

This is known as a randomised block design. The markets are blocked by days of the week. This design is analysed using **two-factor analysis of variance** as explained in section 3.4. One of the factors – in this case the markets – is the object of the investigation. The other factor – in this case the day of the week – is introduced because it is thought that it might have a substantial effect on the results. This is known as the blocking factor. As with the paired comparison, the introduction of the days of the week as a factor will, if the design is successful, reduce the experimental error. It will make it easier to detect a difference between markets, if such a difference exists.

Section 3.5 deals with **Latin squares**, a more sophisticated design, where two blocking factors may be included.

Blocking is used to reduce experimental error by applying treatments (usually more than two) to the same subjects or in the same conditions.

Worked example 1.2

In a comparison of the drying times of three different types of wood preservative, *A*, *B* and *C*, samples of each of four different woods, *W1*, *W2*, *W3* and *W4*, are available.

Three experimental designs are suggested.

Design 1			Design 2			Design 3		
A	**B**	**C**	**A**	**B**	**C**	**A**	**B**	**C**
W1	*W2*	*W3*	*W1*	*W2*	*W1*	*W1*	*W2*	*W3*
W1	*W2*	*W3*	*W2*	*W3*	*W3*	*W3*	*W4*	*W2*
W1	*W2*	*W3*	*W3*	*W1*	*W2*	*W4*	*W1*	*W4*
			W4	*W4*	*W4*	*W2*	*W3*	*W1*
			W1	*W2*	*W3*			

Thus, for example, the first column of **Design 2** indicates preservative *A* is applied to two samples of wood *W1* and one sample each of woods *W2*, *W3* and *W4*; the written order within any column is unimportant.

(a) State **two** disadvantages of **Design 1**.

(b) Write down the name of **Design 3**.

(c) Name the technique used to analyse the results from **Design 3**.

(d) State one advantage of **Design 3** over **Design 2**.

(e) Explain how randomisation might be used in the context of **Designs 1**, **2** and **3**.

Solution

(a) Each type of wood preservative is used on only one wood. Thus if a difference is found it will not be possible to tell whether it is due to the different types of wood preservative or to the different woods (or both). Wood 4 is not used at all.

(b) This is a randomised block design. Each type of wood preservative is used once on each wood.

(c) Two factor analysis of variance.

(d) In **Design 3** each type of wood preservative is used with the same combination of woods. This is not the case with **Design 2** so that a comparison of the mean drying times for **Design 2** may be affected by the different combinations of woods used with each preservative.

(e) In **Design 1** the allocation of wood to wood preservative would be made by a random process. This would not overcome the problem identified in the answer to **(a)**. It would however ensure that the results would not be, deliberately or unconsciously, rigged by selecting a particular wood for the most favoured preservative.

Similarly in **Design 2** a random process could be used to decide which wood was *W1*, which was *W2*, etc. Thus the wood to be used twice with each preservative would be determined by a random process.

The results of **Design 3** are less likely to be affected by bias. However decisions such as the order of carrying out the treatments should ideally be determined by a random process.

1.6 Control groups

In the examples above two or more different markets were compared. Sometimes there are not two or more treatments, but only one. For example, we may wish to observe the effect of a particular medical treatment on arthritis or the effect of a coaching course on students' tennis playing skills. The effect of these treatments cannot be judged in isolation. An arthritis sufferer may improve (or deteriorate) with no treatment. Similarly, a tennis player may improve without attending a coaching course.

It is necessary to have a **control group** and an **experimental group**. These two groups should be matched as closely as possible. That is, the people in one group should be as similar as possible to the people in the other group as far as characteristics relevant to the investigation are concerned. This does not mean that all the people in a particular group must be similar to each other, but that the group as a whole must be similar to the other group.

For example, in the case of the arthritis sufferers the two groups should contain people of similar age, gender, general health and severity of arthritis. In the case of the tennis players, the groups should contain students of similar age, gender, fitness and tennis playing ability.

The groups should be selected and then one group (the experimental group) should be chosen at random to receive the experimental treatment (or tennis coaching). The other group will be the control group. The control group will receive no treatment (or coaching) or will continue with the standard treatment. The effect on the two groups can then be compared.

> If a new treatment is applied to an experimental group, a control group, which receives no treatment or the standard treatment, is needed to act as a measure of the effect of not applying the new treatment.

1.7 Blind and double blind trials

In the case of medical treatment, it is well established that some patients will improve or recover without treatment and that often this improvement will be greater or quicker if they are told they are having treatment. Thus it is standard practice in drugs' tests to give the control group a placebo. This is a harmless substance which looks like the real medication but, in fact, does not contain any drug. Many patients will improve after taking placebos. To show a drug to be effective, significantly more patients who took the drug must show improvement than those who took the placebo. (There are, of course, other issues such as possible side effects to consider as well).

> A placebo is a pill or treatment which contains no active ingredient.

If the patients who took the placebos knew that they were taking placebos the effect would, of course, be lost. It is essential that the patients should not know whether or not they are taking placebos and this is known as a blind trial.

> In a blind trial subjects do not know whether they are receiving the treatment or a placebo.

Although the patient will not know whether they are taking the drug or the placebo, they will have consented to taking part in the trial. They will therefore know that they may be taking the placebo.

Even more subtle effects can be at work. It has been found that, even if the patients do not know whether or not they are taking placebos, the doctor may expect those patients taking the drug to fare better than those taking placebos. This expectation may somehow transmit itself to the patient whose condition may improve as a result. Therefore it is necessary that the doctor does not know which patients are receiving placebos and which are receiving the drugs. Of course, someone must know who is receiving the drugs otherwise it would be impossible to analyse the results. However, it should be someone who has no direct contact with the patient. Trials where neither the patient nor the doctor know who is receiving the drugs are known as double blind trials.

> In a double blind trial neither the subject nor the person administering the treatment knows whether a placebo or an active drug is being given.

It has been suggested that the person carrying out the statistical analysis also should not know which patients took the drug to prevent this influencing the analysis. This would be described as a triple blind trial.

Drug trials are greatly affected by the ethical problems involved. Firstly, it is of course essential that patients taking part should be fully informed of the nature and possible risks of the experiment. Not everyone will agree to take part in a randomised trial and this fact alone means that genuinely random samples are unobtainable. Secondly, once a treatment has been established as beneficial, it would be wrong not to let all the patients taking part in the trial benefit from it even if this interferes with strictly statistical considerations. Thirdly, it is clearly wrong to carry out an experiment, with all the inconvenience it may cause and false hopes it may raise, if it has not been well designed. In the past, clinical trials have suffered from numerous defects including cases where the trial has been too small to establish the effectiveness of a treatment, whatever the results obtained. In other cases, lack of effective design has made the experimental error much larger than it need be, thus making a real effect impossible to detect.

The last 20 years have seen great improvements in this area, with drug companies and organisations, such as the National Institute for Clinical Excellence, employing statisticians to ensure that clinical trials are well designed.

Worked example 1.3

To measure the effectiveness of a drug to relieve breathlessness, 12 subjects, all susceptible to breathlessness, were each administered the drug after one attack of breathlessness and the placebo after a separate attack. One hour after the attacks an index of breathlessness was obtained for each subject, with the following results:

Subject	Drug	Placebo
1	28	32
2	31	33
3	17	23
4	18	26
5	31	34
6	12	17
7	33	30
8	18	19
9	25	23
10	19	21
11	17	24
12	16	49

(a) Explain the role that randomisation could play in carrying out this experiment.

(b) Explain the meaning of a blind and of a double blind trial in the context of this experiment.

(c) Making no assumptions regarding the distribution of these data, investigate the claim (using the 5% significance level) that the drug significantly reduces the breathlessness index.

Solution

(a) It would almost certainly be impossible to obtain a random sample of all sufferers of breathlessness to take part in this trial. However, having identified some suitable and available subjects, it may be possible to make the final selection using random numbers.

The order in which the drug and the placebo are taken could affect the results – the response to the placebo could be different if it is taken after the drug rather than before. The order could be determined by a random process for each subject or alternatively it could be decided that six subjects should take the placebo first and six subjects should take the drug first. The six subjects taking the placebo first should be selected at random from the twelve taking part.

(b) In a blind trial the subjects would not know whether they were taking the drug or the placebo. In a double blind trial the doctor administering the treatment and assessing the breathlessness index, also would not know whether the subject was taking the drug or the placebo.

(c) If no assumptions regarding the distribution are to be made, the sign test is appropriate. (Given the untypically large difference for subject 12 it would be unwise to make any assumptions.)

H_0 Population median difference $= 0$

H_1 Population median difference (drug – placebo) < 0

See S3, chapter 5.

Subject	Drug	Placebo	Drug −Placebo
1	28	32	−
2	31	33	−
3	17	23	−
4	18	26	−
5	31	34	−
6	12	17	−
7	33	30	+
8	18	19	−
9	25	23	+
10	19	21	−
11	17	24	−
12	16	49	−

$10 -$ $2 +$

Binomial $n = 12$ $p = 0.5$ $P(2 \text{ or fewer}) = 0.0193$

Since $0.0193 < 0.05$ reject $\mathbf{H_0}$.

Conclude at the 5% significance level that the drug reduces the breathlessness index.

EXERCISE IA

1 In an investigation of the effect of a new drug in the treatment of acne, a specialist was asked to prescribe the new drug to one group of patients and a placebo to another group.

(a) Which group of patients was the experimental group?

Blind trials were employed in the investigation.

(b) Explain the meaning and purpose of such trials.

2 A doctor wishes to test the effectiveness of a new drug for treating a particular skin disease. Explain to the doctor the meaning and purpose of blind and double blind trials.

3 A manufacturer of bicycle tyres is considering using a new process with the intention of increasing the average distance cycled before puncturing. This is to be tested experimentally. Explain in this context:

(a) the meaning of replicates,

(b) the meaning of experimental error,

(c) the advantages of using a paired design.

4 A road haulage firm moves lorryloads of slate from a quarry to a depot 70 miles away. You are asked to advise the firm how to investigate which of two alternative routes is quicker. Design an experiment to compare the routes efficiently. Explain the role of replication and randomisation in your design. In addition to any features of the design, how would you seek to minimise experimental error?

5 An A level teacher believes that students will be more successful if they work at their own pace using self-learning materials. Tutorials will be provided to deal with particular problems. To test this theory she asks for volunteers from the 40 students who intend to take A level statistics to study in this way. The remaining students will be taught using traditional class teaching. At the end of the course the A level results of the two groups will be compared.

(a) Explain why, whatever the results, this experiment cannot establish which method of teaching is more successful.

(b) Suggest improvements to the experimental design.

6 Pairs of twins, where each twin suffers from moderate asthma, are recruited for the trial of a treatment. The trial is a double blind trial in which the twin selected at random to be in the control group is given a placebo. The percentage improvement after four weeks of treatment was assessed with the following results:

Twin pair	Placebo	New treatment
1	16	21
2	8	16
3	6	9
4	22	25
5	22	20
6	24	28
7	24	26
8	11	15

(a) Explain, in the context of this question, what is meant by a double blind trial.

(b) Explain, in the context of this question, what is meant by a placebo.

(c) Carry out a Wilcoxon's signed-rank test, at the 5% significance level, to determine whether the new treatment appears to result in a twin having a higher percentage improvement of their asthma.

7 A local council claims that the average take-home pay of manual workers in its employment is £190 per week. A sample of 125 such workers had mean take-home pay of £198 and standard deviation of £28.

(a) Test, at the 5% significance level, the hypothesis that the mean take-home pay of all the manual workers employed by the council is £190. Assume that the sample is random and that the distribution of take-home pay is normal.

(b) How would your conclusion be affected if you later discovered that:

   (i) the distribution of take-home pay was not normal but the sample was random,

   (ii) the sample was not random but the distribution of take-home pay was normal?

   Give a brief justification for each of your answers.

8 Ronan, a market trader, sells petfood. He decided to find out whether changing his supplier would increase his takings. He told a friend who was a statistician 'It worked. Yesterday using my old supplier my takings were £280, today with the new supplier my takings were £360.' The statistician persuaded Ronan to carry out a further trial over a two-week period with the following results:

Day	1st week						2nd week					
	Mon	Tue	Wed	Thu	Fri	Sat	Mon	Tue	Wed	Thu	Fri	Sat
Supplier	Old	Old	New	Old	New	New	New	New	Old	New	Old	Old
Takings (£)	265	299	315	270	487	508	283	304	321	268	445	489

   (a) Using the data from the further trial, apply Wilcoxon's signed-rank test at the 5% significance level to test whether Ronan's takings increased when the new supplier was used.

   (b) Explain why the conclusion drawn from his original one-day trial may be invalid and the advantages of the trial designed by the statistician. Include an explanation of experimental error, replication and randomisation in this context.

9 As part of an investigation into the effects of exercise, a sports scientist measured the pulse rate of 15 visitors to a gymnasium. Eight of the visitors had just completed an exercise aimed at increasing upper body strength while the other seven had just completed an exercise aimed at increasing leg strength.

Pulse rate (beats per minute)	
Upper body exercise	Leg exercise
192	129
184	193
217	124
164	135
128	167
182	145
216	173
137	

A second sports scientist asked seven people to take part in a similar investigation. Each of the seven people was asked to attend the gymnasium on two successive days and perform one of the two exercises on each day for exactly three minutes. A random process was used to decide, for each person, which exercise was performed on the first day.

The results were as follows:

	Pulse rate (beats per minute)	
Person	Upper body exercise	Leg exercise
A	149	136
B	194	172
C	124	125
D	148	137
E	152	135
F	168	160
G	196	184

Without carrying out any calculations:

(a) explain, in the context of this question, the advantages of a paired comparison relative to comparing two independent samples,

(b) discuss briefly the use, or otherwise, of randomisation in these two experiments,

(c) excluding anything you have said in answer to **(a)** and **(b)** give a further advantage of the second experiment compared to the first,

(d) state which experiment is more likely to detect a difference in pulse rates if such a difference exists.

10 A manufacturer wishes to compare four different soap powders, **A**, **B**, **C** and **D**. Subjects are to be asked to use a particular soap powder and give it a mark out of 100. Three experimental designs are suggested.

Design 1				Design 2				Design 3			
A	**B**	**C**	**D**	**A**	**B**	**C**	**D**	**A**	**B**	**C**	**D**
S_1	S_4	S_7	S_{10}	S_1	S_2	S_4	S_4	S_1	S_1	S_1	S_1
S_2	S_5	S_8	S_{11}	S_2	S_3	S_1	S_2	S_2	S_2	S_2	S_2
S_3	S_6	S_9	S_{12}	S_3	S_4	S_3	S_1	S_3	S_3	S_3	S_3

In **Design 1** twelve subjects are randomly allocated, three to each soap powder. In **Design 2** only four subjects are used (the order they appear in each column is unimportant) and in **Design 3** only three subjects are used.

(a) Write down the name given to:

   (i) **Design 1**,

   (ii) **Design 3**.

I

(b) Name the technique used to analyse:
   (i) Design 1,
   (ii) Design 3.

(c) Explain why **Design 3** is to be preferred to
   (i) Design 1,
   (ii) Design 2.

Key point summary

I Experimental error is the effect of factors other than those controlled by the experimenter.   *p 2*

2 In a paired comparison, experimental error is reduced by applying both treatments to the same subjects or in the same conditions.   *p 3*

3 The purpose of randomisation is to eliminate bias.   *p 6*

4 Blocking is used to reduce experimental error by applying treatments (usually more than two) to the same subjects or in the same conditions.   *p 8*

5 If a new treatment is applied to an experimental group, a control group, which receives no treatment or the standard treatment, is needed to act as a measure of the effect of not applying the new treatment.   *p 10*

6 A placebo is a pill or treatment which contains no active ingredient.   *p 10*

7 In a blind trial subjects do not know whether they are receiving the treatment or a placebo.   *p 10*

8 In a double blind trial neither the subject nor the person administering the treatment knows whether a placebo or an active drug is being given.   *p 11*

Test yourself	What to review
1 Hedda wishes to compare the time taken to travel to college by bus and by bicycle. Explain to her, in the context of this investigation, the meaning of:	*Section 1.2*
(a) experimental error,	
(b) replicates.	

Test yourself (continued)	**What to review**

2 One hundred and ninety 10-year-old children are given an
arithmetic test. Half the children then have a vitamin
supplement added to their daily diet. After three months
the children take a similar arithmetic test.

Section 1.6

 (a) Identify
   (i) the control group,
   (ii) the experimental group.
 (b) Explain the purpose of the control group.

---

3 A group of patients suffering from stomach ulcers agree to
take part in a randomised trial. Half the patients are
selected at random and treated with an experimental drug.
The other half receive placebos. Explain in this context the
meaning of:

Section 1.7

 (a) placebo,
 (b) blind trial,
 (c) double blind trial.

---

4 As part of a GCSE project a sample of pupils at a large
comprehensive school are to be asked to take part in a
survey. One of the purposes is to estimate the average
disposable income (pocket money plus any earnings) of
pupils.

Section 1.4

 The sample is chosen by standing in a corridor and
asking pupils as they pass to take part. Explain why the
resulting non-random sample could lead to misleading
conclusions.

---

5 A dietitian wishes to examine the effect on pulse rates of
eating unhealthy food. A sample of customers entering a
burger bar are asked to agree to have their pulse rates
measured, as are a second sample of customers leaving
the burger bar.

Section 1.3

 Explain how paired comparisons could have been used to
improve the design of this experiment.

---

6 An experiment is to be carried out to compare six different
layouts of instruments on a control panel. The purpose is to
see which layout leads to the fastest response to an
emergency. Different people will respond at different speeds
and so to reduce experimental error a sample of ten people
will be asked to respond to a simulated emergency on each of
the six layouts. What is the name given to this method of
reducing experimental error?

Section 1.5

Test yourself ANSWERS

1 **(a)** If Hedda makes two journeys to college by bus they will not take exactly the same time. This difference is due to factors other than method of transport and is called experimental error.

   (b) Repeated journeys by bus are identical as far as the factor being investigated is concerned and are called replicates.

2 **(a) (i)** Children who did not have the supplement added.

   (ii) Children who did have the supplement added.

   (b) To enable improvement made by children who had supplement added to be compared with improvement made by children who did not have it added.

3 **(a)** A placebo is a pill or treatment which contains no active ingredient.

   (b) In a blind trial the patient does not know whether or not they are receiving the active ingredient or a placebo.

   (c) In a double blind trial neither the patient nor the person administering the treatment knows whether the patient is receiving the active ingredient or a placebo.

4 The pupils passing at the time might, for example, all be 12-year-olds who would probably have lower average disposable income than the whole population of pupils. (Many other answers possible.)

5 If the same customers had their pulse rates tested before and after eating, the differences could be examined thus eliminating a major source (difference between customers) of experimental error.

6 Blocking.

CHAPTER 2

Analysis of paired comparisons

Learning objectives

After studying this chapter you should be able to:

■ apply the paired t-test to test for the equality of (or for a given difference in) the means of two populations using data from paired samples

■ understand the assumptions of the paired t-test and recognise circumstances where it would be more appropriate to apply a non-parametric test to data from paired samples.

2.1 Introduction

In S7, sections 5.3 and 5.4, tests were considered for the equality of (or for a given difference in) the means of two normal populations using data from two independent samples. In chapter 1 of this book the advantages of using paired comparisons, where appropriate, have been discussed. Provided it is reasonable to assume that the differences between paired samples are normally distributed, the t-distribution may be used to analyse data from paired comparisons.

2.2 Paired samples *t*-test

Assuming that the two populations from which the paired samples of size n are selected are distributed with means μ_1 and μ_2, respectively, then the differences between pairs will also be normally distributed with mean $\mu_1 - \mu_2 = \mu_d$ and variance σ_d^2, say. Thus a test of $\mathbf{H_0}: \mu_1 = \mu_2$ is equivalent to a test of $\mathbf{H_0}: \mu_d = 0$.

> See S7, chapter 1.

Although the two populations may well be normally distributed, the key distributional assumption for the test is that the differences between pairs of values are approximately normally distributed.

Let $\overline{D}$ and S_d^2 denote the mean and variance, respectively, of a sample of n differences.

Then $\overline{D} \sim N\left(\mu_d , \dfrac{\sigma_d^2}{n} \right)$

or $Z = \dfrac{\overline{D} - \mu_d}{\dfrac{\sigma_d}{\sqrt{n}}} \sim N(0, 1)$

> Upper case $\overline{D}$ is used here as it represents a variable. Lower case $\overline{d}$ would be used for a particular value of the variable. You will not be penalised in an examination whichever one you use.
>
> $\overline{D} \sim N\left(\mu_d, \dfrac{\sigma_d^2}{n} \right)$ means $\overline{D}$ is distributed with mean μ_d and variance $\dfrac{\sigma_d^2}{n}$.

Thus, from section 4.2 of S4,

$$\frac{\overline{D} - \mu_d}{\frac{S_d}{\sqrt{n}}} \sim t_{n-1} \text{ (t-distribution with $v = n - 1$ degrees of freedom.)}$$

Tests on paired samples which do not require the differences to be normally distributed (sign test, Wilcoxon's signed-rank test) were studied in S3.

2

This result can be used to test the equality of (or for a given difference in) two population means based upon paired samples providing the differences are normally distributed.

Worked example 2.1

A school mathematics teacher decides to test the effect of using an educational computer package, consisting of geometric designs and illustrations, to teach geometry. Since the package is expensive, the teacher wishes to determine whether using the package will result in an improvement in the pupils' understanding of the topic. The teacher randomly assigns pupils to two groups; a control group receiving standard lessons and an experimental group using the new package. The pupils are selected in pairs of equal mathematical ability, with one from each pair assigned at random to the control group and the other to the experimental group. On completion of the topic the pupils are given a test to measure their understanding. The results, percentage marks, are shown in the table.

Pair	Control	Experimental
1	72	75
2	82	79
3	93	84
4	65	71
5	76	82
6	89	91
7	81	85
8	58	68
9	95	90
10	91	92

Assuming differences in percentage marks to be normally distributed, investigate the claim that the educational computer package produces an improvement in pupils' understanding of geometry.

Solution

$H_0: \mu_d = 0$ Difference = Experimental − Control

$H_1: \mu_d > 0$ (one-tailed)

Significance level, $\alpha = 0.05$ (say)

Degrees of freedom, $v = 10 - 1 = 9$

Critical region, $t > 1.833$

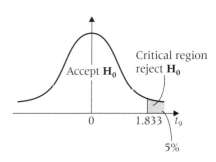

Under $\mathbf{H_0}$, the test statistic is

$$t = \frac{\bar{d}}{\frac{s_d}{\sqrt{n}}}$$

The 10 differences (Experimental − Control) are

$$d: 3 \quad -3 \quad -9 \quad 6 \quad 6 \quad 2 \quad 4 \quad 10 \quad -5 \quad 1$$
$$\bar{d} = 1.5 \quad \text{and} \quad s_d = 5.72$$

Thus $\quad t = \dfrac{1.5}{\dfrac{5.72}{\sqrt{10}}} = 0.829$

This value does not lie in the critical region so $\mathbf{H_0}$ is not rejected. Thus there is no evidence, at the 5% level of significance, to suggest that the educational computer package produces an improvement in pupils' understanding of geometry.

Worked example 2.2

In a comparison of a variety of spring wheat and a variety of winter wheat, one feature of interest was protein content. The two varieties were grown at each of nine locations. The results below are the protein concentrations measured in grams of protein per kilogram of wheat.

Differences in protein concentrations may be assumed to be normally distributed.

Location	Spring wheat	Winter wheat
1	125	83
2	111	84
3	144	116
4	171	145
5	135	100
6	166	150
7	143	114
8	176	149
9	168	137

Investigate, at the 10% level of significance, the claim that the mean protein concentration of the spring wheat exceeds that of the winter wheat by 25 grams of protein per kilogram of wheat.

Solution

$\mathbf{H_0}: \mu_d = 25 \quad (\mu_s - \mu_w = 25)$

$\mathbf{H_1}: \mu_d \neq 25 \quad \text{(two-tailed)}$

Significance level, $\alpha = 0.10$

Degrees of freedom, $v = 9 - 1 = 8$

Critical region, $|t| > 1.860$

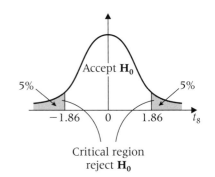

Under $\mathbf{H_0}$, the test statistic is

$$t = \frac{\bar{d} - 25}{\frac{s_d}{\sqrt{n}}}$$

The nine differences (spring − winter) are

d: 42   27   28   26   35   16   29   27   31

$\bar{d} = 29$ and $s_d = 7.0356$

Thus $t = \dfrac{29 - 25}{\dfrac{7.0356}{\sqrt{9}}} = 1.71$.

This value does not lie in the critical region so $\mathbf{H_0}$ is not rejected.

Thus, at the 10% level of significance, there is no evidence to reject the claim that the mean protein concentration of the variety of spring wheat exceeds that of the variety of winter wheat by 25 grams of protein per kilogram of wheat.

Worked example 2.3

Sixteen children participated in a study of the effect of athletic training on heart rate. Eight of the children were trained competitive swimmers. The other eight were normal healthy untrained children selected from a large group of volunteers. An untrained child was chosen to match each trained child with respect to age, height, weight and body surface area. The table below shows the children's resting heart rates in beats per minute.

Pair	Untrained	Trained
1	90	95
2	85	75
3	75	75
4	120	85
5	95	80
6	105	80
7	100	85
8	95	75

(a) Explain why paired rather than independent samples were used in the study.

(b) Using Wilcoxon's signed-rank test, at the 5% significance level, examine whether there is a difference between the heart rates of trained and untrained children.

> This test is in S3. However, the specification of S8 states that Wilcoxon's signed-rank test and the sign test may be required.

(c) What additional assumption would be required in order to carry out a paired t-test? Why might a t-test be preferred?

Solution

(a) Differences between children would be a large source of experimental error in this experiment. By examining the differences between children with similar characteristics, this source of experimental error is reduced. This makes it more likely to detect a difference if one exists.

(b) H_0: population median difference $= 0$

H_1: population median difference $\neq 0$ (two-tailed)

Significance level, $\alpha = 0.05$

Critical region $T \leqslant 2$ ($n = 8 - 1$ (one difference $= 0$))

> As Wilcoxon's signed-rank test assumes the differences are distributed symmetrically, H_0 could refer to the population mean difference.

Pair	Untrained	Trained	Difference	rank +	rank −
1	90	95	−5		1
2	85	75	10	2	
3	75	75	0		
4	120	85	35	7	
5	95	80	15	3.5	
6	105	80	25	6	
7	100	85	15	3.5	
8	95	75	20	5	

> Pair 3, with no difference, is omitted from the ranking.

$T_+ = 27$ $T_- = 1$

Reject H_0, conclude population median difference $\neq 0$. Trained children have lower heart rate than untrained children.

(c) The t-test requires the assumption that the differences are normally distributed. If this assumption is valid then, as the t-test uses the actual differences rather than the ranks, the test has more chance of detecting a difference if one exists.

Worked example 2.4

A large food processing firm is considering introducing a new recipe for its ice cream. In a preliminary trial, a panel of 11 tasters were asked to score ice cream, made from both the existing and the new recipe, for sweetness. The results, on a scale from 0 to 100, with the sweeter ice cream being given the higher score, were as follows:

Taster	Existing recipe	New recipe
A	88	94
B	35	49
C	67	66
D	17	82
E	24	25
F	32	96
G	8	14
H	44	56
I	73	27
J	47	44
K	25	79

(a) Use a sign test, at the 5% significance level, to test whether the new recipe is sweeter than the existing one.

Because of the erratic nature of the scores obtained, it was decided to repeat the trial with a new panel of 10 tasters, this time giving some guidance as to how scores should be allocated. Two other ice creams were tasted first. One was very sweet and the tasters were told that it had a score of 90. The other was not sweet and had a score of 10.

The new trial gave the following results:

Taster	Existing recipe	New recipe
L	52	74
M	44	65
N	57	66
O	49	47
P	61	71
Q	55	55
R	49	62
S	69	66
T	64	73
U	46	59

(b) Use a paired *t*-test, making any necessary assumptions, to test the hypothesis that there is no difference in sweetness between the two recipes at the 1% significance level.

(c) Discuss briefly the suitability of the choice of a sign test for the first set of data and a paired *t*-test for the second. Comment on the suggestion that Wilcoxon's signed-rank test should have been used for both sets of data.

Solution

(a)

Taster	Existing recipe	New recipe	Sign (E–N)
A	88	94	−
B	35	49	−
C	67	66	+
D	17	82	−
E	24	25	−
F	32	96	−
G	8	14	−
H	44	56	−
I	73	27	+
J	47	44	+
K	25	79	−

H_0: population median difference $= 0$

H_1: population median difference < 0 (one-tailed)

8 − signs   3 + signs

Binomial $n = 11$ $p = 0.5$ P(3 or fewer) $= 0.113 > 0.05$ (5%)

Accept population median difference $= 0$.

There is no significant evidence that new recipe is sweeter.

(b)

Taster	Existing recipe	New recipe	Difference (E–N)
L	52	74	−22
M	44	65	−21
N	57	66	−9
O	49	47	2
P	61	71	−10
Q	55	55	0
R	49	62	−13
S	69	66	3
T	64	73	−9
U	46	59	−13

$\mathbf{H_0}: \mu_d = 0$

$\mathbf{H_1}: \mu_d \neq 0$ (two-tailed)

Significance level, $\alpha = 0.01$

Degrees of freedom, $v = 10 - 1 = 9$

Critical region, $|t| > 3.250$

$$\bar{d} = -9.2 \quad s_d = 8.766$$

$$t = \frac{-9.2 - 0}{\frac{8.766}{\sqrt{10}}} = -3.32$$

Reject $\mu_d = 0$

Conclude there is a difference: new recipe sweeter.

(c) In **(a)**, the erratic nature of the scores suggested that the magnitudes of the differences would be an unreliable measure. However, the sign should be reliable since it is very unlikely that a taster would give a lower score to the recipe they regarded as sweeter. Hence the sign test is a good choice. However there is no obvious evidence from the observed differences

$$-6 \quad -14 \quad 1 \quad -65 \quad -1 \quad 64 \quad -6 \quad -12 \quad 46 \quad 3 \quad -54$$

that the assumptions for the paired *t*-test (normal distribution of differences) or for Wilcoxon's signed-rank test (symmetrical distribution of differences) have been violated.

In **(b)**, the training makes it likely that the magnitudes of the differences give a good indication of the tasters' judgement of the difference in sweetness. Since there is nothing in the data to suggest that the assumption of normally distributed differences is unreasonable, the *t*-test is a good choice. This is because it uses the magnitudes of the differences and so is the most likely, of the three tests, to detect a difference if one exists.

Wilcoxon's signed-rank test would be unsuitable in **(a)** as the magnitudes (and therefore the ranks) of the differences are unreliable. It would be suitable in **(b)** but as already stated the *t*-test is preferable.

> A large outlier or an obviously skewed distribution of values would cast doubts on these assumptions. The assumptions cannot be proved to be true, we can only say whether or not they are plausible.

EXERCISE 2A

Note that the sign of the test statistic and, for one-sided tests, the critical value will depend on whether $y - x$ or $x - y$ is calculated. Where the significance level has not been stated in the question, use 5%.

1 A random sample of eleven students sat a Chemistry examination consisting of one theory paper and one practical paper. Their marks out of 100 are given in the table below.

Student	Theory mark	Practical mark
A	30	52
B	42	58
C	49	42
D	50	67
E	63	94
F	38	68
G	43	22
H	36	34
I	54	55
J	42	48
K	26	17

Assuming differences in pairs to be normally distributed, test, at the 5% level of significance, the hypothesis of no difference in mean mark on the two papers. [A]

2 A convenience food, known as 'Quicknosh', was introduced into the British market in January 1992. After a poor year for sales, the manufacturers initiated an intensive advertising campaign during January 1993. The table records the sales, in thousands of pounds, for a one-month period before and a one-month period after the advertising campaign, for each of eleven regions.

Region	Sales before campaign	Sales after campaign
A	2.4	3.0
B	2.6	2.5
C	3.9	4.0
D	2.0	4.1
E	3.2	4.8
F	2.2	2.0
G	3.3	3.4
H	2.1	4.0
I	3.1	3.3
J	2.2	4.2
K	2.8	3.9

Determine, at the 5% significance level, whether an increase in mean sales has occurred by using the t-test for paired values. [A]

3 In an investigation to compare the accuracy of Crackshot and Fastfire 12-bore shotguns in clay pigeon shooting, ten competitors each fired 100 shots with each make of gun. Their scores are shown in the table.

Competitor	Crackshot	Fastfire
A	93	87
B	99	91
C	90	86
D	86	87
E	85	78
F	94	95
G	87	89
H	91	84
I	96	88
J	79	74

It may be assumed that the differences between pairs of scores are approximately normally distributed. Examine the claim that the Crackshot shotgun is the more accurate for clay pigeon shooting. [A]

4 In a study of memory recall, 12 students were given ten minutes to try to memorise a list of 20 nonsense words. Each student was then asked to list as many of the words as he or she could remember both one hour and twenty-four hours later. The numbers of words recalled correctly by each student are shown below.

Student	1 hr later	24 hrs later
A	14	10
B	9	6
C	18	14
D	12	6
E	13	8
F	17	10
G	16	12
H	16	10
I	19	14
J	8	5
K	15	10
L	7	5

Stating any necessary assumptions, use a paired *t*-test to determine whether there is evidence, at the 5% level of significance, that, for all such students, the mean number of words recalled after one hour exceeds that recalled after twenty-four hours by five words. [A]

5 The temperature of the earth may be measured either by thermometers on the ground (x), which is an accurate but tedious method, or by sensors mounted in space satellites (y), which is a less accurate method and may be biased. The following table gives readings (°C) taken by both methods at eleven sites.

Site	Ground therm, x	Satellite sensors, y
1	4.6	4.7
2	17.3	19.5
3	12.2	12.5
4	3.6	4.2
5	6.2	6.0
6	14.8	15.4
7	11.4	14.9
8	14.9	17.8
9 '	9.3	9.7
10	10.4	10.5
11	7.2	7.4

Given that all readings are normally distributed, investigate the hypothesis that satellite sensors give, on average, significantly higher readings than the ground thermometers.

[A]

6 Two analysers are used in a hospital laboratory to measure blood creatinine levels. (These are used as a measure of kidney function.) To compare the performance of the two machines, a technician took eight specimens of blood and measured the creatinine level (in micromoles per litre) of each specimen using each machine. The results were as follows:

Specimen	Analyser A	Analyser B
1	119	106
2	173	153
3	100	83
4	99	95
5	77	69
6	121	123
7	84	84
8	73	67

The technician carried out a paired t-test and reported that there was a difference between analysers at the 5% significance level. Verify that this is in fact the case, assuming a normal distribution.

7 Two trainee estate agents, I and II, each valued independently a random sample of eight small properties. Their valuations, in £000s, are shown below.

Property	Trainee I	Trainee II
A	83.7	79.6
B	58.8	59.2
C	77.7	75.8
D	85.1	84.3
E	91.9	90.1
F	66.4	65.2
G	69.8	66.9
H	48.5	53.8

Stating any assumptions necessary, use a paired *t*-test to investigate whether there is evidence that the two trainees differ in their valuations.

8 As part of an investigation into the effects of alcohol on the human body at high altitude, ten male subjects were taken to a simulated altitude of 8000 m and given several tasks to perform. Each subject was carefully observed for deterioration in performance due to lack of oxygen, and the time, in seconds, at which useful consciousness ended was recorded. Three days later, the experiment was repeated one hour after the same ten subjects had unknowingly consumed 1 ml of 100%-proof alcohol per 5 kg of body weight. The time, in seconds, of useful consciousness was again recorded. The resulting data are given below.

Subject	No alcohol	Alcohol
1	260	185
2	565	375
3	900	310
4	630	240
5	280	215
6	365	420
7	400	405
8	735	205
9	430	255
10	900	900

Using an appropriate parametric test, determine whether or not these data support the hypothesis that the consumption of the stated amount of alcohol reduces the mean time of useful consciousness at high altitudes. [A]

9 Trace metals in drinking water affect the flavour of the water and high concentrations can pose a health hazard. The following table shows the zinc concentrations, in milligrams per 1000 litres, of water on the surface and on the river bed at each of twelve locations on a river.

Location	Surface	Bed
1	387	435
2	515	532
3	721	817
4	341	366
5	689	827
6	599	735
7	734	812
8	541	669
9	717	808
10	523	622
11	524	576
12	445	487

Differences in zinc concentrations of water in this river may be assumed to be normally distributed.

Examine the claim that zinc concentration of water in this river is more than 50 milligrams per 1000 litres greater on the river bed than on the surface.

10 A sample of topsoil and a sample of subsoil were taken from each of eight randomly selected agricultural locations in a particular county.

Each soil sample was analysed to determine its pH value with the following results.

Location	Topsoil pH	Subsoil pH
A	6.58	6.78
B	5.98	6.14
C	5.69	5.80
D	5.91	6.07
E	5.98	6.10
F	6.19	6.01
G	6.23	6.18
H	5.68	5.88

(a) Use a paired *t*-test, at the 5% level of significance, to investigate for a mean difference in pH between topsoil and subsoil in the county.

It is suggested that an *F*-test could be used to compare the variability in pH between topsoil and subsoil.

(b) State why such a test would **not** be appropriate if applied to the above data. [A]

11 The following data are the third and fourth round scores of a random sample of five competitors in an open golf tournament.

Competitor	3rd round	4th round
A	76	70
B	75	73
C	72	71
D	75	68
E	79	76

(a) (i) Use a paired *t*-test and the 5% significance level to test whether there is a difference in the mean score of all the competitors on the two rounds.

(ii) State the distributional assumption you have made in order to apply a paired *t*-test. Comment on its plausibility.

(b) Repeat **(a) (i)** using a sign test and comment.

(c) Repeat **(a) (i)** using a Wilcoxon's signed-rank test. Comment on the plausibility of any necessary assumption.

(d) In view of your comments in **(a) (ii)**, **(b)** and **(c)**, which test do you recommend in these circumstances?

12 Eight joints of meat were each cut in half. One half was frozen and wrapped using a standard process and the other half using a new process. The sixteen halves were placed in a freezer and the number of days to spoilage (which can be detected by a discolouration of the package) was noted for each.

Joint	Standard process	New process
1	146	167
2	254	240
3	199	266
4	235	926
5	262	313
6	212	296
7	265	260
8	218	307

(a) Use the sign test, at the 5% significance level, to investigate the claim that the halves frozen and wrapped using the new process lasted longer.

The observation on the new process for joint 4 was queried. Investigation showed that the recorded figure was probably incorrect but that the half using the new process had definitely lasted longer to spoilage than the other half.

(b) (i) Why do you think the observation on the new process for joint 4 was queried?

(ii) Does the result of the investigation affect the validity of the sign test carried out in **(a)**? Give a reason.

(iii) Would Wilcoxon's signed-rank test be a suitable test to apply to the data? Give a reason.

(c) A paired *t*-test was applied to the data for joints 1, 2, 3, 5, 6, 7 and 8. The *t*-statistic was calculated to be 2.65. Use this result, at the 5% significance level, to investigate the claim that the halves frozen and wrapped by the new process lasted longer. (You may assume that the sample is random and the differences are normally distributed.)

(d) Compare the conclusions reached in **(a)** and **(c)**. Comment.

13 The blood clotting times for five people were measured before and after they had consumed a fixed amount of alcohol. The times (seconds) are given below.

Person	Before	After
1	124	117
2	134	120
3	169	136
4	785	176
5	182	163

A statistician queried the observation on person 4 before alcohol. The experimenter agreed that an error must have been made but said that he was certain that, for this person the blood clotting time was shorter after than before alcohol. He had used the sign test on the five people and had accepted, at the 5% significance level, that there was no difference in the median blood clotting times before and after alcohol.

(a) **(i)** Confirm, by making any necessary calculations, that the sign test applied to these data does lead to the experimenter's conclusion.

(ii) Use a paired *t*-test on persons 1, 2, 3 and 5 to test whether there is a difference, at the 5% significance level, in the mean blood clotting time.

(b) Comment on:

(i) the validity and advisability of using each of the tests on these data,

(ii) the suggestion that Wilcoxon's signed-rank test should be used on the five people.

Key point summary

1 If $\overline{D}$ and S_d denote the mean and standard deviation, respectively, of a random sample of n differences that can be assumed to be normally distributed with mean μ_d, then

$$\frac{\overline{D} - \mu_d}{\frac{S_d}{\sqrt{n}}} \sim t_{n-1}.$$

p 21

Test yourself

What to review

1 (a) Find the 5% lower critical value for a *t*-statistic having 12 degrees of freedom.

Section 2.2

(b) Find the 1% critical values for a two-tailed test of a *t*-statistic having 7 degrees of freedom.

Test yourself (continued)	What to review

2 The winning margin in many competitive swimming events is less than 0.01 s. Consequently, any technique that may give a competitive swimmer even a slight advantage is given careful consideration. To investigate the possible effect of two different starts, the *hole entry* and the *flat entry*, on swimming times, eight competitive swimmers were selected at random. For each starting technique, the time, in seconds, to water entry was recorded for each swimmer with the following results:

Section 2.2

Swimmer	Hole entry	Flat entry
1	1.07	1.13
2	1.03	1.11
3	1.21	1.18
4	1.33	1.34
5	1.42	1.44
6	1.11	1.08
7	1.35	1.41
8	1.24	1.29

Use the paired differences to test whether there is evidence that, for competitive swimmers, the two techniques differ with respect to time to water entry. State clearly your null and alternative hypotheses and any distributional assumptions which you make.

3 A hospital is experimenting with a newly-developed drug that controls the blood pressure of hypertensive patients who have a history of elevated blood pressure. The diastolic blood pressure, in mm of Hg, is measured before and after administration of the drug to each of a sample of nine such patients, with the following results.

Section 2.2

Patient	Before drug	After drug
1	117	94
2	95	81
3	91	82
4	101	88
5	115	97
6	89	85
7	103	77
8	104	89
9	141	110

(a) Explain why it would **not** be correct here to calculate a pooled estimate of variance and then a t-statistic to test the difference in means.

(b) Investigate the claim that the drug produces a decrease of more than 10 mm of Hg in the mean diastolic blood pressure of hypertensive patients who have a history of elevated blood pressure. Use the 5% significance level.

Test yourself (*continued*)

4 Trainee estate agent, T, and qualified estate agent, Q, each valued independently a random sample of ten properties. Their valuations, in thousands of pounds, are shown below.

Section 2.2

Property	Estate Agent	
	T	Q
G	90.2	96.7
H	72.6	72.1
I	88.7	93.4
J	106.2	115.0
K	50.3	48.7
L	67.5	74.6
M	123.7	132.5
N	97.6	100.1
O	47.8	43.2
P	168.6	171.4

(a) Stating the necessary distributional assumption, use a paired t-test at the 1% level of significance to investigate whether T's valuations of properties are, on average, lower than Q's valuations.

(b) Explain why a paired t-test might be preferred to a sign test for this data.

(c) It is suggested that an F-test could be used to compare the variability in valuations between T and Q.

Explain why such a test would **not** be appropriate if applied to the above data.

Test yourself ANSWERS

(c) These are not independent samples and so the F-test is not appropriate.

(b) The assumption of normal distribution appears plausible and so the paired t-test is preferred as it has more chance of detecting a difference between valuations if such a difference exists;

4 (a) Assume differences follow a normal distribution.
$t = 2.38$, cv 2.821, accept no difference;

(b) $t = 2.47$, cv 1.860, difference greater than 10 mm of Hg.

3 (a) Pooled estimate of variance requires two independent random samples;

2 $t = 1.85$, cv $\mp$ 2.365 (5%), accept no difference.

1 (a) -1.782; **(b)** ± 3.499.

CHAPTER 3

Analysis of variance (ANOVA)

Learning objectives

After studying this chapter you should be able to:

- appreciate the need for analysing data from more than two samples
- understand the underlying models for the analysis of variance
- identify the correct analysis to apply to a given situation
- carry out a one-way analysis of variance
- carry out a two-way analysis of variance (without replicates)
- carry out an analysis of a Latin square.

3.1 Introduction

Consider the following two investigations.

(a) A car magazine wishes to compare the average petrol consumption of THREE similar models of car and has available six vehicles of each model.

(b) A teacher is interested in a comparison of the average percentage marks attained in the examinations of FIVE different subjects and has available the marks of eight students who all completed each examination.

In both these investigations, interest is centred on a comparison of **more than two populations**; THREE models of car, FIVE examinations.

In **(a)**, six vehicles of each of the three models are available so there are three **independent samples**, each of size six. This example requires an extension of the test considered in S7 section 5.4, which was for two normal population means using independent samples and a pooled estimate of variance.

See also section 1.5.

In **(b)** however, there is the additional feature that the same eight students each completed the five examinations, so there are five **dependent samples**, each of size eight. This example requires an extension of the test considered in the previous chapter, which was for two normal population means using dependent (paired) samples.

This chapter will show that an appropriate method of investigation for **(a)** is a **one-way** ANOVA to test for differences between the three models of car. For **(b)**, an appropriate method is a **two-way** ANOVA to test for differences between the five subjects and, if required, for differences between the eight students.

Subsequently, consideration will be given to the analysis of a particular extension of **(b)** when the number of subjects is equal to the number of students, say 5, and, additionally for example, each student falls into one of five age categories.

3.2 Factors and factor levels

Two new terms for analysis of variance need to be introduced at this stage.

Factor – a characteristic under consideration, thought to influence the measured observations.

Level – a value of the factor.

In **(a)** above, there is one factor (model of car) at THREE levels.

In **(b)** above, there are two factors (subjects and students) at FIVE and EIGHT levels, respectively.

In the extension to **(b)**, there would be three factors (subjects, students and age) each at FIVE levels.

3.3 One-way (factor) ANOVA

In general, one-way analysis of variance techniques can be used to study the effect of $k(> 2)$ levels of a single factor.

To determine if different levels of the factor affect measured observations differently, the following hypotheses are tested.

$$\mathbf{H_0}: \mu_i = \mu \quad \text{all} \quad i = 1, 2, \ldots, k$$
$$\mathbf{H_1}: \mu_i \neq \mu \quad \text{some} \quad i = 1, 2, \ldots, k$$

where μ_i is the population mean for level i.

Assumptions

When applying one-way analysis of variance there are three key assumptions that should be satisfied. They are essentially the same as those assumed in section 5.4 of S7 for $k = 2$ levels, and are that:

A the observations are obtained independently and randomly from the populations defined by the factor levels,

B the population at each factor level is (approximately) normally distributed,

C these normal populations have a common variance, σ^2.

Thus for factor level i, the population is assumed to have a distribution which is $N(\mu_i, \sigma^2)$.

Worked example 3.1

The table below shows the lifetimes under controlled conditions, in hours in excess of 1000 hours, of samples of 60 W electric light bulbs of three different brands.

	Brand	
1	**2**	**3**
16	18	26
15	22	31
13	20	24
21	16	30
15	24	24

Assuming all lifetimes to be normally distributed with common variance, test, at the 1% significance level, the hypothesis that there is no difference between the three brands with respect to mean lifetime.

Solution

Here there is one factor (brand) at three levels (1, 2 and 3). Also the sample sizes are all equal (to 5), although as you will see later this is not necessary.

$\mathbf{H_0}$: $\mu_i = \mu$ all $i = 1, 2, 3$
$\mathbf{H_1}$: $\mu_i \neq \mu$ some $i = 1, 2, 3$

The sample mean and variance estimate for each level are as follows:

	Brand		
	1	**2**	**3**
Sample size	5	5	5
Mean	16	20	27
Variance estimate	9	10	11

Since each of these three variance estimates is an estimate of the common population variance, σ^2, a pooled estimate may be calculated in the usual way as follows.

$$s_W^2 = \frac{(5-1) \times 9 + (5-1) \times 10 + (5-1) \times 11}{5 + 5 + 5 - 3} = 10$$

This quantity is called the **variance within samples**. It is an estimate of σ^2 based on $v = 5 + 5 + 5 - 3 = 12$ degrees of freedom. This is irrespective of whether or not the null hypothesis is true, since differences between levels (brands) will have no effect on the within sample variances.

The variability between samples may be estimated from the three sample means as follows:

	Brand		
	1	**2**	**3**
Sample mean	16	20	27
Mean		21	
Variance		21	

This variance estimate, denoted by $s_{\bar{B}}^2$ is called the **variance between sample means**. Since it is calculated using sample means, it is an estimate of

$$\frac{\sigma^2}{5} \quad \left(\text{that is } \frac{\sigma^2}{n} \text{ in general}\right)$$

based upon $(3 - 1) = 2$ degrees of freedom, but only if the null hypothesis is true. If $\mathbf{H_0}$ is false, then the subsequent 'large' differences between the sample means will result in $5s_{\bar{B}}^2$ being an inflated estimate of σ^2.

The two estimates of σ^2, s_W^2 and $5s_{\bar{B}}^2$ may be tested for equality using the F-test in section 5.2 of S7 with

$$F = \frac{5s_{\bar{B}}^2}{s_W^2}$$

as lifetimes may be assumed to be normally distributed.

Recall that the F-test requires the two variances to be independently distributed (from independent samples). Although this is by no means obvious here (both were calculated from the same data), s_W^2 and $s_{\bar{B}}^2$ are in fact independently distributed.

The test is always one-sided, upper-tail, since if $\mathbf{H_0}$ is false, $5s_{\bar{B}}^2$ is inflated whereas s_W^2 is unaffected.

Thus in analysis of variance, the convention of placing the larger variance estimate in the numerator of the F-statistic is **not** applied.

The solution is thus summarised and completed as follows.

$\mathbf{H_0}: \mu_i = \mu$ all $i = 1, 2, 3$

$\mathbf{H_1}: \mu_i \neq \mu$ some $i = 1, 2, 3$

Significance level, $\alpha = 0.01$

Degrees of freedom, $v_1 = 2$, $v_2 = 12$

Critical region, $F > 6.927$

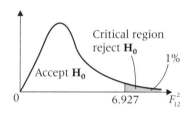

Test statistic is $F = \dfrac{5s_{\bar{B}}^2}{s_W^2} = \dfrac{155}{10} = 15.5$

This value does lie in the critical region. There is evidence, at the 1% significance level, that the true mean lifetimes of the three brands of bulb do differ.

At this point it is useful to note that, although the above calculations were based on (actual lifetimes − 1000), the same value would have been obtained for the test statistic (F) using actual lifetimes. This is because F is the ratio of two variances, both of which are unaffected by subtracting a working mean from all the data values. Additionally, in analysis of variance, data values may also be scaled by multiplying or dividing by a constant without affecting the value of the F-ratio. This is because each variance involves the square of the constant which then cancels in the ratio. Scaling of data values can make the subsequent analysis of variance less cumbersome and, sometimes, more accurate.

Notation and computational formulae

The calculations undertaken in the previous example are somewhat cumbersome, and are prone to inaccuracy with non-integer sample means. They also require considerable changes when the sample sizes are unequal. Equivalent computational formulae are available which cater for both equal and unequal sample sizes.

First, some notation.

Number of samples (or levels)	$= k$
Number of observations in ith sample	$= n_i, \quad i = 1, 2, \ldots, k$
Total number of observations	$= n = \sum_i n_i$
Observation j in ith sample	$= x_{ij}, \quad j = 1, 2, \ldots, n_i$
Sum of n_i observations in ith sample	$= T_i = \sum_j x_{ij}$
Sum of all n observations	$= T = \sum_i T_i = \sum_i \sum_j x_{ij}$

The computational formulae are as follows.

Total sum of squares,	$SS_T = \sum_i \sum_j x_{ij}^2 - \dfrac{T^2}{n}$
Between samples sum of squares,	$SS_B = \sum_i \dfrac{T_i^2}{n_i} - \dfrac{T^2}{n}$
Within samples sum of squares,	$SS_W = SS_T - SS_B$

> The formulae for SS_T and SS_B are given in the AQA booklet of formulae and tables.

A mean square (or unbiased variance estimate) is given by

(sum of squares) ÷ (degrees of freedom)

$$\left[\text{cf.} \quad s^2 = \frac{\sum (x - \bar{x})^2}{n - 1} \right].$$

Hence

Total mean square,	$MS_T = \dfrac{SS_T}{n-1}$
Between samples mean square,	$MS_B = \dfrac{SS_B}{k-1}$
Within samples mean square,	$MS_W = \dfrac{SS_W}{n-k}$

Note that for the degrees of freedom:
$$(k-1) + (n-k) = (n-1).$$

ANOVA table

It is convenient to summarise the results of an analysis of variance in a table. For a one-way analysis this takes the following form.

Source of variation	Sum of squares	Degrees of freedom	Mean square	F-ratio
Between samples	SS_B	$k-1$	MS_B	$\dfrac{MS_B}{MS_W}$
Within samples	SS_W	$n-k$	MS_W	
Total	SS_T	$n-1$		

The within sample degrees of freedom can be found by subtracting the between sample degrees of freedom from the total degrees of freedom (as for the sum of squares).

Worked example 3.2

A reworking of Worked example 3.1 using the above computational formulae and ANOVA table.

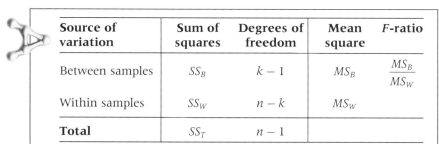

	Brand			
1	**2**	**3**		
16	18	26		$k = 3$
15	22	31		$n_1 = n_2 = n_3 = 5$
13	20	24		$n = 15$
21	16	30		
15	24	24		
T_i 80	100	135	$315 = T$	

$$\Sigma\Sigma x_{ij}^2 = 7045$$

$$SS_T = 7045 - \frac{315^2}{15} = 430$$

$$SS_B = \left(\frac{80^2}{5} + \frac{100^2}{5} + \frac{135^2}{5}\right) - \frac{315^2}{15} = 310$$

$$SS_W = 430 - 310 = 120$$

Thus, the ANOVA table is as follows:

Source of variation	Sum of squares	Degrees of freedom	Mean square	F-ratio
Between brands	310	2	155	15.5
Within brands	120	12	10	
Total	430	14		

This *F*-ratio value is precisely the same as that determined in Worked example 3.1.

Worked example 3.3

In a comparison of the cleaning action of four detergents, 20 pieces of white cloth were first soiled with Indian ink. The cloths were then washed under controlled conditions with five pieces washed by each of the four detergents. Unfortunately three pieces of cloth were 'lost' in the course of the experiment. Whiteness readings, made on the 17 remaining pieces of cloth, are shown below.

	Detergent		
A	**B**	**C**	**D**
77	74	73	76
81	66	78	85
61	58	57	77
76		69	64
69		63	

Assuming all whiteness readings to be normally distributed with common variance, test the hypothesis of no difference between the four brands' mean whiteness readings after washing.

Solution

H_0: no difference in mean readings $\mu_i = \mu$ all i
H_1: a difference in mean readings $\mu_i \neq \mu$ some i
Significance level, $\alpha = 0.05$
Degrees of freedom, $v_1 = k - 1 = 3$
        and $v_2 = n - k = 17 - 4 = 13$
Critical region, $F > 3.411$

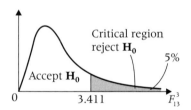

	A	**B**	**C**	**D**	**Total**
n_i	5	3	5	4	$n = 17$
T_i	364	198	340	302	$T = 1204$

$$\Sigma\Sigma x_{ij}^2 = 86\,362$$

$$SS_T = 86\,362 - \frac{1204^2}{17} = 1090.47$$

$$SS_B = \left(\frac{364^2}{5} + \frac{198^2}{3} + \frac{340^2}{5} + \frac{302^2}{4}\right) - \frac{1204^2}{17} = 216.67$$

$$SS_W = 1090.47 - 216.67 = 873.80$$

The ANOVA table is now as follows:

Source of variation	Sum of squares	Degrees of freedom	Mean square	F-ratio
Between detergents	216.67	3	72.22	1.07
Within detergents	873.80	13	67.22	
Total	1090.47	16		

The F-ratio of 1.07 does not lie in the critical region.

Thus there is no evidence, at the 5% significance level, to suggest a difference between the four brands' mean whiteness after washing.

Model

From the three assumptions for one-way ANOVA, listed previously,

$$x_{ij} \sim N(\mu_i, \sigma^2) \quad \text{for} \quad j = 1, 2, \ldots, n_i \text{ and } i = 1, 2, \ldots, k$$

Hence $\quad x_{ij} - \mu_i = \varepsilon_{ij} \sim N(0, \sigma^2)$

where ε_{ij} denotes the variation of x_{ij} about its mean μ_i and so represents the inherent random variation in the observations.

If $\quad \mu = \dfrac{1}{k} \displaystyle\sum_{i=1}^{k} \mu_i$, then $\displaystyle\sum_{i=1}^{k} (\mu_i - \mu) = 0$.

Writing $\mu_i - \mu = \alpha_i$ results in $\mu_i = \mu + \alpha_i$ where $\displaystyle\sum_{i=1}^{k} \alpha_i = 0$.

Hence α_i can be interpreted as the mean effect of factor level i relative to the overall mean μ.

Combining $x_{ij} - \mu_i = \varepsilon_{ij}$ with $\mu_i - \mu = \alpha_i$ results in

$$x_{ij} = \mu + \alpha_i + \varepsilon_{ij} \quad \text{for} \quad j = 1, 2, \ldots, n_i \text{ and } i = 1, 2, \ldots, k$$

This formally defines a model for one-way (factor) analysis of variance, where

$x_{ij} = j$th observation at ith level (in ith sample),

μ = overall factor mean,

α_i = mean effect of ith level of factor relative to μ, where $\displaystyle\sum_{i=1}^{k} \alpha_i = 0$,

ε_{ij} = inherent random variation $\sim N(0, \sigma^2)$.

Note that as a result,

$$\mathbf{H_0}: \mu_i = \mu \text{ (all } i) \quad \Rightarrow \quad \mathbf{H_0}: \alpha_i = 0 \text{ (all } i)$$

Estimates of μ, α_i and ε_{ij} can be calculated from observed measurements. When all the samples are of equal sizes, these are

$$\frac{T}{n}, \quad \left(\frac{T_i}{n_i} - \frac{T}{n}\right) \quad \text{and} \quad \left(x_{ij} - \frac{T_i}{n_i}\right), \text{ respectively.}$$

When all the samples are not of equal size $\dfrac{T}{n}$ is replaced by

$\dfrac{1}{k}\displaystyle\sum \dfrac{T_i}{n_i}$. This will not be

required in an examination.

Thus for the example on 60 W electric light bulbs for which the observed measurements (x_{ij}) were

| | Brand | |
1	2	3
16	18	26
15	22	31
13	20	24
21	16	30
15	24	24

with $n = 15$, $n_1 = n_2 = n_3 = 5$, $T = 315$, $T_1 = 80$, $T_2 = 100$ and $T_3 = 135$.

Hence, estimates of μ, α_1, α_2 and α_3 are 21, -5, -1 and $+6$, respectively.

Estimates of the ε_{ij} are best tabulated as shown below.

| | Brand (estimates of ε_{ij}) | |
1	2	3
0	-2	-1
-1	2	4
-3	0	-3
5	-4	3
-1	4	-3

Notice that, relative to the original measurements, these values representing inherent random variation are quite small.

EXERCISE 3A

Assume a significance level of 5% if a level has not been stated in the question. Use interpolation for critical values where appropriate.

1 Four treatments for fever blisters, including a placebo, A, were randomly assigned to 20 patients. The data below show, for each treatment, the numbers of days from initial appearance of the blisters until healing is complete.

Treatment	Number of days				
A	5	8	7	7	8
B	4	6	6	3	5
C	6	4	4	5	4
D	7	4	6	6	5

Test the hypothesis, at the 5% significance level, that there is no difference between the four treatments with respect to mean time of healing.

2 The following data give the lifetimes, in hours, of three types of battery.

	Type	
I	**II**	**III**
50.1	51.0	49.5
49.9	50.8	50.1
49.8	50.9	50.2
49.7	50.9	49.8
50.0	50.6	49.3

Analyse these data for a difference between mean lifetimes. (Use a 5% significance level.)

3 Three different brands of magnetron tubes (the key component in microwave ovens) were subjected to stress testing. The number of hours each operated before needing repair was recorded.

	Brand	
A	**B**	**C**
36	49	71
48	33	31
5	60	140
67	2	59
53	55	424

Although these times may not represent lifetimes, they do indicate how well the tubes can withstand stress.

Use a one-way analysis of variance procedure to test the hypothesis that the mean lifetime under stress is the same for the three brands.

What assumptions are necessary for the validity of this test? Is there reason to doubt these assumptions for the given data?

4 Three special ovens in a metal working shop are used to heat metal specimens. All the ovens are supposed to operate at the same temperature. It is known that the temperature of an oven varies, and it is suspected that there are significant mean temperature differences between ovens. The table below shows the temperatures, in degrees centigrade, of each of the three ovens on a random sample of heatings.

Oven	Temperature (°C)				
1	494	497	481	496	487
2	489	494	479	478	475
3	489	483	487	472	474

Stating any necessary assumptions, test for a difference between mean oven temperatures.

Estimate the values of μ (1 value), α_i (3 values) and ε_{ij} (15 values) for the model (temperature)$_{ij} = x_{ij} = \hat{\mu} + \alpha_i + \varepsilon_{ij}$. Comment on what they reveal.

5 Eastside Health Authority has a policy whereby any patient admitted to a hospital with a suspected coronary heart attack is automatically placed in the intensive care unit. The table below gives the number of hours spent in intensive care by such patients at five hospitals in the area.

		Hospital		
A	**B**	**C**	**D**	**E**
30	42	65	67	70
25	57	46	58	63
12	47	55	81	80
23	30	27		
16				

Use a one-way analysis of variance to test, at the 1% level of significance, for differences between hospitals. [A]

6 An experiment was conducted to study the effects of various diets on pigs. A total of 24 similar pigs were selected and randomly allocated to one of the five groups such that the control group, which was fed a normal diet, had eight pigs and each of the other groups, to which the new diets were given, had four pigs each. After a fixed time the gains in mass, in kilograms, of the pigs were measured. Unfortunately by this time two pigs had died, one which was on diet A and one which was on diet C. The gains in mass of the remaining pigs are recorded below.

Diets	**Gain in mass (kg)**			
Normal	23.1	9.8	15.5	22.6
	14.6	11.2	15.7	10.5
A	21.9	13.2	19.7	
B	16.5	22.8	18.3	31.0
C	30.9	21.9	29.8	
D	21.0	25.4	21.5	21.2

Use a one-way analysis of variance to test, at the 5% significance level, for a difference between diets.

What further information would you require about the dead pigs and how might this affect the conclusions of your analysis? [A]

3.4 Two-way (factor) ANOVA

This is an extension of the one factor situation to take account of a second factor. The levels of this second factor are often determined by groupings of subjects or units used in the investigation. As such it is often called a **blocking factor** because it places subjects or units into homogeneous groups called **blocks**. The design itself is then called a **randomised block design**.

Worked example 3.4

A computer manufacturer wishes to compare the speed of four of the firm's compilers. The manufacturer can use one of two experimental designs.

(a) Use 20 similar programs, randomly allocating five programs to each compiler.

(b) Use four copies of any five programs, allocating one copy of each program to each compiler.

Which would you recommend, and why?

Solution

In **(a)**, although the 20 programs are similar, any differences between them may affect the compilation times and hence perhaps any conclusions. Thus in the 'worst scenario', the five programs allocated to what is really the fastest compiler could be the five requiring the longest compilation times, resulting in the compiler appearing to be the slowest! If used, the results would require a one factor analysis of variance; the factor being compiler at 4 levels.

See also section 1.5.

In **(b)**, since all five programs are run on each compiler, differences between programs should not affect the results. Indeed it may be advantageous to use five programs that differ markedly so that comparisons of compilation times are more general. For this design, there are two factors; compiler (4 levels) and program (5 levels). The factor of principal interest is compiler, whereas the other factor, program, may be considered as a blocking factor as it creates five blocks each containing four copies of the same program.

Thus **(b)** is the better designed investigation.

The actual compilation times, in milliseconds, for this two factor (randomised block) design are shown in the following table.

Program	Compiler			
	1	**2**	**3**	**4**
A	29.21	28.25	28.20	28.62
B	26.18	26.02	26.22	25.56
C	30.91	30.18	30.52	30.09
D	25.14	25.26	25.20	25.02
E	26.16	25.14	25.26	25.46

Assumptions and interaction

The three assumptions for a two-way analysis of variance when there is only one observed measurement at each combination of levels of the two factors are as follows.

A   The population at each factor level combination is (approximately) normally distributed.

B   These normal populations have a common variance, σ^2.

C   The effect of one factor is the same at all levels of the other factor.

Hence, from assumptions **A** and **B**, when one factor is at level i and the other is at level j, the population has a distribution which is $N(\mu_{ij}, \sigma^2)$.

Assumption **C** is equivalent to stating that there is **no interaction** between the two factors.

Interaction exists when the effect of one factor depends upon the level of the other factor. For example, consider the effects of the two factors:

       sugar (levels none and 2 teaspoons),

and   stirring (levels none and 1 minute),

on the sweetness of a cup of tea.

Stirring has no effect on sweetness if sugar is not added but certainly does have an effect if sugar is added. Similarly, adding sugar has little effect on sweetness unless the tea is stirred.

Hence factors sugar and stirring are said to interact.

Interaction can only be assessed if more than one measurement is taken at each combination of the factor levels. Since such situations are beyond the scope of this text, it will always be assumed that interaction between the two factors does not exist.

Thus, for example, since it would be most unusual to find one compiler particularly suited to one program, the assumption of no interaction between compilers and programs appears reasonable.

Notation and computational formulae

As illustrated earlier, the data for a two-way ANOVA can be displayed in a two-way table. It is convenient, in general, to label the factors as a **row factor** and a **column factor**.

Notation, similar to that for the one factor case, is then as follows:

Number of levels of row factor	$= m$
Number of levels of column factor	$= n$
Total number of observations	$= mn$
Observation in (ij)th cell of table	$= x_{ij}$
(ith level of row factor and	$i = 1, 2, \ldots, m$
jth level of column factor)	$j = 1, 2, \ldots, n$

$$\text{Sum of } n \text{ observations in } i\text{th row} = R_i = \sum_j x_{ij}$$

$$\text{Sum of } m \text{ observations in } j\text{th column} = C_j = \sum_i x_{ij}$$

$$\text{Sum of all } mn \text{ observations} = T = \sum_i \sum_j x_{ij} = \sum_i R_i = \sum_j C_j$$

These lead to the following computational formulae which again are similar to those for one-way ANOVA except that there is an additional sum of squares, etc., for the second factor.

Total sum of squares, $$SS_T = \sum_i \sum_j x_{ij}^2 - \frac{T^2}{mn}$$

Between rows sum of squares, $$SS_R = \sum_i \frac{R_i^2}{n} - \frac{T^2}{mn}$$

Between columns sum of squares, $$SS_C = \sum_j \frac{C_j^2}{m} - \frac{T^2}{mn}$$

Error (residual) sum of squares, $$SS_E = SS_T - SS_R - SS_C$$

The formulae for SS_T, SS_R and SS_C are given in the AQA booklet of formulae and tables.

ANOVA table and hypothesis tests

A two-way analysis of variance table takes the following form:

Source of variation	Sum of squares	Degrees of freedom	Mean square	F-ratio
Between rows	SS_R	$m-1$	MS_R	$\frac{MS_R}{MS_E}$
Between columns	SS_C	$n-1$	MS_C	$\frac{MS_C}{MS_E}$
Error (residual)	SS_E	$(m-1)(n-1)$	MS_E	
Total	SS_T	$mn-1$		

The error sum of squares and degrees of freedom (but **not** mean square) may be found by subtracting 'Between rows' and 'Between columns' from the 'Total'.

Note that for the degrees of freedom,

$$(m-1)+(n-1)+(m-1)(n-1)=(mn-1).$$

Using the F-ratios, tests for significant row effects and for significant column effects can be undertaken.

H$_0$: no effect due to row factor

H$_1$: an effect due to row factor

Test statistic, $$F_R = \frac{MS_R}{MS_E}$$

Critical region, $$F_R > F_{[(m-1),\,(m-1)(n-1)]}$$

H$_0$: no effect due to column factor

H$_1$: an effect due to column factor

Test statistic, $$F_C - \frac{MS_C}{MS_E}$$

Critical region, $$F_C > F_{[(n-1),\,(m-1)(n-1)]}$$

Worked example 3.5

Returning to the compilation times, in milliseconds, for each of five programs, run on four compilers.

Test, at the 1% significance level, the hypothesis that there is no difference between the performance of the four compilers.

Has the use of programs as a blocking factor proved worthwhile? Explain.

The data, given earlier, are reproduced below.

Program	Compiler 1	2	3	4
A	29.21	28.25	28.20	28.62
B	26.18	26.02	26.22	25.56
C	30.91	30.18	30.52	30.09
D	25.14	25.26	25.20	25.02
E	26.16	25.14	25.26	25.46

Solution

To ease computations, these data have been transformed (coded) by

$$x = 100 \times (\text{time} - 25)$$

to give the following table of values and totals.

Program	Compiler 1	2	3	4	Row total (R_i)
A	421	325	320	362	1428
B	118	102	122	56	398
C	591	518	552	509	2170
D	14	26	20	2	62
E	116	14	26	46	202
Column total (C_j)	1260	985	1040	975	$T = 4260$

$$\Sigma\Sigma x_{ij}^2 = 1\,757\,768$$

$$m = 5 \quad n = 4$$

The sums of squares are now calculated as follows:

(Rows = Programs,   Columns = Compilers)

$$SS_T = 1\,757\,768 - \frac{4260^2}{20} = 850\,388$$

$$SS_R = \frac{1}{4}\left(1428^2 + 398^2 + 2170^2 + 62^2 + 202^2\right) - \frac{4260^2}{20} = 830\,404$$

$$SS_C = \frac{1}{5}\left(1260^2 + 985^2 + 1040^2 + 975^2\right) - \frac{4260^2}{20} = 10\,630$$

$$SS_E = 850\,388 - 830\,404 - 10\,630 = 9354$$

The ANOVA table is:

Source of variation	Sum of squares	Degrees of freedom	Mean square	F-ratio
Between programs	830 404	4	207 601.0	266.33
Between compilers	10 630	3	3543.3	4.55
Error (residual)	9354	12	779.5	
Total	850 388	19		

H_0: no effect on compilation times due to compilers

H_1: an effect on compilation times due to compilers

Significance level, $\alpha = 0.01$

Degrees of freedom, $v_1 = n - 1 = 3$

$$\text{and} \quad v_2 = (m - 1)(n - 1) = 4 \times 3 = 12$$

Critical region, $F > 5.953$

Test statistic $\quad F_C = 4.55$

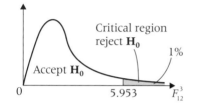

This value does **not** lie in the critical region. Thus there is no evidence, at the 1% significance level, to suggest a difference in compilation times between the four compilers.

The use of programs as a blocking factor has been very worthwhile. From the ANOVA table

(a) SS_R accounts for $\dfrac{830\,404}{850\,388} \times 100 = 97.65\%$ of the total variation in the observations, much of which would have been included in SS_E had not programs been used as a blocking variable,

(b) $F_R = 266.33$ which indicates significance at any level!

Model

With x_{ij} denoting the one observation in the ith row and jth column, (ij)th cell, of the table, then

$$x_{ij} \sim N\left(\mu_{ij}, \sigma^2\right) \quad \text{for} \quad i = 1, 2, \ldots, m \text{ and } j = 1, 2, \ldots, n$$

or $\quad x_{ij} - \mu_{ij} = \varepsilon_{ij} \sim N\left(0, \sigma^2\right)$.

However, it is assumed that the two factors do not interact but simply have an additive effect, so that

$$\mu_{ij} = \mu + \alpha_i + \beta_j \quad \text{with} \quad \sum_i \alpha_i = \sum_j \beta_j = 0, \text{ where}$$

μ = overall mean

α_i = mean effect of ith level of row factor relative to μ

β_j = mean effect of jth level of column factor relative to μ

ε_{ij} = inherent random variation.

As a result, when testing for an effect due to rows, the hypotheses may be written as

$$\mathbf{H_0}: \alpha_i = 0 \quad \text{(all } i\text{)}$$
$$\mathbf{H_1}: \alpha_i \neq 0 \quad \text{(some } i\text{)}$$

Similarly, when testing for an effect due to columns, the hypotheses may be written as

$$\mathbf{H_0}: \beta_j = 0 \quad \text{(all } j\text{)}$$
$$\mathbf{H_1}: \beta_j \neq 0 \quad \text{(some } j\text{)}$$

If required, estimates of μ, α_i, β_j and ε_{ij} can be calculated from the observed measurements by

$$\frac{T}{mn}, \quad \left(\frac{R_i}{n} - \frac{T}{mn}\right), \quad \left(\frac{C_j}{m} - \frac{T}{mn}\right), \quad \left(x_{ij} - \frac{R_i}{n} - \frac{C_j}{m} + \frac{T}{mn}\right),$$

respectively.

EXERCISE 3B

Assume a significance level of 5% if a level has not been stated in the question. Use interpolation for critical values where appropriate.

1 Prior to submitting a quotation for a construction project, companies prepare a detailed analysis of the estimated labour and materials costs required to complete the project. A company which employs three project cost assessors, wished to compare the mean values of these assessors' cost estimates. This was done by requiring each assessor to estimate independently the costs of the same four construction projects. These costs, in £0000s, are shown below.

	Assessor		
Project	A	B	C
1	46	49	44
2	62	63	59
3	50	54	54
4	66	68	63

Perform a two-way analysis of variance on these data to test the hypothesis, at the 5% significance level, that there is no difference between the assessors' mean cost estimates.

2 In an experiment to investigate the warping of copper plates, the two factors studied were the temperature and the copper content of the plates. The response variable was a measure of the amount of warping. The resultant data are as follows:

Temp (°C)	Copper content (%)			
	40	**60**	**80**	**100**
50	17	19	23	29
75	12	15	18	27
100	14	19	22	30
125	17	20	22	30

Stating all necessary assumptions, analyse for significant effects.

3 In a study to compare the body sizes of silkworms, three genotypes were of interest: heterozygous (HET), homozygous (HOM) and wild (WLD). The length, in millimetres, of a separately reared cocoon of each genotype was measured at each of five randomly chosen sites with the following results:

Genotype	Site				
	1	**2**	**3**	**4**	**5**
HOM	29.87	28.24	32.27	31.21	29.85
HET	32.51	30.82	34.46	34.01	32.99
WLD	35.76	34.14	36.54	34.95	36.11

Identify the blocking factor. Has it proved useful? Explain.

Investigate, at the 1% significance level, for a difference in mean lengths between the three genotypes.

4 Four different washing solutions were being compared to study their effectiveness in retarding bacteria growth in milk containers. The study was undertaken in a laboratory, and only four trials could be run on any one day. As days could represent a potential source of variability, the experimenter decided to use days as a blocking factor. Observations were made for five days with the following (coded) results.

Solution	Day				
	1	**2**	**3**	**4**	**5**
A	12	21	17	38	29
B	15	23	16	43	35
C	6	11	7	32	28
D	18	27	23	43	35

Stating any necessary assumptions, analyse for significant differences between solutions.

Was the experimenter wise to use days as a blocking factor? Justify your answer.

5 The marathon of the South West took place in Bristol in April 1982. The following table gives the times taken to complete the course, in hours, by twelve competitors, together with their type of occupation and training method used.

Training method	Type of occupation		
	Office worker	Manual worker	Professional sportsperson
A	5.7	2.9	3.6
B	4.5	4.8	2.4
C	3.9	3.3	2.6
D	6.1	5.1	2.7

Carry out an analysis of variance and investigate, at the 5% level of significance, for differences between types of occupation and between training methods.

The age and gender of each of the above competitors are subsequently made available to you. Is this information likely to affect your conclusions? Explain your answer.

6 Information about the current state of a complex industrial process is displayed on a control panel which is monitored by a technician. In order to find the best display for the instruments on the control panel, three different arrangements were tested by simulating an emergency and observing the reaction times of five different technicians. The results, in seconds, are given below.

Arrangement	Technician				
	P	**Q**	**R**	**S**	**T**
A	2.4	3.3	1.9	3.6	2.7
B	3.7	3.2	2.7	3.9	4.4
C	4.2	4.6	3.9	3.8	4.5

Carry out an analysis of variance and investigate for differences between technicians and between arrangements at the 5% significance level.

Currently arrangement C is used and it is suggested that this be replaced by arrangement A. Comment, briefly, on this suggestion and on what further information you would find useful before coming to a definite decision.

3.5 Latin square designs

Construction

Consider a randomised block design in which

number of blocks = number of treatments = n (say).

This is equivalent to a two-way ANOVA in which

number of rows = number of columns = n,

so the total number of observations is n^2.

In such situations, it is possible to introduce a second blocking factor (with n levels) without increasing the number of observations from n^2 to n^3.

Consider the following example.

In a comparison of three wood priming paints, A, B and C, atmospheric temperature was considered, not unreasonably, to be a key blocking factor. Hence the following (simple) randomised block design.

	Temperature	
15°C	**20°C**	**25°C**
A	C	B
B	B	C
C	A	A

(Each paint appears once only at each temperature.)

However, it was then suggested that wood surface could also be a source of (unwanted) variation and so could be a second blocking factor with three levels, rough (R), medium (M), smooth (S). Rather than extend the design to $3^3 = 27$ observations, this second blocking factor can be introduced as follows in $3^2 = 9$ observations.

	Temperature		
Wood surface	**15°C**	**20°C**	**25°C**
R	A	B	C
M	B	C	A
S	C	A	B

(Each paint now appears once only at each temperature **and** once only on each wood surface.)

This carefully planned design enables an assessment of paint differences whilst at the same time removing two potential sources of variation; temperature and wood surface. We shall see that it is also possible to assess the significance of these two blocking factors, and that, in some situations, they are actual factors of interest.

The design above is an example of a 3×3 Latin square design.

Below are examples of 4×4 and 5×5 Latin squares.

	Column			
Row	**1**	**2**	**3**	**4**
1	A	C	D	B
2	B	D	A	C
3	C	A	B	D
4	D	B	C	A

	Column				
Row	**1**	**2**	**3**	**4**	**5**
1	D	A	B	C	E
2	E	B	C	D	A
3	A	C	D	E	B
4	B	D	E	A	C
5	C	E	A	B	D

Assumptions

The Latin square design assumptions are simply an extension of those for the two-way ANOVA.

A The population at each factor level combination is (approximately) normally distributed.

B These normal populations have a common variance, σ^2.

C There is no interaction between the three factors.

Notation and computational formulae

Again this follows from the two-way ANOVA.

Number of levels of row factor	$= n$
Number of levels of column factor	$= n$
Number of levels of **letter** factor	$= n$
Total number of observations	$= n^2$ (**not** n^3)
Observation for row i, column j, letter k	$= x_{ij(k)}$
with i, j, k	$= 1, 2, \ldots, n.$

Sum of observations in row i	$= R_i$
Sum of observations in column j	$= C_j$
Sum of observations for letter k	$= L_k$
Sum of all n^2 observations	$= T$

$$\left(T = \sum_i R_i = \sum_j C_j = \sum_k L_k\right)$$

These lead to the following computational formulae:

Total sum of squares,

$$SS_T = \sum_i \sum_j x_{ij(k)}^2 - \frac{T^2}{n^2}$$

Between rows sum of squares,

$$SS_R = \sum_i \frac{R_i^2}{n} - \frac{T^2}{n^2}$$

Between column sum of squares,

$$SS_C = \sum_j \frac{C_j^2}{n} - \frac{T^2}{n^2}$$

Between letters sum of squares,

$$SS_L = \sum_k \frac{L_k^2}{n} - \frac{T^2}{n^2}$$

Error (residual) sum of squares,

$$SS_E = SS_T - SS_R - SS_C - SS_L$$

Note that these formulae are **not** provided in the AQA booklet of formulae and tables. However, they are a simple extension to those for a two-way ANOVA which are provided. ($m = n$, plus formula for SS_L and additional subtraction of SS_L in finding SS_E.)

ANOVA table and hypothesis tests

The ANOVA table for a Latin square design takes the following form:

Source of variation	Sum of squares	Degrees of freedom	Mean square	F-ratio
Between rows	SS_R	$n - 1$	MS_R	$\dfrac{MS_R}{MS_E}$
Between columns	SS_C	$n - 1$	MS_C	$\dfrac{MS_C}{MS_E}$
Between letters	SS_L	$n - 1$	MS_L	$\dfrac{MS_L}{MS_E}$
Error (residual)	SS_E	$(n - 1)(n - 2)$	MS_E	
Total	SS_T	$n^2 - 1$		

Note that for the degrees of freedom,

$$3(n - 1) + (n - 1)(n - 2) = n^2 - 1.$$

Using the above F-ratios, tests for significant row effects, column effects and letter effects can be undertaken by a comparison of each ratio with

$$F_{[(n-1),\,(n-1)(n-2)]}.$$

Remember that for all F-tests in analysis of variance, they are one-tailed with MS_E in the denominator.

At this point it is worthwhile consolidating the above ideas on analysis of a Latin square using a simple example.

Worked example 3.6

A 4×4 Latin square design.

Row	Column 1	Column 2	Column 3	Column 4	R_i
1	A 3	B 2	C 3	D 2	10
2	B 0	A 4	D 1	C 1	6
3	C 6	D 4	A 8	B 4	22
4	D 1	C 2	B 2	A 5	10
C_j	10	12	14	12	$T = 48$

$$L_1(A) = 20 \quad L_2(B) = 8 \quad L_3(C) = 12 \quad L_4(D) = 8$$

$$\sum_i \sum_j x_{ij(k)}^2 = 210$$

$$SS_T = 210 - \frac{48^2}{4^2} = 66$$

$$SS_R = \frac{1}{4}(10^2 + 6^2 + 22^2 + 10^2) - \frac{48^2}{4^2} = 36$$

$$SS_C = \frac{1}{4}(10^2 + 12^2 + 14^2 + 12^2) - \frac{48^2}{4^2} = 2$$

$$SS_L = \frac{1}{4}(20^2 + 8^2 + 12^2 + 8^2) - \frac{48^2}{4^2} = 24$$

$$SS_E = 66 - 36 - 2 - 24 = 4$$

The ANOVA table is:

Source of variation	Sum of squares	Degrees of freedom	Mean square	F-ratio
Between rows	36	3	12	18
Between columns	2	3	$\frac{2}{3}$	1
Between letters	24	3	8	12
Error (residual)	4	6	$\frac{2}{3}$	
Total	66	15		

For tests at the 5% level of significance,

$$F_{[3,6]}(0.95) = 4.757$$

Thus, there is:

- evidence of an effect due to row factor,
- no evidence of an effect due to column factor,
- evidence of an effect due to letter factor.

Model

With $x_{ij(k)}$ denoting the one observation in the ith row and jth column, with letter k, then

$$x_{ij(k)} \sim N\left(\mu_{ij(k)}, \sigma^2\right) \quad \text{for} \quad i, j, k = 1, 2, \ldots, n$$

or $\quad x_{ij(k)} - \mu_{ij(k)} = \varepsilon_{ij(k)} \sim N\left(0, \sigma^2\right).$

Due to the assumption of no interaction between the three factors,

$$\mu_{ij(k)} = \mu + \alpha_i + \beta_j + \gamma_k$$

with $\quad \sum_i \alpha_i = \sum_j \beta_j = \sum_k \gamma_k = 0,$ where

μ = overall mean

α_i = mean effect of ith level of row factor relative to μ

β_j = mean effect of jth level of column factor relative to μ

γ_k = mean effect of kth level of letter factor relative to μ

$\varepsilon_{ij(k)}$ = inherent random variation.

Thus, for example,

H$_0$: no effect due to letter factor $\Rightarrow \gamma_k = 0$ (all k)

H$_1$: an effect due to letter factor $\Rightarrow \gamma_k \neq 0$ (some k)

Finally, if required, estimates of the parameters in the model can be found using the following formulae:

$$\hat{\mu} = \frac{T}{n^2}$$

$$\hat{\alpha}_i = \frac{R_i}{n} - \frac{T}{n^2}$$

$$\hat{\beta}_j = \frac{C_j}{n} - \frac{T}{n^2}$$

$$\hat{\gamma}_k = \frac{L_k}{n} - \frac{T}{n^2}$$

$$\hat{\varepsilon}_{ij(k)} = x_{ij(k)} - \frac{R_i}{n} - \frac{C_j}{n} - \frac{L_k}{n} + \frac{2T}{n^2}$$

Worked example 3.7

In a comparison of three brands of petrol, A, B and C, three makes of car, 1, 2 and 3, were used. Each car was driven at a steady speed, either $50\,\mathrm{km\,h^{-1}}$, $75\,\mathrm{km\,h^{-1}}$ or $100\,\mathrm{km\,h^{-1}}$, around an oval track. The cars were each filled with 30 litres of petrol and driven until this was used up. The distances travelled were recorded to the nearest 100 m as follows:

Car	Speed	Fuel	Distance
1	50	B	347.8
1	75	C	331.4
1	100	A	275.8
2	50	A	365.4
2	75	B	339.8
2	100	C	298.9
3	50	C	318.9
3	75	A	302.2
3	100	B	271.8

Investigate for a difference between the three brands of petrol.

Solution

First rearrange the data into a Latin square, using rows for cars, columns for speeds and letters for fuel brands.

Car	Speed 50		Speed 75		Speed 100		R_i
1	B	347.8	C	331.4	A	275.8	955.0
2	A	365.4	B	339.8	C	298.9	1004.1
3	C	318.9	A	302.2	B	271.8	892.9
C_j	1032.1		973.4		846.5		$T = 2852.0$

$$L_1(A) = 943.4 \quad L_2(B) = 959.4 \quad L_3(C) = 949.2$$

$$\sum_i \sum_j x_{ij(k)}^2 = 912\,076.14$$

Hence, using the computational formulae,

$$SS_T = 8309.03$$
$$SS_R = 2070.30 \quad \text{(cars)}$$
$$SS_C = 5999.63 \quad \text{(speeds)}$$
$$SS_L = 43.74 \quad \text{(brands)}$$
$$SS_E = 195.36$$

Source of variation	Sum of squares	Degrees of freedom	Mean square	F-ratio
Between cars	2070.30	2	1035.15	10.60
Between speeds	5999.63	2	2999.81	30.71
Between brands	43.74	2	21.87	0.22
Residual	195.36	2	97.68	
Total	8309.03	8		

$$F_{[2,2]}(0.95) = 19.00$$

Thus, at the 5% level of significance, there is no evidence that fuel consumption is dependent on the brand of petrol.

Notes

- The (blocking) factor 'speed' has proved to be significant, at the 5% level.

- Whilst the (blocking) factor 'car' is not significant at the 5% level, it, nevertheless, has markedly reduced the residual sum of squares.

- The large critical value is due, in part, to only two residual degrees of freedom. For this reason, Latin squares usually need to be at least of size 4×4 unless a prior estimate of the residual mean square is available.

EXERCISE 3C

Assume a significance level of 5% if a level has not been stated in the question. Use interpolation for critical values where appropriate.

1 (a) Construct a 6×6 Latin square.

(b) State the residual degrees of freedom in a
  (i) 5×5 Latin square,
  (ii) 6×6 Latin square,
  (iii) 7×7 Latin square.

2 Complete the following analysis of variance table resulting from the analysis of a 4×4 Latin square design.

Source of variation	Sum of squares	Degrees of freedom	Mean square	F-ratio
Between rows	360			
Between columns	630			
Between letters	150			
Residual				
Total	1260			

Hence test, at the 1% level, for significant effects.

3 A steel company wishes to investigate the influence of the type of paint and of the drying time on the surface finish of different qualities of their rolled steel sections.

Three drying times, 20, 30 and 40 minutes, and three types of paint, A, B and C, are chosen.

The company conducts the experiment by measuring the degree of abrasion on a sample of each of three qualities, I, II and III, of steel section using each combination of drying time and paint with the following (coded) results.

Paint	Drying time					
	20		30		40	
A	III	6	I	5	II	10
B	I	7	II	9	III	11
C	II	11	III	13	I	12

(a) Assuming no interaction between the three factors, and using the 5% level of significance, analyse the data for significant effects.

(b) State the other assumptions necessary for analysing such information using analysis of variance.

4 In an investigation of fluid flow through four different types of nozzle, A, B, C and D, a Latin square design was used involving four operators and four temperatures.

The coded results are as follows:

Temperature (°C)	Operator							
	1		2		3		4	
5	B	17	A	18	C	16	D	19
10	C	20	D	21	A	20	B	18
15	A	26	B	22	D	25	C	20
20	D	31	C	26	B	24	A	23

(a) Investigate, at the 1% level of significance, for a difference between the four nozzle types.

(b) Assess the effectiveness of each of the two blocking factors, operator and temperature.

5 The abrasion resistance of rubber can be changed by treating the rubber with a chlorinating agent.

In order to study the effects of five such agents, A, B, C, D and E, five different types of rubber 1, 2, 3, 4 and 5, were made available, as were five machines, a, b, c, d and e, on which to perform the tests.

The design and results, abrasion loss, are shown below.

Rubber	Machine									
	a		b		c		d		e	
1	D	20.8	A	20.1	B	20.2	E	21.0	C	21.3
2	B	19.2	C	19.6	E	16.7	A	18.8	D	18.4
3	E	17.1	D	16.5	A	15.3	C	19.8	B	16.6
4	A	16.4	B	15.8	C	15.8	D	15.2	E	18.8
5	C	20.8	E	18.1	D	17.1	B	19.5	A	16.2

(a) Determine, at the 5% level, whether there are significant differences in abrasion resistance due to the five chlorinating agents.

(b) Assess whether rubber and machine have been suitable blocking factors.

MIXED EXERCISE

Assume a significance level of 5% if a level has not been stated in the question. Use interpolation for critical values where appropriate.

1 After completing a six month typing course with the Speedyfingers Institute, four people, A, B, C and D, had their typing speed measured, in words per minute, on each of five kinds of work. The results are given in the table below.

People	Legal	Business	Numeric	Prose I	Prose II
A	40	47	42	45	53
B	34	32	14	36	44
C	33	40	31	48	44
D	24	26	25	27	45

Carry out an analysis of variance and investigate, at the 5% level of significance, for differences between the people and between kinds of work.

Subsequently it transpired that A and C used electric typewriters, whilst B and D used manual typewriters. Does this information affect your conclusions and why?   [A]

2 A batch of bricks was randomly divided into three parts and each part was stored by a different method. After one week the percentage water content of a number of bricks stored by each method was measured.

Method of storage	% water content					
1	7.4	8.5	7.1	6.2	7.8	
2	5.5	7.1	5.6			
3	4.8	5.1	6.2	4.9	6.1	7.1

Making any necessary assumptions, use a one-way analysis of variance to investigate, at the 5% significance level, for differences between methods of storage.

If low water content is desirable, state which method of storage you would recommend, and calculate a 95% confidence interval for its mean percentage water content after one week. [You may assume that the estimated variance of a sample mean is given by (within samples mean square) ÷ (sample size).] [A]

3 A textile factory produces a silicone-proofed nylon cloth for making into rainwear. The chief chemist thought that a silicone solution of about 12% strength would yield a cloth with a maximum waterproofing index. It was also suspected that there might be some batch to batch variation because of slight differences in the cloth.

To test this, five different strengths of solution were tested on each of three different batches of cloth. The following values of the waterproofing index were obtained.

| | Strength of silicone solution (%) | | | | |
Cloth	6	9	12	15	18
A	20.8	20.6	22.0	22.6	20.9
B	19.4	21.2	21.8	23.9	22.4
C	19.9	21.1	22.7	22.7	22.1

[You may assume that the total sum of squares of the observations $(\Sigma x^2) = 7022.79$.]

Carry out an analysis of variance to investigate, at the 5% significance level, for differences between strengths of silicone solution and between cloths.

Comment on the chief chemist's original beliefs in the light of these results and suggest what actions the chief chemist might take. [A]

4 A catering firm wishes to buy a meat tenderiser, but was concerned with the effect on the weight loss of meat during cooking. The following results were obtained for the weight loss of steaks of the same pre-cooked weight when three different tenderisers were used.

Tenderiser	Weight loss (g)				
A	36	28	42	58	
B	17	59	33		
C	36	74	29	55	55

(a) Carry out a one-way analysis of variance and test, at the 5% significance level, the hypothesis that there is no difference in weight loss between tenderisers.

Time and temperature are important factors in the weight loss during cooking. As these had not been taken account of during the first trial, a further set of results was obtained where all the steaks were cooked at the same temperature. Cooking times of 20, 25 and 30 minutes were used. An analysis of these data led to the following table:

Source of variation	Sum of squares	Degrees of freedom
Between tenderisers	321	2
Between times	697	2
Error	85	4
Total	1103	8

(b) Test at the 5% significance level for differences between tenderisers and between times.

(c) Contrast the results obtained in **(a)** and **(b)** and comment on why the two sets of data can lead to different conclusions. [A]

5 In a 6 × 6 Latin square experimental design the sums of squares corresponding to the various sources of variation are shown in the table below:

Source of variation	Sum of squares	Degrees of freedom	Mean square	F-ratio
Between rows	55.0			
Between columns	78.5			
Between letters	96.5			
Residual				
Total	310.0			

(a) Copy and complete the table.

(b) Hence test, at the 5% level of significance, the hypothesis of:

    (i) no row effects,

    (ii) no column effects,

    (iii) no letter effects.

6 In a comparison of the drying times, in hours, of five different paints, each paint was applied to six different surfaces and allowed to dry under identical conditions. An analysis of the results provided the following information:

Source	Sum of squares
Between paints	4.698
Between surfaces	5.691
Error	
Total about the mean	11.023

(a) Assuming all drying times to be normally distributed with a common variance, investigate, at the 1% level of significance, for a difference between the mean drying times of the five paints.

(b) Suggest a possible next step in the analysis of the original data. [A]

7 A commuter in a large city can travel to work by car, bicycle or bus. She times four journeys by each method with the following results, in minutes.

Car	Bicycle	Bus
27	34	26
45	38	41
33	43	35
31	42	46

(a) Carry out an analysis of variance and investigate, at the 5% significance level, whether there are differences in the mean journey times for the three methods of transport.

(b) The time of day at which she travels to work varies. Bearing in mind that this is likely to affect the time taken for the journey, suggest a better design for her experiment and explain briefly why you believe it to be better.

(c) Suggest a factor other than leaving time which is likely to affect the journey time and two factors other than journey time which might be considered when choosing a method of transport. [A]

8 As part of a project to improve the steerability of trucks, a manufacturer took three trucks of the same model and fitted them with soft, standard and hard front springs, respectively. The turning radius (the radius of the circle in which the truck could turn a full circle) was measured for each truck using a variety of drivers, speeds and surface conditions.

(a) Use the following information to test for a difference between springs at the 5% significance level.

Source	Sum of squares	Degrees of freedom
Between springs	37.9	2
Within springs	75.6	18
Total	113.5	20

A statistician suggested that the experiment would be improved if the same truck was used all the time with the front springs changed as necessary and if the speed of the truck was controlled.

The following results for turning circle, in metres, were obtained.

Speed	Soft	Springs Standard	Hard
15 km/h	42	43	39
25 km/h	48	50	48

(b) Carry out a two-way analysis of variance and investigate, at the 5% significance level, for differences between springs and between speeds. [You may assume that the total sum of squares about the mean (SS_T) is 92.]

(c) Compare the two experiments and suggest a further improvement to the design. [A]

9 A lecturer travels from home to work by car on Mondays, Wednesdays and Fridays. She leaves home at the same time each day and always travels by the same route. However, she feels that the journey nearly always takes longer on Mondays.

To investigate this feeling, she records her journey times on each of five randomly chosen Mondays, Wednesdays and Fridays, during April, May and June. Her recorded times, in minutes, are shown below.

Day	Journey time (x)	Sum (Σx)	Sum of squares (Σx^2)
Monday	28 34 29 34 30	155	4837
Wednesday	24 27 25 25 22	123	3039
Friday	25 28 27 26 21	127	3255

(a) Stating any necessary assumptions, carry out an analysis of variance to investigate for differences between mean journey times on Mondays, Wednesdays and Fridays.

(b) Calculate the sample mean journey time for Monday. Calculate also the sample mean journey time for Wednesday and Friday combined.

(c) Hence, using the value for your mean square within groups, calculated in **(a)**, as a pooled estimate of variance, investigate the lecturer's feeling that her mean journey time for Monday exceeds that for Wednesday and Friday combined. [A]

10 In a study of the diesel consumption of town buses, four buses, A, B, C and D, were tested. In the first journey of the day over a specified route, drivers a, b, c and d were used. For the second journey, the drivers were reassigned to the buses, and so on, for all four journeys as shown in the following Latin square design. (The results are in miles per gallon.)

	Bus			
Journey	A	B	C	D
1	10.4 a	10.8 b	10.0 c	10.7 d
2	10.6 b	10.2 d	10.4 a	9.8 c
3	10.1 d	10.0 c	10.9 b	9.9 a
4	9.7 c	10.0 a	10.2 d	10.7 b

(a) Complete an analysis of variance table for these data.

(b) Test, at the 5% level of significance, the hypothesis of no effect due to drivers.

(c) Estimate the four driver effects.

(d) Assess the effectiveness of the two *nuisance* factors, bus and journey.

11 A drug is produced by a fermentation process. An experiment was run to compare three similar chemical salts, X, Y and Z, in the production of the drug. Since there were only three of each of four types of fermenter A, B, C and D available for use in the production, three fermentations were started in each type of fermenter, one containing salt X, another salt Y and the third salt Z. After several days, samples were taken from each fermenter and analysed. The results, in coded form, were as follows:

	Fermenter type		
A	**B**	**C**	**D**
X 67	Y 73	X 72	Z 70
Z 68	Z 65	Y 80	X 68
Y 78	X 69	Z 73	Y 69

State the type of experimental design used.

Test, at the 5% level of significance, the hypothesis that the type of salt does not affect the fermentation.

Comment on what assumption you have made about the interaction between type of fermenter and type of salt.   [A]

12 A factory is to introduce a new product which will be assembled from a number of components. Three different designs are considered and four employees are asked to compare their speed of assembly. The trial is carried out one morning and each of the four employees assembled design A from 8.30 a.m. to 9.30 a.m., design B from 10.00 a.m. to 11.00 a.m. and design C from 11.30 a.m. to 12.30 p.m. The number of products completed by each of the employees is shown in the following table.

Design	Employee			
	1	2	3	4
A	17	4	38	8
B	21	6	52	20
C	28	9	64	22

(a) Carry out a two-way analysis of variance and investigate, at the 5% significance level, for differences between designs and between employees. [You may assume that the total sum of squares about the mean (SS_T) is 3878.9.]

(b) Comment on the fact that all employees assembled the designs in the same order. Suggest a better way of carrying out the experiment.

(c) The two-way analysis assumes that the effects of design and employee may be added. Comment on the suitability of this model for these data. [A]

13 In a hot, Third World country, milk is brought to the capital city from surrounding farms in churns carried on open lorries. The keeping quality of the milk is causing concern. The lorries could be covered to provide shade for the churns relatively cheaply or refrigerated lorries could be used but these are very expensive. The different methods were tried and the keeping quality measured. (The keeping quality is measured by testing the pH at frequent intervals and recording the time taken for the pH to fall by 0.5. A high value of this time is desirable.)

Transport method	Keeping quality (hours)					
Open	16.5	20.0	14.5	13.0		
Covered	23.5	25.0	30.0	33.5	26.0	
Refrigerated	29.0	34.0	26.0	22.5	29.5	30.5

(a) Carry out a one-way analysis of variance and investigate, at the 5% level, for differences between methods of transport.

(b) Examine the method means and comment on their implications.

(c) Different farms have different breeds of cattle and different journey times to the capital, both of which could have affected the results. How could the data have been collected and analysed to allow for these differences? [A]

14 Trace metals in water affect the water's flavour and high concentrations can pose a health risk.

The following table shows, at each of five locations on a river, the zinc concentrations, in milligrams per 100 litres, of the water on the surface, at half depth and on the river bed.

Location	Surface	Half Depth	River Bed	Totals
1	26	25	30	81
2	41	55	63	159
3	32	39	49	120
4	67	73	91	231
5	44	48	67	159
Totals	210	240	300	750

(a) Carry out a two-way analysis of variance and hence test, at the 1% level of significance, the hypothesis that the mean zinc concentration is the same at all three depths.

You may assume that the sum of squares of the 15 observations $\left(\sum_i \sum_j x_{ij}^2 \right)$ is $42\,650$.

(b) Has the use of *location* as the blocking factor proved effective? Justify your answer. [A]

15 As part of an investigation into the effect of different teaching techniques, a group of 28 students of similar IQ was used. Each student was assigned, at random, to one of four different groups so that each group contained seven students.

Each group of students was then subjected to one of four different teaching techniques. At the end of a prescribed period of time, all students remaining in the groups were given a common test and their percentage scores are shown below.

	Teaching technique			
	I	**II**	**III**	**IV**
	77	75	69	69
	80	79	75	77
Percentage scores	76	83	70	71
	71	80	73	75
	76	73	68	
		78		
Sum	380	468	355	292
Sum of squares	28\,922	36\,568	25\,239	21\,356

(a) Investigate, at the 5% level of significance, for differences between the mean scores on the four teaching techniques.

Later it transpired that techniques I and II were simply variations of one technique, A, and techniques III and IV were simply variations of another, technique B.

(b) Using the value of your mean square within groups, calculated in (a), as a pooled estimate of variance, or otherwise, investigate, at the 5% level of significance, for a difference between the mean scores on the two teaching techniques A and B. [A]

16 In a pilot study of the effect of five different formulations, A, B, C, D and E, of a propellant on an observed burning rate, each formulation is mixed from a batch of raw material that is only large enough for five formulations to be tested. Furthermore, the formulations are prepared by several operators and there may be substantial differences in their skills and experience.

Hence, in order to cater for the two *nuisance factors*, batch and operator, a Latin square design was employed as shown below. The values represent burning rate.

Batch	Operator 1	2	3	4	5
1	E 33	D 24	C 31	B 38	A 44
2	A 40	E 31	D 33	C 36	B 50
3	B 32	A 46	E 36	D 31	C 30
4	C 35	B 45	A 42	E 32	D 26
5	D 25	C 39	B 33	A 48	E 40

(a) Investigate, at the 1% level of significance for a difference between the five formulations with respect to burning rate.

(b) Assess the importance of the two *nuisance factors*.

Key point summary

1 The assumptions for the three models considered, one and two factor ANOVAs, and Latin square designs, are that: *p 37* *p 47*

  A the observations are obtained independently and randomly from populations at each factor level (combination), *p 56*

  B these populations are (approximately) normally distributed with common variance, σ^2,

  C when two or more factors are involved, there is no interaction between them.

2 One way ANOVA table *p 41*

Source of variation	Sum of squares	Degrees of freedom	Mean square	F-ratio
Between samples	SS_B*	$k-1$	$MS_B = \dfrac{SS_B}{k-1}$	$\dfrac{MS_B}{MS_W}$
Within samples	$SS_W = SS_T - SS_B$	$n-k$	$MS_W = \dfrac{SS_W}{n-k}$	
Total	SS_T*	$n-1$		

* Provided in the AQA booklet of formulae and tables.

3 Two-way ANOVA table   p 49

Source of variation	Sum of squares	Degrees of freedom	Mean square	F-ratio
Between rows	SS_R*	$m-1$	$MS_R = \dfrac{SS_R}{m-1}$	$\dfrac{MS_R}{MS_E}$
Between columns	SS_C*	$n-1$	$MS_C = \dfrac{SS_C}{n-1}$	$\dfrac{MS_C}{MS_E}$
Error	$SS_E = SS_T - SS_R - SS_C$	$(m-1)(n-1)$	$MS_E = \dfrac{SS_E}{(m-1)(n-1)}$	
Total	SS_T*	$mn-1$		

* Provided in the AQA booklet of formulae and tables.

4 Latin square ANOVA table   p 57

Source of variation	Sum of squares	Degrees of freedom	Mean square	F-ratio
Between rows	SS_R†	$n-1$	$MS_R = \dfrac{SS_R}{n-1}$	$\dfrac{MS_R}{MS_E}$
Between columns	SS_C†	$n-1$	$MS_C = \dfrac{SS_C}{n-1}$	$\dfrac{MS_C}{MS_E}$
Between letters	SS_L*	$n-1$	$MS_L = \dfrac{SS_L}{n-1}$	$\dfrac{MS_L}{MS_E}$
Error	$SS_E = SS_T - SS_R - SS_C - SS_L$	$(n-1)(n-2)$	$MS_E = \dfrac{SS_E}{(n-1)(n-2)}$	
Total	SS_T†	n^2-1		

† As in Key Point 3 above with $m = n$.

* $SS_L = \sum\limits_{k} \dfrac{L_k^2}{n} - \dfrac{T^2}{n^2}$

Test yourself	**What to review**

1 In an investigation of the effect of study method on learning, college students were assigned to one of three different methods; reading only, reading and underlining, and reading and making notes. One week after studying a particular article, the students were given a test on the article's contents with the following results:

Section 3.3

	Reading only	Reading and underlining	Reading and making notes
		Study method	
	15	16	18
	14	20	17
	18	18	23
Test score	13	17	16
	11	14	19
	14		22
	13		20
			25

Test yourself (continued)	**What to review**

(a) Carry out a one-way analysis of variance to investigate for differences between the three methods of study.

(b) State **two** key assumptions made when carrying out a one-way analysis of variance.

(c) Suggest **one** possible flaw in the design of the above investigation. Outline a better designed investigation and state the method you would then use to analyse the results.

---

2 In an investigation of five different sources of pine seed, seeds from each source were planted in each of four types of soil. The table below shows the percentage survival rates recorded as part of the investigation.

Section 3.4

Sources of seed	Type of soil				
	I	**II**	**III**	**IV**	**Total**
A	62.2	47.5	50.8	60.3	220.8
B	60.0	40.0	54.7	57.3	212.0
C	98.8	87.2	87.5	86.9	360.4
D	86.9	68.6	68.9	75.2	299.6
E	66.3	40.1	44.5	56.3	207.2
Total	374.2	283.4	306.4	336.0	1300.0

(a) Carry out a two-way analysis of variance and hence test the null hypothesis of no difference in the true mean percentage survival rates for the five seed sources.

You may assume that the sum of squares of the twenty observations $\left(\sum_i \sum_j x_{ij}^2 \right)$ is $90\,203.80$.

(b) Interpret your conclusion by making reference to the five seed source means.

(c) Has the use of *type of soil* as the blocking factor proved effective? Justify your answer.

(d) In analysing the data above an assumption of *no interaction* had to be made. Explain what this implies.

---

3 A commuter, who drives to work each weekday morning, can travel by one of five routes, A, B, C, D and E. In a comparison of travelling times, the commuter chooses day and time of departure as blocking factors in the following 5×5 Latin square, where the response is travelling time, in minutes.

Section 3.5

Test yourself (*continued*) | What to review

Day	Time	Route	Response
Mon	6.50	C	19
Tue	6.50	D	16
Wed	6.50	A	23
Thu	6.50	E	19
Fri	6.50	B	14
Mon	7.10	A	21
Tue	7.10	E	20
Wed	7.10	C	18
Thu	7.10	B	17
Fri	7.10	D	13
Mon	7.30	B	17
Tue	7.30	C	21
Wed	7.30	D	17
Thu	7.30	A	20
Fri	7.30	E	18
Mon	7.50	D	18
Tue	7.50	B	19
Wed	7.50	E	23
Thu	7.50	C	19
Fri	7.50	A	20
Mon	8.10	E	23
Tue	8.10	A	26
Wed	8.10	B	21
Thu	8.10	D	17
Fri	8.10	C	18

(a) Investigate, at the 1% level of significance, for a difference between the five routes with respect to travelling time.

(b) Assess the suitability of the two blocking factors, day and time.

Test yourself ANSWERS

1 **(a)** $SS_T = 250.55$, $SS_B = 134.55$, $F = 9.86$, cv = 3.61 difference between methods;
(b) Responses are random/independent.
Responses are distributed normally at each level.
Responses have same variance at all levels.
(c) Effect of student differences.
Use characteristic of students as blocking variable.
Two-way analysis of variance.

2 **(a)** $SS_T = 5703.8$, $SS_R = 4569.2$, $SS_C = 923.6$, $F_R = 65.0$,
cv = 3.259 difference between sources;
(b) Means: 55.2 53.0 90.1 74.9 51.8
A, B and E similar, D higher, C best;
(c) Yes, as clear differences in soil totals and/or $F_C = 17.5$;
(d) Effect of the soil is the same for all seed types.

3 **(a)** $SS_T = 201.84$, $SS_{Days} = 51.84$, $SS_{Times} = 34.24$, $SS_{Routes} = 106.64$,
$F_{Routes} = 35.1$, cv = 5.412 difference between routes;
(b) Both suitable as $F_{Days} = 17.1$ and $F_{Times} = 11.3$.

CHAPTER 4

Statistical process control

Learning objectives

After studying this chapter you should be able to:

- understand the purpose of statistical process control
- set up and use charts for means, ranges, standard deviations and proportion non-conforming
- use an appropriate method to estimate short-term standard deviation.

4.1 Introduction

Statistical process control may be used when a large number of similar items – such as chocolate bars, jars of jam or car doors – are being produced. Every process is subject to variability. It is not possible to put exactly the same amount of jam in each jar or to make every car door of exactly the same width. The variability present when a process is running well is called the short-term or inherent variability. It is usually measured by the standard deviation.

Most processes will have a target value. Too much jam in a jar will be uneconomical for the manufacturer but too little will lead to customer complaints. A car door which is too wide or too narrow will not close smoothly.

When the mean value of the items produced is equal to the target value and the variability is equal to the short-term variability the process is said to be under statistical control.

The purpose of statistical process control is to give a signal when the process mean has moved away from the target or when item-to-item variability has increased. In both cases appropriate action must be taken by a machine operator or an engineer. Statistics can only give the signal for action, deciding on and taking the appropriate action needs other skills.

> Samples are taken and tested while production is in progress so that action can be taken before too many unsatisfactory items have been produced.

> Statistical process control may be used when a large number of similar items are being produced. Its purpose is to give a signal when the process mean has moved away from the target value or when item-to-item variability has increased.

4.2 Control charts

The most common method of statistical process control is to take samples at regular intervals and to plot the sample mean on a control chart. An example is shown in the diagram below.

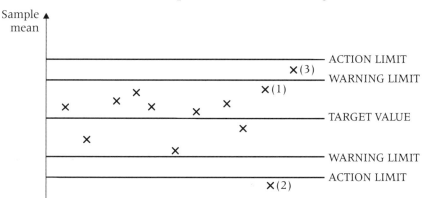

If the sample mean lies within the warning limits (as point 1) the process is assumed to be on target. If it lies outside the action limits (as point 2) the process is off target and the machine must be reset or other action taken. If the mean is between the warning and action limits (as point 3) this is a signal that the process may be off target. In this case another sample is taken immediately. If the mean of the new sample is outside the warning limits action is taken. If, however, the second sample mean is within the warning limits production is assumed to be on target.

> For control charts for means:
> - Sample mean between warning limits – no action.
> - Sample mean between warning and action limits – take another sample immediately. If new sample mean outside warning limits take action.
> - Sample mean outside action limits – take action.

4.3 Setting the limits

If the limits are too far from the target value small deviations from the target may go undetected, but if the limits are too close to the target value there will be a large number of false alarms (that is, there will be a signal for action when the process mean is on target and no action is necessary). To decide where to set the limits a measure of short-term variability is needed. This is generally found by taking a large sample when the process is believed to be performing satisfactorily. (This is known as a process capability study.)

Failure to detect a deviation from target corresponds to a Type 2 error. A false alarm corresponds to a Type 1 error.

For example, 100 chocolate bars were taken from a production line shortly after the machinery had been overhauled and reset, and at a time when there was no reason to think that anything further could be done to make the production more consistent.

The weights, in grams, of 100 chocolate bars (unwrapped) were found:

59.55 62.33 63.68 67.10 56.85 57.84 64.40 60.26 62.05 64.29
64.57 60.14 62.51 62.02 60.16 61.45 58.42 58.19 65.65 65.90
63.34 60.01 59.11 62.57 58.48 60.25 61.42 63.25 63.46 63.33
58.55 65.36 63.03 61.71 62.26 62.05 60.42 58.77 62.69 66.20
59.80 61.45 60.78 61.89 63.91 58.53 59.29 62.24 61.12 60.60
61.82 58.98 62.63 59.68 62.79 63.90 62.64 61.96 64.14 60.70
59.90 57.73 67.08 63.25 64.20 61.16 61.03 65.79 62.43 62.75
62.17 61.29 69.01 63.31 62.92 64.13 62.46 60.61 61.58 60.71
68.11 65.46 57.81 64.73 63.27 64.63 59.70 54.59 61.83 59.21
60.46 59.05 61.06 55.08 61.60 63.85 64.42 62.91 63.54 60.69

You can use your calculator to check that the standard deviation is 2.60 g. This value will be used when setting up the charts.

If the target weight for a chocolate bar is 61.5 g and production is to be controlled by weighing samples of size 5 at regular intervals then the sample means will have a standard deviation of

$$\frac{2.60}{\sqrt{5}} = 1.16 \text{ g}.$$

In practice, it has been found to be convenient to set the warning limits so that, if the mean is on target, 95% of sample means will lie within them. The action limits are set so that 99.8% of sample means lie within them when the mean is on target. Since we are dealing with sample means it is reasonable to assume they are normally distributed. Hence, in this case, the warning limits will be set at

$$61.5 \pm \left(1.96 \times \frac{2.60}{\sqrt{5}} \right)$$

$$\Rightarrow \quad 61.5 \pm 2.28$$

$$\Rightarrow \quad 59.22 \text{ and } 63.78$$

The action limits will be set at

$$61.5 \pm \left(3.09 \times \frac{2.60}{\sqrt{5}} \right)$$

$$\Rightarrow \quad 61.5 \pm 3.59$$

$$\Rightarrow \quad 57.91 \text{ and } 65.09$$

If the mean is on target 1 in 20 sample means will lie outside the warning limits and 1 in 500 sample means will lie outside the action limits.

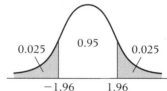

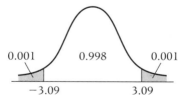

The warning limits are set at $\mu \pm 1.96 \dfrac{\sigma}{\sqrt{n}}$ and the action limits at $\mu \pm 3.09 \dfrac{\sigma}{\sqrt{n}}$, where μ is the target value, σ is the short-term standard deviation, and n is the sample size.

In practice, the value of the standard deviation will only be an estimate and 95% and 99.8% are somewhat arbitrary figures. For these reasons, and for simplicity, the limits are often set at $\mu \pm 2\dfrac{\sigma}{\sqrt{n}}$ and $\mu \pm 3\dfrac{\sigma}{\sqrt{n}}$.

Samples of size 5 were taken and weighed every hour as the chocolate bars were being produced. The first ten samples are shown below.

Sample	1	2	3	4	5	6	7	8	9	10
	59.55	64.57	63.34	58.55	59.80	61.82	59.90	62.17	68.11	60.46
	62.33	60.14	60.01	65.36	61.45	58.98	57.73	61.22	65.46	59.05
	63.68	62.51	59.11	63.03	60.78	62.63	66.03	69.01	57.81	65.05
	67.10	62.02	62.57	60.72	61.89	59.68	64.25	63.31	64.72	55.08
	56.85	60.16	58.48	62.26	63.91	62.70	65.20	62.92	63.27	61.60
mean	**61.90**	**61.88**	**60.70**	**61.98**	**61.57**	**61.16**	**62.62**	**63.73**	**63.87**	**60.25**

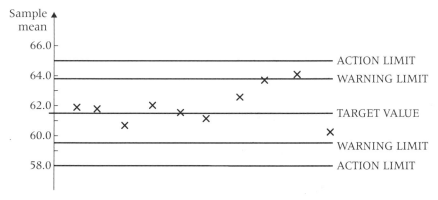

According to the chart production proceeded satisfactorily until the ninth sample where the sample mean went outside the warning limits. The tenth sample was therefore taken immediately instead of waiting another hour. The mean of this sample was within the warning limits and so production was allowed to continue.

Worked example 4.1

A machine filling packets of breakfast cereal is known to operate with a standard deviation of 3 g. The target is to put 500 g of cereal in each packet. Production is to be controlled by taking four packets at regular intervals and weighing their contents.

(a) Set up a control chart for means.

(b) What action, if any, would you recommend if the next sample weighed:
    (i) 503 497 499 496,
    (ii) 501 491 492 492,
    (iii) 502 500 507 505,
    (iv) 500 502 505 501?

Solution

(a) Warning limits

$$500 \pm \left(1.96 \times \frac{3}{\sqrt{4}}\right)$$

$$500 \pm 2.94$$

497.1 and 502.9

Action limits

$$500 \pm \left(3.09 \times \frac{3}{\sqrt{4}}\right)$$

$$500 \pm 4.635$$

495.4 and 504.6

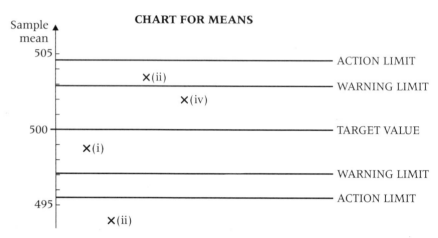

CHART FOR MEANS

(i) mean 498.75 – within warning limits – no action,
(ii) mean 494.0 – outside action limits – take action,
(iii) mean 503.5 – between warning and action limits –
take another sample immediately; if mean of new
sample outside warning limits take action,
(iv) mean 502.0 – within warning limits – no action.

EXERCISE 4A

1 In the production of bolts with nominal length 5.00 cm, the
standard deviation of the lengths is 0.03 cm. Production is to
be controlled by taking samples of size 4 every two hours and
measuring the lengths.

(a) Calculate, upper and lower, warning (95%) and action
(99.8%) limits for a control chart for means and draw
the chart.

(b) What action, if any, would you recommend in each of
the following cases when the lengths of the next sample
are:
(i)   5.01 5.03 4.97 4.96,
(ii) 4.92 4.90 5.00 4.92,
(iii) 4.99 5.10 5.03 5.04,
(iv) 4.99 4.97 4.96 4.99,
(v)   5.03 4.91 4.92 5.00?

2 A company manufactures panels for use in making baths. The panels have a target width of 700 mm. When production is satisfactory the widths are normally distributed with a standard deviation of 2 mm. Production is to be controlled by taking a sample of five panels at regular intervals and measuring their widths.

(a) Calculate, upper and lower, warning (95%) and action (99.8%) limits for a control chart for means and draw the chart.

(b) What action, if any, would you recommend in each of the following cases when the widths of the next sample are:
  (i)   701.2 698.2 704.4 699.4 695.5,
  (ii) 700.2 697.5 695.1 696.0 698.9,
  (iii) 699.5 707.1 704.9 703.9 706.4?

3 From previous investigations of a production process of rivets, it has been established that their head diameters are normally distributed. Also when head diameters have a mean of 14.5 mm and a standard deviation of 0.16 mm, the production process is in a satisfactory state of statistical control.

(a) Using these values as standards for future production, calculate, but do not graph, for samples of size 6, upper and lower, warning and action control limits for means.

(b) What action, if any, would you recommend, in each of the following cases when a sample gave the following head diameters:
  (i)   14.98 14.72 14.36 14.53 14.61 14.46,
  (ii) 14.57 14.67 14.49 14.41 14.62 14.58,
  (iii) 14.28 14.47 14.19 14.18 14.29 14.12?

4.4 Target values

In some cases the target value is not defined or is uattainable. For example, the target for strength of malleable iron castings is *as large as possible*. The target value for percentage impurity is probably zero but it will be recognised that this is unattainable (and even if it was attainable it would be nonsense to set up charts with lower limits set at negative values of impurity). In these cases a large sample should be taken when the process is believed to be running satisfactorily and the sample mean used as a target value. For example, tests on the tensile strength of malleable iron castings at a foundry at a time when production was thought to be satisfactory gave a mean of 148.0 and a standard deviation of 2.0; the units are GN m^{-2}.

The process is to be controlled by testing the strength of samples of size 5 at regular intervals.

Warning limits are $\qquad 148 \pm \left(1.96 \times \dfrac{2}{\sqrt{5}} \right)$

$\qquad\qquad\qquad$ 146.2 and 149.8

Action limits are $\qquad 148 \pm \left(3.09 \times \dfrac{2}{\sqrt{5}} \right)$

$\qquad\qquad\qquad$ 145.2 and 150.8

A sample mean less than 145.2 would lead to action being taken in the usual way. A sample mean greater than 150.8 would indicate that the average strength had increased. This would not, of course, lead to action to reduce the mean but might lead to an investigation to see how the improvement may be maintained.

> The first thing to do in this case would be to check for errors in the testing or calculation.

4.5 Control of variability

In the chocolate bar example in section 4.3 the warning limits were 59.22 and 63.78. If the next sample was

$\qquad$ 59.35 $\quad$ 62.46 $\quad$ 48.67 $\quad$ 68.79 $\quad$ 71.23

then the sample mean is 62.1 which is comfortably within the warning limits and no action is signalled. However, closer examination of this sample shows that something has gone drastically wrong with production. Although the mean is acceptable the variability within the sample has increased alarmingly. Although an increase in variability would make it more likely that action would be signalled on the chart for means, this chart is not an effective way of monitoring variability. An additional chart is needed for this purpose.

The best measure of variability is the standard deviation. However, since the sample range is easier to understand and calculate, traditionally it has been used as a measure of variability in statistical process control. With the ready availability of calculators there is now little reason for not using the standard deviation as a measure of variability. However operators using the charts may have little statistical knowledge so there could still be advantages in using an easily understood concept like range rather than the more complex concept of standard deviation. Whichever measure is chosen the charts are constructed in the same way. They depend on an estimate of standard deviation being available. They also assume that the data are normally distributed. It is no longer enough only to assume that the sample means are normally distributed. No target value is shown on the charts. The target for variability is zero but this is an unrealistic value to use on the charts.

> This is exactly comparable with charts for percentage impurity where the target of zero is unrealistic.

4.6 Charts for ranges

The limits for the range are found by multiplying the short-term standard deviation by the appropriate value of D found from table 12 in the appendix.

Table 12 can also be found in the AQA formulae and tables book.

In the case of the chocolate bars with samples of size 5 and a short-term standard deviation of 2.6:

- the upper action limit is $5.484 \times 2.6 = 14.3$,
- the upper warning limit is $4.197 \times 2.6 = 10.9$,
- the lower warning limit is $0.850 \times 2.6 = 2.21$
- the lower action limit is $0.367 \times 2.6 = 0.95$.

The first ten samples are shown below:

Sample	1	2	3	4	5	6	7	8	9	10
	59.55	64.57	63.34	58.55	59.80	61.82	59.90	62.17	68.11	60.46
	62.33	60.14	60.01	65.36	61.45	58.98	57.73	61.22	65.46	59.05
	63.68	62.51	59.11	63.03	60.78	62.63	66.03	69.01	57.81	65.05
	67.10	62.02	62.57	60.72	61.89	59.68	64.25	63.31	64.72	55.08
	56.85	60.16	58.48	62.26	63.91	62.70	65.20	62.92	63.27	61.60
range	10.25	4.43	4.86	6.81	4.11	3.72	8.30	7.79	10.30	9.97

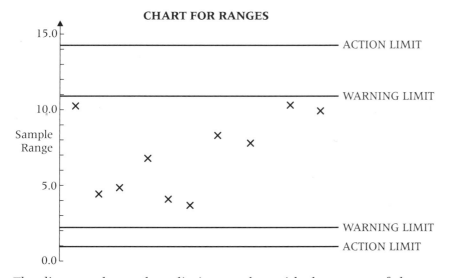

CHART FOR RANGES

The diagram shows these limits together with the ranges of the samples. All the ranges lie within the warning limits and there is no indication that any action to reduce variability is needed.

No target value is shown. The limits are not symmetrical about a centre line.

Note 1. When the sample is taken a point will be plotted on the chart for means and on the chart for ranges. Both these points must be within the warning limits for production to be regarded as satisfactory.

Note 2. Lower limits are sometimes omitted from these charts. A point below the lower limits indicates that the variability has probably been reduced. Clearly action to increase the variability would be ridiculous as one of the purposes of statistical process control is to minimise variability. However, it may still be worth including the lower limits so that any decrease in variability can be investigated with a view to maintaining the improvement.

4.7 Charts for standard deviations

These are calculated and operated in exactly the same way as the charts for ranges. The only difference being that the appropriate factor to select from table 12 is E. The standard deviation chart gives a slightly better chance of detecting an increase in the variability when one exists. The risk of a false alarm is the same for both charts.

For the chocolate bar example:

- the upper action limit is $2.15 \times 2.6 = 5.59$,
- the upper warning limit is $1.67 \times 2.6 = 4.34$,
- the lower warning limit is $0.35 \times 2.6 = 0.91$,
- the lower action limit is $0.15 \times 2.6 = 0.39$.

Sample	1	2	3	4	5	6	7	8	9	10
	59.55	64.57	63.34	58.55	59.80	61.82	59.90	62.17	68.11	60.46
	62.33	60.14	60.01	65.36	61.45	58.98	57.73	61.22	65.46	59.05
	63.68	62.51	59.11	63.03	60.78	62.63	66.03	69.01	57.81	65.05
	67.10	62.02	62.57	60.72	61.89	59.68	64.25	63.31	64.72	55.08
	56.85	60.16	58.48	62.26	63.91	62.70	65.20	62.92	63.27	61.60
s	3.92	1.85	2.14	2.55	1.53	1.73	3.61	3.06	3.82	3.64

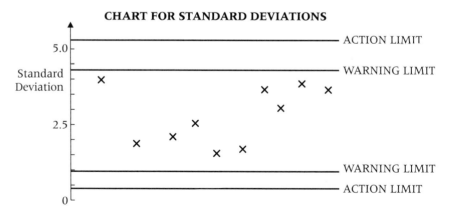

The standard deviations

$$s = \sqrt{\frac{\Sigma(x - \bar{x})^2}{n - 1}}$$

should be plotted on the chart.

As with the range chart all the points lie within the warning limits and there is no indication that action is necessary to reduce the variability. Standard deviation charts and range charts will usually, but not always, give the same signal.

You should use a range chart or a standard deviation chart – not both.

As with the range charts the lower limits can be useful but are often not included.

Variability may be controlled by plotting the sample ranges or standard deviations on control charts. The limits for these charts are found by multiplying the process short-term standard deviation by factors found in table 12.

Worked example 4.2

(a) Set up a chart for standard deviations for the packets of breakfast cereal given in Worked example 4.1.

(b) What action, if any, would you recommend if the next sample weighed:
   (i)   502 496 499 496,
   (ii) 506 494 496 496,
   (iii) 499 490 505 505,
   (iv) 506 510 508 508,
   (v)   497 498 498 497?

Solution

(a) The short term standard deviation is 3 g.
The upper action limit is $2.33 \times 3 = 6.99$.
The upper warning limit is $1.76 \times 3 = 5.28$.
The lower warning limit is $0.27 \times 3 = 0.81$.
The lower action limit is $0.09 \times 3 = 0.27$.

(b) For this part you need to remember the limits for the chart for means as well as for the chart for standard deviations. The limits for the chart for means calculated in Worked example 4.1 were:

Warning limits 497.1 and 502.9

Action limits   495.4 and 504.6

   (i) $\bar{x} = 498.25$ $s = 2.87$ – both within warning limits – no action,

   (ii) $\bar{x} = 498.0$ $s = 5.42$ – mean okay, warning signal on standard deviation chart – take another sample immediately; if s above upper warning limit on new chart take action; if not, no action necessary,

   (iii) $\bar{x} = 499.75$ $s = 7.09$ – mean okay but action signal on standard deviation chart – take action,

   (iv) $\bar{x} = 508.0$ $s = 1.63$ – variability okay but action signal on mean chart – take action,

(v) $\bar{x} = 497.5$ $s = 0.58$ – mean within warning limits, s below lower warning limit – no action needed. Some indication that variability may have been reduced. This is good. Could take another sample immediately to check, with a view to maintaining improvement.

EXERCISE 4B

1 A company manufactures panels for use in making baths. The panels have a target width of 700 mm. When production is satisfactory the widths are normally distributed with a standard deviation of 2 mm. Production is to be controlled by taking a sample of five panels at regular intervals and measuring their widths.

   (a) Calculate, upper and lower, warning (95%) and action (99.8%) limits for a control chart for means and draw the chart. (You should already have done this in exercise 4A, question 2.)

   (b) Calculate upper and lower warning limits for a control chart for standard deviations and draw the chart.

   (c) What action, if any, would you recommend if the next sample measured is:
   (i)   701.2 698.2 704.4 699.4 695.5,
   (ii) 700.2 697.5 695.1 696.0 698.9,
   (iii) 699.5 707.1 704.9 703.9 706.4?   [A]

2 Raw material used in a chemical process contains some impurity. In order to ensure that the percentage impurity does not become too large or too variable samples of size 3 are tested at regular intervals. When the process is running satisfactorily the mean percentage impurity was found to be 16.7 with a standard deviation of 3.4.

   (a) Set up control charts for means and for standard deviations.

   (b) What action, if any, would you recommend if the next sample was:
   (i)   16.9 19.3 20.2,
   (ii) 24.2 25.6 22.0,
   (iii) 14.2 19.1 5.2,
   (iv) 22.7 19.3 23.1,
   (v)   9.3 12.2 8.1?   [A]

3 From previous investigations of a production process for rivets, it has been established that their head diameters are normally distributed. Also when the head diameters have a mean of 14.5 mm and a standard deviation of 0.16 mm, the production process is in a satisfactory state of statistical control.

(a) Using these values as standards for future production, calculate, but do not graph, for samples of size 6, upper and lower, warning and action control limits for:

    (i) means (you should already have done this in exercise 4A, question 3),

    (ii) standard deviations.

(b) What action, if any, would you recommend, in each of the following cases when a sample gave the following head diameters:

    (i)   14.88 14.72 14.46 14.53 14.61 14.49,

    (ii) 14.54 14.99 14.16 14.22 14.77 14.49,

    (iii) 14.09 14.51 14.07 14.32 14.21 14.04,

    (iv) 14.17 13.81 14.56 14.87 14.72 14.55,

    (v)   14.57 14.60 14.49 14.48 14.62 14.58,

    (vi) 14.28 14.47 14.19 14.18 14.29 14.12?   [A]

4 An electrical firm is asked to manufacture a particular type of resistor which has a nominal resistance of 120 Ω. Historical data have revealed that, irrespective of the nominal resistance, the standard deviation of the manufacturing process when under control is 1.5 Ω. The production manager proposes to set the process mean at 120 Ω and to control the quality by taking samples of size 5 at regular intervals.

(a) Calculate, but do not graph:

    (i) upper and lower, warning (95%) and action (99.8%), control lines for sample means,

    (ii) upper, warning (95%) and action (99.8%), control lines for sample ranges.

(b) What action, if any, would you take if a sample gave resistances of 124, 118, 126, 125 and 117 Ω?

(c) What action, if any, would you take if a sample gave resistances of 123, 119, 126, 125 and 121 Ω?   [A]

4.8 Estimating the short-term standard deviation

The best way of estimating the short-term standard deviation is to take a large sample when the process is running well and calculate the standard deviation using the formula

$$\sqrt{\frac{\Sigma(x - \bar{x})^2}{(n - 1)}}.$$

This is how the standard deviation was estimated for the chocolate bars. The same sample may also be used for estimating a suitable target value when one is required. This procedure is called a process capability study.

Data for statistical process control purposes are often collected in small samples. For this reason the short-term standard deviation is often estimated from a number of small samples rather than from one large sample. If the process is running well, at the time, the standard deviation should be constant but it may be that there have been some small changes in the mean. If this is the case pooling the small samples and regarding them as one large sample will tend to over estimate the short-term standard deviation. It is better to make an estimate of variability from each sample individually and then take the mean. This estimate may be the sample range or the sample standard deviation.

For example, a company manufactures a drug with a nominal potency of 5.0 mg cm^{-3}. For prescription purposes it is important that the mean potency of tablets should be accurate and the variability low. Ten samples, each of four tablets, were taken at regular intervals during a particular day when production was thought to be satisfactory. The potency of the tablets was measured.

Sample	1	2	3	4	5	6	7	8	9	10
	4.97	4.98	5.13	5.03	5.19	5.13	5.16	5.11	5.07	5.11
	5.09	5.15	5.05	5.18	5.12	4.96	5.15	5.07	5.11	5.19
	5.08	5.08	5.12	5.06	5.10	5.02	4.97	5.09	5.01	5.13
	5.06	4.99	5.11	5.05	5.04	5.09	5.09	5.08	4.96	5.17

The ranges of the ten samples are

    0.12 0.17 0.08 0.15 0.15 0.17 0.19 0.04 0.15 0.08

giving a mean sample range of 0.13. This mean range can be converted to a standard deviation by multiplying by an appropriate factor from the column headed b in table 12. For samples of size 4 the estimated standard deviation would be

    $0.4857 \times 0.13 = 0.063.$

The factors in the table assume that the data is normally distributed.

Alternatively, the standard deviations for the ten samples are

    0.0548 0.0804 0.0359 0.0678 0.0619

    0.0753 0.0873 0.0171 0.0660 0.0365.

For mathematical reasons, the best way of estimating the standard deviation is to find the mean of the ten variances and take the square root, i.e.,

$$\sqrt{\frac{0.0548^2 + 0.0804^2 + 0.0359^2 + 0.0678^2 + 0.0619^2 + 0.0753^2 + 0.0873^2 + 0.0171^2 + 0.0660^2 + 0.0365^2}{10}} = 0.062$$

As can be seen, there is little difference in the two estimates. Although the second method is mathematically preferable the first method is perfectly adequate for most purposes.

> When the standard deviation must be estimated from a number of small samples the average sample range can be calculated and a factor from table 12 applied. Alternatively s_i can be calculated for each sample and the formula $s = \sqrt{\Sigma s_i^2 / n}$ evaluated.

Here n is the number of samples and **not** the sample size.

Worked example 4.3

In the production of bank notes samples are taken at regular intervals and a number of measurements made on each note. The following table shows the width (mm) of the top margin in eight samples each of size 4. The target value is 9 mm.

Sample	1	2	3	4	5	6	7	8
	9.0	10.4	8.2	7.9	8.2	8.4	7.4	7.6
	8.1	9.0	9.2	7.7	9.0	8.1	8.0	8.5
	8.7	7.9	7.9	7.7	7.4	8.4	8.9	8.1
	7.5	7.2	7.7	9.3	8.6	8.7	9.8	8.8

(a) Calculate the mean sample range and, assuming a normal distribution, use it to estimate the standard deviation of the process.

(b) Use the estimate made in **(a)** to draw a control chart for means showing 95% warning limits and 99.8% action limits. Plot the eight means.

(c) Draw a control chart for ranges showing the upper and lower action and warning limits. Plot the eight ranges.

(d) Comment on the current state of the process.

(e) What action, if any, would you recommend in each of the following cases, where the next sample is:
(i) 9.1 10.2 8.9 9.7,
(ii) 7.3 6.9 8.8 7.1,
(iii) 10.4 10.1 9.2 6.8,
(iv) 10.9 9.8 8.8 11.1,
(v) 9.3 9.2 9.3 9.3?

(f) Suggest two methods, other than the one used in **(a)**, to estimate the short-term standard deviation of the process. Compare the relative merits of these three methods in the context of control charts.

Solution

Sample	1	2	3	4	5	6	7	8
mean	8.325	8.625	8.25	8.15	8.30	8.40	8.525	8.25
range	1.5	3.2	1.5	1.6	1.6	0.6	2.4	1.2

(a) The mean range $= 13.6/8 = 1.7$ and the estimated standard deviation $= 0.4857 \times 1.7 = 0.826$.

(b) The chart for means is plotted as follows:

Warning limits $9.00 \pm \left(1.96 \times \dfrac{0.826}{\sqrt{4}}\right) \quad \Rightarrow \quad 8.19$ and 9.81

Action limits $\quad 9.00 \pm \left(3.09 \times \dfrac{0.826}{\sqrt{4}}\right) \quad \Rightarrow \quad 7.72$ and 10.28

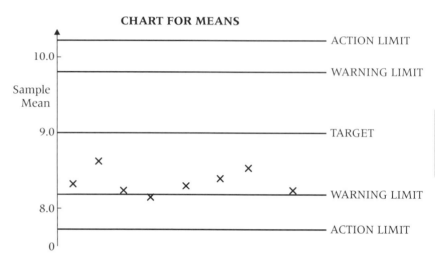

CHART FOR MEANS

Only one point is outside the warning limits but all eight points are well below the target value.

(c) The chart for ranges is plotted as follows:
Upper action limit $5.309 \times 0.826 = 4.39$
Upper warning limit $3.984 \times 0.826 = 3.29$
Lower warning limit $0.595 \times 0.826 = 0.49$
Lower action limit $0.199 \times 0.826 = 0.16$

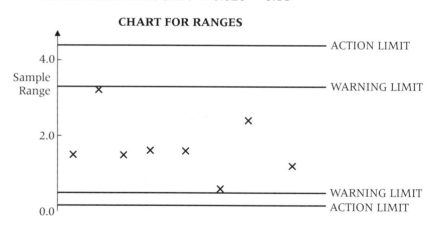

CHART FOR RANGES

(d) All ranges are within warning limits. Variability appears to be under control. One mean is below lower warning limit. This is not in itself a problem. Since 95% of sample means lie within the warning limits when the process is on target, 5% or 1 in 20, will lie outside warning limits if the mean is on target. However, as all the sample means are below the target it appears that the machine needs resetting to increase the mean.

In this case, looking at the chart as a whole is more informative than examining each point separately.

(e) (i) mean 9.475 range 1.3 – no action,

(ii) mean 7.525 range 1.9 – below action limit on mean chart – action is needed to increase mean, probably by resetting machine,

(iii) mean 9.125 range 3.6 – outside warning limit on range chart – take another sample immediately; if still outside the warning limit take action to reduce variability, probably by overhauling the machine,

(iv) mean 10.15 range 2.3 – outside warning limit on mean chart – take another sample immediately; if still outside warning limit take action to increase mean,

(v) mean 9.275 range 0.1 – below lower action limit on range chart – check data; if correct take no action but investigate how variability has been reduced with a view to maintaining the improvement.

> Changing the mean is likely to be easier than reducing the variability.

(f) An alternative method of estimating the standard deviation is to regard the 32 observations as a single sample and to estimate the standard deviation using the formula

$$\sqrt{\frac{\Sigma(x - \bar{x})^2}{(n - 1)}}.$$ This would be a satisfactory method if the mean had not changed while the eight samples were taken but would tend to overestimate the short-term standard deviation if it had. In this case the eight plotted means suggest that the mean has remained constant (although below target).

Another alternative is to calculate the standard deviation separately for each sample. If these values are $s_1, s_2, \ldots, s_8$ the estimate of the standard deviation will be

$$\sqrt{(s_1{}^2 + s_2{}^2 + \ldots + s_8{}^2)/8}.$$

Another alternative is to use

$$(s_1 + s_2 + \ldots + s_8)/8.$$

These last two methods will be satisfactory even if the mean has changed and/or the data is not normally distributed.

EXERCISE 4C

1 Nine samples, each of size 5, from a production process have ranges (cm) of

  2.3 2.9 1.8 3.4 2.0 3.6 2.9 2.1 1.1.

Calculate the mean range and, assuming a normal distribution, estimate the standard deviation of the process.

2 Eight samples, each of size 7, from a production process give estimates of standard deviation (mm) of

  4.8 3.7 4.2 1.9 4.2 3.0 3.6 2.7.

Estimate the standard deviation of the process using the formula $s = \sqrt{\Sigma s_i^2/n}$.

3 Charts are to be used to control the width of a slot on a Duralumin forging used in aircraft production. The table below gives the width of slot on eight samples each of size 5 taken when production was thought to be satisfactory. The units are 0.001 cm above 1.800 cm.

Sample	1	2	3	4	5	6	7	8
	77	76	76	74	80	78	75	72
	80	79	77	78	73	81	77	71
	78	73	72	75	75	79	75	75
	72	74	76	77	76	76	76	74
	78	73	74	77	74	76	77	77

(a) Estimate the standard deviation of the process:
   (i) by finding the mean range of the eight samples and applying a suitable factor from table 12,
   (ii) by calculating the standard deviation of each sample and applying the formula $s^2 = \Sigma s_1^2/n$. Compare the two estimates and comment.

(b) Using the estimate of standard deviation made in (a)(ii) calculate action and warning limits for a chart for means and a chart for ranges.

As production is satisfactory use the overall mean as the target value.

(c) If the next sample was

   76 80 79 74 77

what action, if any, would you take? [A]

4 A steel maker supplies sheet steel to a manufacturer whose machines are set on the assumption that the thickness is 750 (the units are thousandths of a millimetre). The supplier decides to set up control charts to ensure that the steel is as close to 750 as possible. Eight samples each of five measurements are taken when production is thought to be satisfactory. The sample means and ranges are as follows:

Sample	1	2	3	4	5	6	7	8
mean	738	762	751	763	757	754	762	761
range	14	21	17	53	29	49	71	62

(a) Assuming the thicknesses are normally distributed estimate the standard deviation of the process.

(b) Using the target value as a centre line draw a control chart for means showing 95% and 99.8% control lines. Plot the eight means.

(c) Draw a control chart for the range showing the upper action and warning limits. Plot the eight ranges.

(d) Comment on the patterns revealed by the charts and advise the manufacturer how to proceed. [A]

5 The following data show the lengths (cm) of samples of four bolts taken at regular intervals from a production process. The drawing dimension (target value) is 5.00 cm.

Sample	1	2	3	4	5	6	7	8	9	10
	5.01	4.99	5.00	4.995	5.01	5.005	5.02	5.01	4.995	5.02
	5.015	5.01	4.99	5.015	5.02	4.99	5.00	4.995	4.99	4.995
	4.995	4.985	4.995	5.00	4.99	5.00	5.01	4.99	4.99	4.99
	4.985	5.005	5.015	4.99	5.01	5.00	5.005	4.99	5.00	4.99

> The measurement is to the nearest 0.005 cm. If all measurements had been written to 3 d.p. (e.g. 5.010), this would have incorrectly implied measurement to the nearest 0.001 cm.

(a) Estimate the standard deviation of the process:
   (i) by finding the mean range of the samples and applying a suitable factor from table 12,
  (ii) by calculating the standard deviation of each sample and applying the formula $s^2 = \Sigma s_i^2/n$. Compare the two estimates and comment.

(b) Using the estimate of standard deviation made in **(a)(ii)** set up a chart for means. Plot the ten sample means and comment.

(c) Using the estimate of standard deviation made in **(a)(ii)** set up a chart for standard deviations. Plot the standard deviations from the ten samples and comment. [A]

4.9 Tolerance limits

Many processes have tolerance limits within which the product must lie. The purpose of statistical process control is to ensure that a process functions as accurately, and with as little variability, as possible. In setting up the charts no account is taken of any tolerances. A process which is under statistical control may be unable to meet the tolerances consistently. Alternatively, it may be able to meet the tolerances easily.

In the example of drug potency in section 4.8 the standard deviation was estimated to be about 0.063. How would the process perform if the tolerances were 4.9 to 5.1?

It is generally reasonable to assume that mass-produced items will follow a normal distribution. If we also assume that the mean is exactly on target, i.e. 5.00, we can calculate the proportion outside the tolerances.

$$z_1 = (4.9 - 5.0)/0.063 = -1.587$$
$$z_2 = (5.1 - 5.0)/0.063 = 1.587$$

The proportion outside the tolerances is $2 \times (1 - 0.9437) = 0.113$. Hence, even in the best possible case with the mean exactly on target, about 11% of the tablets would be outside the tolerances.

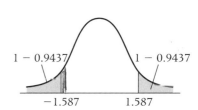

This process cannot meet these tolerances however well statistical process control is applied. A better and almost certainly more expensive process is needed to meet these tolerances.

Almost all of a normal distribution lies within three standard deviations of the mean. So if the tolerance width exceeds six standard deviations the process should be able to meet the tolerances consistently, provided the mean is kept on target. In the example above the tolerance width is $5.1 - 4.9 = 0.2$ which is $0.2/0.063 = 3.2$ standard deviations.

> If the tolerance width exceeds six standard deviations the process should be able to meet the tolerances consistently, provided the mean is kept on target.

In some cases the tolerance width may greatly exceed six standard deviations and the tolerances will be easily met. It can be argued that in these cases statistical process control is unnecessary. However, to produce a high quality product, it is better to have the process exactly on target than just within the tolerances. A car door which is exactly the right width is likely to close more smoothly than one which is just within the acceptable tolerances.

Worked example 4.4

The copper content of bronze castings has a target value of 80%. The standard deviation is known to be 4%. During the production process, samples of size 6 are taken at regular intervals and their copper content measured.

(a) Calculate upper and lower warning and action limits for control charts for:
  (i) means,
  (ii) standard deviations.

(b) The following results were obtained from samples on three separate occasions:
  (i)   82.0 83.5 79.8 84.2 80.3 81.0,
  (ii) 75.8 68.4 80.3 78.2 79.9 73.5,
  (iii) 79.5 80.0 79.9 79.6 79.9 80.4.

  For each sample, calculate the mean and standard deviation and recommend any necessary action.

(c) If the process currently has a mean of 76% with a standard deviation of 4%, what is the probability that the mean of the next sample will lie within the warning limits on the chart for means?

(d) The tolerance limits are 73% and 87%. A process capability index, C_p, is defined to be $\dfrac{\text{tolerance width}}{6\sigma}$.

(i) Calculate C_p, for this process.

(ii) Explain why a C_p value less than 1 is regarded as unsatisfactory.

(iii) Explain why, if the mean is off target, a C_p value greater than 1 may still be unsatisfactory.

Solution

(a) The Control chart for means:

Warning limits $80 \pm \left(1.96 \times \dfrac{4}{\sqrt{6}}\right) \quad\Rightarrow\quad$ 76.8 and 83.2

Action limits $\quad 80 \pm \left(3.09 \times \dfrac{4}{\sqrt{6}}\right) \quad\Rightarrow\quad$ 74.95 and 85.05

The Control chart for standard deviations:

Upper action limit $2.03 \times 4 = 8.12$

Upper warning limit $1.60 \times 4 = 6.40$

Lower warning limit $0.41 \times 4 = 1.64$

Lower action limit $0.20 \times 4 = 0.80$

(b) **(i)** mean $= 81.8 \quad s = 1.77$ – no action,

(ii) mean $= 76.0 \quad s = 4.53$ – mean below warning limit – you should take another sample immediately; if mean still outside warning limits, take action,

(iii) mean $79.9 \quad s = 0.32$ – standard deviation below action limit – variability has been reduced; try to find out why so that improvement may be maintained.

The probability of a sample mean above the upper warning limit is negligible.

(c) $z_1 = (76.8 - 76.0)/(4/\sqrt{6}) = 0.490$

$z_2 = (83.2 - 76.0)/(4/\sqrt{6}) = 4.409$

Probability within warning limits $= 1 - 0.6879$
$$= 0.3121$$

(d) **(i)** $C_p = (87 - 73)/(6 \times 4) = 0.583$

(ii) C_p less than 1 indicates that the tolerance width is less than 6σ. Hence the process is unlikely to be able to meet the tolerances consistently even if the mean is exactly on target.

(iii) Even if the C_p is more than 1 the tolerances may not be consistently met if the mean is off target.

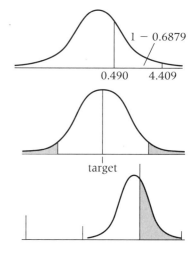

EXERCISE 4D

1 A packaging process is operating with a standard deviation of 1.2 g. Comment on its ability to consistently meet tolerances of:

(a) 440.0 ± 2.0 g,

(b) 440.0 ± 3.6 g,

(c) 440.0 ± 6.0 g.

2 Reels of wire are wound automatically from a continuous source of wire. After each reel is wound the wire is cut and a new reel started. The target is to wind 10 m onto each reel. The lengths of wire on ten samples, each of four reels, are measured with the following results. The units are centimetres above 9 m 50 cm.

Sample	1	2	3	4	5	6	7	8	9	10
	42	64	53	62	26	27	16	17	48	41
	57	76	7	31	54	37	54	44	72	59
	36	52	41	17	62	69	32	46	76	80
	8	40	56	44	51	61	48	49	64	68

(a) Use these samples to estimate the standard deviation and to calculate limits for control charts for means and for standard deviations. Draw the charts and plot the points.

(b) What action, if any, would you take if the next sample was:
(i) 54 64 70 48,
(ii) 9 99 42 58,
(iii) 84 106 99 93?

(c) The tolerance for the length of wire on a reel is 50 ± 70. Comment on the ability of the process to meet these limits.

> As the units are in centimetres above 9 m 50 cm, negative values of length are possible.

(d) If the current mean is 55 and the standard deviation is 18, what is the probability that the next sample mean will be within:
(i) the warning limits,
(ii) the action limits? [A]

3 A biscuit factory produces cream crackers. Packets are sampled at hourly intervals and the weight, in grams, of the contents measured. The results below are from seven samples each of size 5, taken at a time when production was thought to be satisfactory. The target value is 210 g.

Sample	1	2	3	4	5	6	7
	209.0	214.5	204.5	217.5	211.0	224.0	210.0
	211.0	210.0	209.0	216.0	198.0	220.0	208.0
	213.5	212.0	198.5	217.0	209.5	224.0	210.0
	205.0	203.5	203.0	214.0	213.5	218.5	220.0
	210.0	214.0	213.5	209.5	213.5	210.0	211.0

(a) Estimate the standard deviation of the process.

(b) Calculate, upper and lower, warning and action limits for a control chart for:
(i) means,
(ii) standard deviations.

(c) Draw the two control charts and plot the points. Comment on the current state of the process.

(d) What action, if any, would you recommend if the next sample was:
   (i) 196.0 202.5 189.0 197.5 197.0,
   (ii) 204.5 214.0 206.0 207.0 211.0,
   (iii) 188.5 212.5 220.0 215.0 208.0,
   (iv) 206.0 214.5 208.5 209.0 211.0?

(e) The upper specification limit (USL) is 220 g and the lower specification limit (LSL) is 200 g. Estimate C_p, where

$$C_p = (USL - LSL)/6\sigma.$$

Comment on the ability of the process to meet this specification.   [A]

4 Reels of plastic piping are wound automatically from a continuous source. After each reel is wound the piping is cut and a new reel started. The aim is to wind 100 m onto each reel. The length of piping on twelve samples, each of five reels, was measured. The mean and standard deviation of each of the samples are given below:

Sample	1	2	3	4	5	6	7	8	9	10	11	12
Mean	99.8	101.4	100.4	101.9	101.2	100.6	101.7	100.9	100.2	101.4	101.5	101.0
s	3.6	2.4	1.1	3.2	2.3	2.5	1.7	0.9	1.9	2.2	2.3	1.6

(a) Use the data to estimate the standard deviation of the process and to calculate 95% and 99.8% control lines for the sample means. Draw a control chart for means and plot the twelve points.

(b) Draw a control chart for standard deviations. Plot the twelve points and comment on the current state of the process.

(c) If the next sample measured

   97.3 100.6 103.3 100.1 100.9 m

what action would you recommend and why?

Reels containing less than 95 m of piping are unacceptable to customers and reels containing more than 105 m make the process uneconomical.

(d) Comment on the ability of the process to produce reels which lie consistently within these limits.   [A]

5 When steel is hot-rolled for car door hinges, one dimension of interest is the bulb diameter. The table shows the mean, $\bar{x}$ mm, and the standard deviation, s mm, of each of 16 random samples of 5 measurements of bulb diameter.

Sample	1	2	3	4	5	6	7	8	9	10	11	12	13	14	15	16
$\bar{x}$	15.21	15.13	14.88	15.24	15.15	14.84	15.20	15.25	15.17	15.15	15.10	14.93	15.10	15.06	15.14	15.05
s	0.22	0.34	0.40	0.35	0.27	0.48	0.31	0.33	0.49	0.32	0.29	0.21	0.35	0.26	0.42	0.41

(a) Calculate an estimate of the current process mean.

(b) Calculate an estimate of the current process standard deviation using the formula

$$s^2 = (s_1^2 + s_2^2 + \ldots + s_n^2)/n.$$

(c) Given that the target value for bulb diameter is 15.0 mm, draw a control chart for the sample means showing the 95% (warning) and 99.8% (action) control lines.

(d) Draw a control chart for the standard deviations showing the 95% (warning) and 99.8% (action) control lines.

(e) By plotting the above sample means and standard deviations on your charts, comment on the current state of the process.

(f) The tolerance for bulb diameter is (15.0 ± 0.5) mm. Use your estimates of the current process mean, calculated in **(a)**, and of standard deviation calculate in **(b)**, to estimate the expected percentage of output from the process with unsatisfactory bulb diameter. What overall conclusion can be drawn about the current state of the process? [A]

6 The process in exercise 4C question 3 has tolerances of 1.875 ± 0.008 cm. Comment on its ability to meet these tolerances.

4.10 Control charts for proportion non-conforming

Control charts may also be applied when, instead of measuring a variable such as weight or length, items are classified as conforming or non-conforming (defective and non-defective used to be common terms but are rarely used now).

> For a further discussion of non-conforming items, see chapter 5.

Samples of 100 components are taken from a production line at regular intervals and the number non-conforming counted. At a time when production was thought to be satisfactory 12 samples contained the following numbers of non-conforming items:

    10 13 12 19 8 14 17 16 10 18 9 16

The total number of non-conforming items found is 162 out of 1200 components examined. This gives an estimate of the proportion non-conforming, p, of $162/1200 = 0.135$.

> In some cases, instead of estimating p from observed values, an acceptable proportion non-conforming may be given.

If p is constant the number non-conforming in the samples will follow a binomial distribution. As n is large (100) and np is reasonably large ($100 \times 0.135 = 13.5$) the binomial distribution may be approximated by a normal distribution with mean np and standard deviation $\sqrt{np(1-p)}$. Control charts may be set up in the usual way.

> For charts for proportion non-conforming, providing n is reasonably large:
> - the warning limits are $p \pm 1.96\sqrt{p(1-p)/n}$
> - the action limits are $p \pm 3.09\sqrt{p(1-p)/n}$.

In this example the warning limits for p are

$$0.135 \pm 1.96\sqrt{0.135 \times 0.865/100}$$
$$\Rightarrow \quad 0.068 \text{ and } 0.202$$

The action limits for p are

$$0.135 \pm 3.09\sqrt{0.135 \times 0.865/100}$$
$$\Rightarrow \quad 0.029 \text{ and } 0.241$$

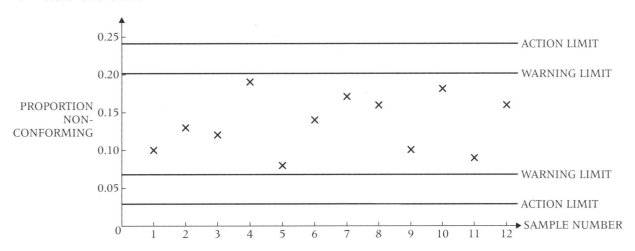

There are several points to note about this chart.
- Only one chart is necessary. The only way a signal can be given is if there are too many non-conforming items.
- 0.135 is not the target value. The target value is zero. However, in this case 0.135 is thought to be a reasonable level. The real purpose of these charts is to ensure that the proportion non-conforming does not rise above 0.135.
- The lower limits are not needed but as with charts for standard deviations it may be useful to retain them as a check on errors in the data or to indicate that an improvement has occurred.
- Charts for the number non-conforming could be plotted as an alternative to the proportion non-conforming. There may be

an advantage in plotting the proportion if the number of items inspected is likely to vary slightly from sample to sample.

- Any variable such as weight or length may be treated in this way by defining limits outside which the item is classified as non-conforming. It is usually easier to decide whether or not an item lies within given limits rather than to make an exact measurement. However, to get equivalent control of the process much larger samples are needed.

- If the samples are too small the normal approximation will not be valid. It would be necessary to use exact binomial probabilities to calculate the limits. However, as small samples do not give good control using proportion defective this problem is not likely to arise. Small values of p would also cause the normal approximation to be invalid. Good control cannot be maintained for small values of p. This problem can be overcome by tightening up the definition of non-conforming.

Worked example 4.5

At a factory making ball-bearings, a scoop is used to take a sample at regular intervals. All the ball-bearings in the scoop are classified as conforming or non-conforming according to whether or not they fit two gauges. This is a very quick and easy test to carry out. Here is the data from ten samples when the process was thought to be performing satisfactorily.

Sample	1	2	3	4	5	6	7	8	9	10
Number in scoop	95	99	115	120	84	107	97	119	92	112
Number non-conforming	16	6	11	10	11	5	13	14	10	13

(a) Use the data to estimate p, the proportion non-conforming, and n, the average number in a scoop. Use these estimated values of n and p to set up control charts for proportion non-conforming. Plot the 10 samples on the chart and comment.

(b) The following samples occurred on separate occasions when the chart was in operation:
  (i) 115 in scoop, 21 non-conforming,
  (ii) 94 in scoop, 8 non-conforming,
  (iii) 92 in scoop, 20 non-conforming,
  (iv) 12 in scoop, 3 non-conforming,
  (v) 104 in scoop, 1 non-conforming.

  For each of the samples comment on the current state of the process and on what action, if any, is necessary.

Solution

(a) The total number non-conforming observed is

$$16 + 6 + 11 + 10 + 11 + 5 + 13 + 14 + 10 + 13 = 109.$$

The total number of ball bearings observed is

$$95 + 99 + 115 + 120 + 84 + 107 + 97 + 119 + 92 + 112 = 1040.$$

$$\overline{n} = 1040/10 = 104 \qquad \hat{p} = 109/1040 = 0.1048$$

> $\overline{n}$ is the mean sample size and $\hat{p}$ is the estimated proportion non-conforming.

This gives warning limits

$$0.1048 \pm 1.96\sqrt{0.1048 \times 0.8952/104}$$
$$\Rightarrow \quad 0.046 \text{ and } 0.164$$

and action limits

$$0.1048 \pm 3.09\sqrt{0.1048 \times 0.8952/104}$$
$$\Rightarrow \quad 0.012 \text{ and } 0.198$$

The proportions non-conforming in samples are

0.168 0.061 0.096 0.083 0.131
0.047 0.134 0.118 0.109 0.116

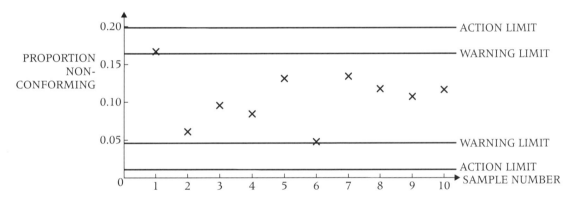

One point is just outside the warning limits. As one point in 20 is expected to lie outside the warning limits this is acceptable and does not cast doubt on the state of the process when these samples were taken. (If the process was unstable when the samples were taken they would be unsuitable for estimating a value of p for use in calculating limits for the chart. It would be necessary to take new samples when the process was running well and use these for estimating p.)

(b) **(i)** $21/115 = 0.183$ – between upper warning and action limits – take another scoop immediately; if this also gives a point above upper warning limit take action.

(ii) $8/94 = 0.085$ – below upper warning limit – production satisfactory.

(iii) $20/92 = 0.217$ – above upper action limit – take action.

(iv) The limits on these charts depend on the sample size n; a small amount of variability in n will make little difference but the limits are unsuitable for use with samples as small as 12 – take another scoop and start again.

(v) $1/104 = 0.0096$ – below lower action limit; process appears to have improved – try to maintain the improvement.

EXERCISE 4E

1 Lengths of cloth produced at a mill often have to be 'mended' by hand before being saleable. In sets of 50 the numbers needing mending were as follows:

17 14 13 16 14 16 22 19 15 16 12

Set up control charts based on this data.

2 To control a process producing components for washing machines 75 components are tested every hour and the number non-conforming recorded. The numbers recorded in eight hours when production was regarded as satisfactory were:

6 16 12 9 14 19 7 13

(a) Use this data to set up a control chart for proportion non-conforming.

(b) What action if any would you recommend if the number non-conforming in the next sample was:
(i) 27, (ii) 15, (iii) 20, (iv) 3?

3 A manufacturer of fishing line takes samples of 60 lengths at regular intervals and counts the number that break when subjected to a strain of 38 N. During a period when production was satisfactory the results for ten samples were as follows:

Sample	1	2	3	4	5	6	7	8	9	10
number breaking	14	9	7	15	10	8	13	12	6	7

(a) Draw a control chart for proportion breaking showing approximate 95% and 99.8% control lines, and plot the ten points.

(b) What action would you recommend if the number breaking in the next sample was:
(i) 18, (ii) 24, (iii) 1?

(c) Give two advantages and one disadvantage of the manufacturer's method of control compared to measuring the actual breaking strength and setting up control charts for mean and range.   [A]

4 In a sweet factory a scoop is used to take a sample of beans, at regular intervals, from a machine making jelly beans. A count is then made of the number of beans in the scoop together with the number with an incomplete coating.

The results for 12 such samples are shown below.

Scoop	Number of beans in scoop	Number of beans with incomplete coating
1	65	8
2	59	5
3	73	9
4	70	14
5	64	10
6	66	17
7	57	12
8	68	8
9	61	9
10	71	12
11	67	7
12	59	6

(a) Use these data to estimate n, the mean number of beans in a scoop, and p, the proportion of jelly beans with an incomplete coating.

(b) Use your estimates found in (a) to calculate the 95% (warning) and 99.8% (action) control lines for a control chart for the proportion of jelly beans with an incomplete coating.

(c) By calculating the proportion of beans with an incomplete coating for each sample comment on the current state of the machine's production. [A]

5 A company owns a large number of supermarkets. Deliveries are made each day from a central warehouse to the supermarkets. Each week 80 deliveries are monitored and the number which are unsatisfactory (either late or incomplete) is recorded. During a period when the service as a whole was regarded as satisfactory the following data were collected.

Week	1	2	3	4	5	6	7	8	9	10
Number unsatisfactory	14	9	12	15	8	10	18	11	19	15

(a) Use the data to estimate p, the proportion of unsatisfactory deliveries. Use this estimate to calculate, upper and lower, warning and action limits for a control chart for p. There should be a chance of approximately 1 in 40 of violating each warning limit and approximately 1 in 1000 of violating each action limit if p remains unchanged. Draw the control chart and plot the 10 points corresponding to the data in the table. (Allow space for at least 14 points and for values of p up to 0.4.)

(b) The following numbers of unsatisfactory deliveries were recorded on separate weeks when the chart was in use. **(i)** 22, **(ii)** 18, **(iii)** 27, **(iv)** 2. For each of these occasions plot a point on your chart and comment on the current state of deliveries.

(c) If, in a particular week, the probability of each delivery being unsatisfactory is 0.32, what is the probability of the number recorded exceeding the upper action limit? [A]

Key point summary

1 Statistical process control may be used when a large number of similar items are being produced. Its purpose is to give a signal when the process mean has moved away from the target value or when item-to-item variability has increased. *p 74*

2 For control charts for means: *p 75*
  • Sample mean between warning limits – no action.
  • Sample mean between warning and action limits – take another sample immediately. If new sample mean outside warning limits take action.
  • Sample mean outside action limits – take action.

3 The warning limits are set at $\mu \pm 1.96 \dfrac{\sigma}{\sqrt{n}}$ *p 76*

and the action limits at $\mu \pm 3.09 \dfrac{\sigma}{\sqrt{n}}$, where μ is the target value, σ is the short-term standard deviation, and n is the sample size.

4 Variability may be controlled by plotting the sample ranges or standard deviations on control charts. The limits for these charts are found by multiplying the process short-term standard deviation by factors found in table 12. *p 83*

5 When the standard deviation must be estimated from a number of small samples the average sample range can be calculated and a factor from table 12 applied. Alternatively s_i can be calculated for each sample and the formula $s = \sqrt{\Sigma s_i^2 / n}$ evaluated. *p 87*

6 If the tolerance width exceeds six standard deviations the process should be able to meet the tolerances consistently, provided the mean is kept on target. *p 92*

7 For charts for proportion non-conforming providing n is reasonably large: *p 97*
  • the warning limits are $p \pm 1.96 \sqrt{p(1-p)/n}$
  • the action limits are $p \pm 3.09 \sqrt{p(1-p)/n}$.

Test yourself	**What to review**
1 A process has a target value 90.0 cm and a short-term standard deviation 2.4 cm. The process is to be controlled by taking samples of size 4 at regular intervals. Calculate warning and action limits for a chart for means.	*Section 4.3*
2 What action if any would you recommend if a sample from the process in question 1 measured 91.2 94.2 96.8 89.8 cm?	*Section 4.3*
3 Why might a sample from the process in question 1 measuring 78.9 94.2 101.3 85.7 cm cause concern?	*Section 4.3*
4 Calculate warning and action limits for a chart for standard deviations for the process in question 1. What do these limits indicate about the process in **(a)** question 2, **(b)** question 3?	*Section 4.7*
5 Samples of size 5 taken from a process which is performing satisfactorily have a mean range of 0.22 mm. Could this process consistently meet tolerances of 50.00 ± 0.30 mm? Explain your answer.	*Section 4.9*
6 What assumption was it necessary to make to answer question 5?	*Section 4.9*
7 A process is controlled by taking samples of 75 at regular intervals and counting the number non-conforming. Calculate warning and action limits for charts for proportion non-conforming if a proportion of 0.16 non-conforming is regarded as satisfactory.	*Section 4.10*
8 What action, if any, would you recommend if, for the process in question 7, the next sample contained: **(a)** 22 non-conforming, **(b)** 1 non-conforming?	*Section 4.10*

1 Warning limits 87.65 and 92.35,
Action limits 86.29 and 93.71.

2 Take another sample immediately; if mean of new sample outside warning limits take action.

3 Although the mean is within the warning limits, there is a large amount of within sample variability.

4 Warning limits 0.648 and 4.22,
Action limits 0.216 and 5.59.

(a) no action; (b) action.

5 Estimated standard deviation 0.0946 cm; tolerance width 6.3 standard deviations. Should be able to meet tolerances consistently provided process mean is exactly on target.

6 Normal distribution.

7 Warning limits 0.077 and 0.243,
Action limits 0.029 and 0.291.

8 (a) Take action;

(b) Process appears to be performing better than satisfactorily; continue production, try to maintain improvement.

CHAPTER 5

Acceptance sampling

Learning objectives

After studying this chapter you should be able to:

■ understand the operation of acceptance sampling schemes
■ draw an operating characteristic for single sampling plans using attributes, double sampling plans using attributes, and single sampling plans using variables
■ select appropriate plans to meet particular conditions.

5

5.1 Introduction

A large supermarket sells prepacked sandwiches in its food department. The sandwiches are bought in large batches from a catering firm. The supermarket manager wishes to test the sandwiches to make sure they are fresh and of good quality. In order to test them they must be unwrapped and tasted. After the test it will be no longer possible to sell them. A decision as to whether or not the batch is acceptable must be based on testing a relatively small sample of sandwiches. This is known as **acceptance sampling**.

Acceptance sampling may be applied where large quantities of similar items or large batches of material are being bought or are being transferred from one part of an organisation to another. Unlike statistical process control where the purpose is to check production as it proceeds, acceptance sampling is applied to large batches of goods which have already been produced.

> Acceptance sampling is designed for use when batches are received regularly from the same supplier and when it is expected that most batches will be accepted.

> Acceptance sampling may be applied to large batches of similar items. It is the process of deciding whether or not the batch is acceptable by testing a small sample of the items.

The test on the sandwiches is called a destructive test because after the test has been carried out the sandwich is no longer saleable. Other reasons for applying acceptance sampling are that when buying large batches of components it may be too expensive or too time consuming to test them all. In other cases, when dealing with a well-established supplier, the customer may be quite confident that the batch will be satisfactory but will still wish to test a small sample to make sure.

5.2 Acceptance sampling by attributes

In acceptance sampling by attributes each item tested is classified as conforming or non-conforming. (Items used to be classified as defective or non-defective but these days no self-respecting manufacturing firm will admit to making defective items.)

A sample is taken and if it contains too many non-conforming items the batch is rejected, otherwise it is accepted. For this method to be effective, batches containing some non-conforming items must be acceptable. If the only acceptable percentage of non-conforming items is zero every item must be examined and any non-conforming items must be removed. This is known as 100% inspection and is not acceptance sampling. However, the definition of non-conforming may be chosen as required. For example, if the contents of jars of jam are required to be between 453 and 461 g, it would be possible to define a jar with contents outside the range 455 to 459 g as non-conforming. Batches containing up to, say, 5% non-conforming items could then be accepted in the knowledge that, unless there was something very unusual about the distribution, this would ensure that virtually all jars in the batch contained between 453 and 461 g.

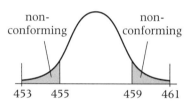

5.3 Operating characteristic

For any particular plan the operating characteristic is a graph of the probability of accepting a batch against the proportion non-conforming in the batch. Provided the sample is small compared to the size of the batch and the sampling is random, the probability of each member of the sample being non-conforming may be taken to be constant. In this case the number of non-conforming items in a batch will follow a binomial distribution.

> The operating characteristic for an acceptance sampling by attributes plan is a graph of probability of acceptance against proportion non-conforming in the batch.

> The probabilities may be found from the binomial distribution provided the sample is random and the sample size is small compared to the batch.

An example of an acceptance sampling plan is to take a sample of size 50 and to reject the batch if three or more non-conforming items are found. If two or fewer non-conforming items are found the batch will be accepted. This plan is often denoted by $n = 50$, $r = 3$ or $n = 50$, $a = 2$. For a batch containing a given proportion of non-conforming items the

r is the rejection number and a is the acceptance number.

probability of the sample containing two or fewer non-conforming items may be read directly from tables of the binomial distribution (or may be calculated). For example, if the batch contained 4% non-conforming items, the probability of any particular item in the sample being classified non-conforming is 0.04 and the probability of the batch containing two or fewer non-conforming items, and therefore being accepted, is 0.6767. The table below shows the probability of acceptance for a range of other cases.

Proportion non-conforming in batch	Probability of accepting batch
0.00	1.000
0.01	0.986
0.02	0.922
0.04	0.677
0.06	0.416
0.08	0.226
0.10	0.112
0.15	0.014
0.20	0.001

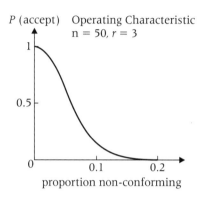

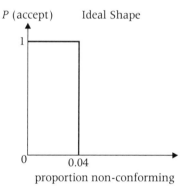

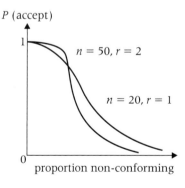

Ideally, if up to 4% non-conforming is acceptable, the probability of accepting a batch containing less than 4% non-conforming should be one and the probability of accepting a batch containing more than 4% non-conforming should be zero. If this were the case, the shape of the operating characteristic would be as shown opposite.

The next diagram shows the operating characteristic for the plan $n = 20$, $r = 1$, drawn on the same axes as the operating characteristic for $n = 50$, $r = 2$. As you can see the plan with the larger sample size, n, has the steeper graph. It is closer to the ideal shape and discriminates better between good batches (i.e. batches with a small proportion of non-conforming items) and bad batches (i.e. batches with a large proportion of non-conforming items).

Note that provided the batch is large enough for the binomial distribution to give a good approximation to the probabilities, it is the number of items inspected which determines how good the sampling plan is. The proportion of the batch inspected is not important. Provided the sampling is random it will be much better to test, say, 100 items from a batch of 5000 than to test 10 items from a batch of 500.

The operating characteristic shows that for all acceptance sampling plans there is some risk of rejecting a good batch (this is equivalent to making a Type 1 error in hypothesis testing) and some risk of accepting a bad batch (Type 2 error).

These risks used to be called manufacturer's risk and customer's risk, the idea being that only the manufacturer was concerned if a good batch was rejected and only the customer was concerned if a bad batch was accepted. These terms are rarely used today as it is recognised that it is in no one's interest for mistakes to be made. If bad batches are accepted the manufacturer will be faced with customer complaints which are expensive to deal with and, in the long run, business will suffer. If good batches are rejected, the cost of unnecessarily replacing them – or at the least the cost of extensive extra testing – will eventually be borne by the customer.

Worked example 5.1

A manufacturer receives large batches of components daily and decides to institute an acceptance sampling scheme. Three possible plans are considered, each of which requires a sample of 30 components to be tested.

Plan A: Accept the batch if no non-conforming components are found, otherwise reject.

Plan B: Accept the batch if not more than one non-conforming component is found, otherwise reject.

Plan C: Accept the batch if two or fewer non-conforming components are found, otherwise reject.

(a) For each plan, calculate the probability of accepting a batch containing:
  (i) 2% non-conforming,
  (ii) 8% non-conforming.

(b) Without further calculation sketch on the same axes the operating characteristic of each plan.

(c) Which plan would be most appropriate in each of the circumstances listed below?
  (i) There should be a high probability of accepting batches containing 2% non-conforming.
  (ii) There should be a high probability of rejecting batches containing 8% non-conforming.
  (iii) A balance is required between the risk of accepting batches containing 8% defective and the risk of rejecting batches containing 2% non-conforming.

Solution

(a) The probability may be calculated or be obtained directly from tables of the binomial distribution.

For a batch containing 2% non-conforming, the probability of any member of the sample being a non-conforming component is 0.02.

From tables of binomial distribution with $n = 30$, $p = 0.02$, the probability of a sample of size 30 containing no non-conforming items is 0.5455 and this is the probability of the batch being accepted if Plan A is used.

If Plan B is used the batch will be accepted if the sample contains 0 or 1 non-conforming items and the probability of this is 0.8795.

If Plan C is used the batch will be accepted if the sample contains 0, 1 or 2 non-conforming components. The probability of this is 0.978.

Similarly if the batch contains 8% non-conforming components, the binomial distribution with $n = 30$, $p = 0.08$, gives the following results for the probability of acceptance when a sample of size 30 is taken:

Plan A: 0.0822   Plan B: 0.296   Plan C: 0.565

(b) From **(a)** we have two points on the operating characteristic for each plan. In addition, all operating characteristics go through the point $(0, 1)$ because if the batch contains no non-conforming components, every sample will contain no non-conforming components and this must lead to the batch being accepted. Every operating characteristic will also pass through the point $(1, 0)$. However this part of the curve is of no interest. It corresponds to batches which contain only non-conforming items. Acceptance sampling would not be used if there was any possibility of this occurring. The graphs may now be sketched as shown opposite.

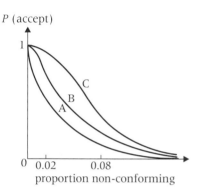

(c) (i) Plan C would be the most suitable as it has the highest probability (0.978) of accepting a batch containing 2% non-conforming.

(ii) Plan A has the lowest probability (0.082) of accepting a batch containing 8% non-conforming. Plan A is therefore the most suitable as the probability of rejecting a batch containing 8% non-conforming is $1 - 0.082 = 0.918$, and this is highest of the three plans.

(iii) Plan B would be the most suitable in this case. It can be seen from the graph that it has a lower probability than A of rejecting a batch containing 2% non-conforming and a lower probability than C of accepting a batch containing 8% non-conforming.

Worked example 5.2

An engine component is defective if its length (in 0.001 mm) is outside the range 19 950 to 20 050. An acceptance sampling scheme consists of taking a sample of size 50 from each batch and accepting the batch if the sample contains two or fewer defective components. If the sample contains three or more defective components the batch is rejected.

(a) Find the probability of accepting batches containing 2%, 5%, 10% and 15% defective components.

The customer complains that the plan has far too high a risk of accepting batches containing a large proportion of defective components. The customer regards a batch containing 1 in 1000 defective components as bad but will agree that a batch containing 1 in 10 000 defective components is good.

(b) (i) If the lengths of components are normally distributed with mean 20 000 and standard deviation 12.8, what proportion are defective?

(ii) It is decided to define components outside the range $20\,000 \pm k$ as non-conforming. Find the value of k to two significant figures which will give 5% non-conforming items for the distribution in **(b) (i)**.

(iii) If the distribution of lengths in a batch is normal with mean 20 010 and standard deviation 12.8 about 1 component in 1000 will be defective. What proportion will be non-conforming? If the plan in **(a)** is applied to non-conforming instead of defective components find from your operating characteristic the probability of accepting this batch.

(c) Explain why the plan in **(b) (iii)** should satisfy the customer.

> In this question a distinction is made between 'defective' meaning a component which will not fulfil its function and 'non-conforming' meaning outside agreed limits.

Solution

(a) From binomial tables, $n = 50$
2% defective $\Rightarrow p = 0.02$ $P(2 \text{ or fewer}) = 0.922$
5% defective $\Rightarrow p = 0.05$ $P(2 \text{ or fewer}) = 0.5405$
10% defective $\Rightarrow p = 0.10$ $P(2 \text{ or fewer}) = 0.112$
15% defective $\Rightarrow p = 0.15$ $P(2 \text{ or fewer}) = 0.014$
(The operating characteristic is identical to the one drawn in section 5.3.)

(b) (i) $z_1 = (19\,950 - 20\,000)/12.8 = -3.906$
$z_2 = (20\,050 - 20\,000)/12.8 = 3.906$

The proportion defective $= (1 - 0.999\,95) + (1 - 0.999\,95)$
$$= 0.0001$$

(ii) $k = 1.96 \times 12.8 = 25$

(iii) If $k = 25$ the limits for non-conforming items are
$20\,000 - 25 = 19\,975$
and $20\,000 + 25 = 20\,025$

$z_1 = (19\,975 - 20\,010)/12.8 = -2.734$
$z_2 = (20\,025 - 20\,010)/12.8 = 1.172$

The proportion non-conforming $= 1 - 0.879\,40 + (1 - 0.996\,87)$
$$= 0.124$$

The probability of accepting this batch if $n = 50$, $r = 3$, is applied to non-conforming items is 0.044 from the operating characteristic.

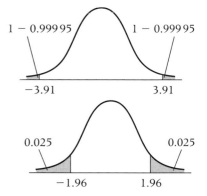

$P\,(\text{accept})$ Operating Characteristic
$n = 50, r = 3$

proportion non-conforming

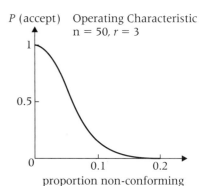

$1 - 0.999\,95$ $1 - 0.999\,95$

-3.91 3.91

0.025 0.025

-1.96 1.96

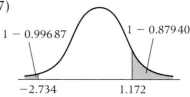

$1 - 0.996\,87$ $1 - 0.879\,40$

-2.734 1.172

(c) The batch contains 0.1% defective components which the customer regards as unsatisfactory. Applying the plan to non-conforming items ensures that there is only a small (less than 5%) chance of accepting this batch.

EXERCISE 5A

1 An acceptance sampling scheme consists of inspecting 25 items and rejecting the batch if two or more non-conforming items are found. Find the probability of accepting a batch containing 15% non-conforming items. Find also the probability of accepting batches containing 2%, 4%, 6%, 8%, 10% and 20% non-conforming items and use your results to draw the operating characteristic.

2 An acceptance sampling scheme consists of taking a random sample of 20 from a large batch of items and accepting the batch if the sample contains two or fewer non-conforming items. Draw the operating characteristic for this scheme.

3 An auditor checks large batches of invoices for errors by selecting a random sample of 50 invoices from each batch. If the number of invoices in the sample with errors is two or fewer, the batch is accepted, otherwise all invoices in the batch are checked.

The proportion of invoices with errors in a batch is p and $P(A)$ denotes the probability that a batch is accepted.

(a) Copy and complete the following table.

p	0.01	0.02	0.03	0.04	0.05	0.06	0.07	0.08	0.09	0.10	0.15	0.20
$P(A)$					0.54	0.42	0.31					0.00

(b) Hence, draw the operating characteristic curve.

(c) Estimate from the operating characterisic the value of p for which
   (i) the probability of accepting a batch is 0.10,
   (ii) the probability of rejecting a batch is 0.05.

4 An acceptance sampling scheme consists of a sample of n components being taken from a batch. The batch is rejected if r or more non-conforming items are found in the sample, otherwise it is accepted.

(a) (i) If $n = 25$ and $r = 3$ find from tables, the probability of accepting a batch containing 1%, 2%, 4%, 7%, 10%, 15% and 20% defective components. Draw the operating characteristic.
   (ii) If $n = 40$ and $r = 4$ draw the operating characteristic.

(b) For each of the acceptance sampling plans in **(a)** find from your operating characteristic the percentage defective in a batch which has a probability of:

  (i) 0.9 of being accepted,
  (ii) 0.98 of being rejected.

5 A pottery produces large batches of breakfast bowls decorated
  with forenames. The pottery has under consideration two
  batch single sampling plans for controlling the quality of
  finished bowls.

  Plan A: Select 20 bowls at random from a batch and accept
  the batch if there are fewer than two defective bowls,
  otherwise reject the batch.

  Plan B: Select 40 bowls at random from a batch and accept
  the batch if there are fewer than four defective bowls,
  otherwise reject the batch.

  (a) Explain why a binomial distribution is appropriate as a
    model for the number of defective bowls in a sample.

  The proportion of defective bowls in a batch is p.

  (b) Copy and complete the following table of probabilities
    that a batch of bowls is accepted.

p	0.00	0.01	0.02	0.03	0.04	0.05	0.06	0.07	0.08	0.09	0.10	0.15	0.20
Plan A						0.74	0.66	0.59	0.52	0.45			
Plan B						0.86	0.78	0.69	0.60	0.51			

  (c) Hence, draw on the same graph the operating
    characteristic curve for each plan.

  (d) If the unit cost of inspecting each bowl is negligible and
    if batches containing 10% defective bowls should be
    rejected, state with a reason which is the better plan.

6 **(a)** An acceptance sampling scheme consists of taking a
    sample of size 50 and rejecting the batch if three or
    more non-conforming items are found. Draw the
    operating characteristic for this scheme.

  (b) A company operates the acceptance sampling scheme
    described in **(a)** when buying components.
    (i) If components with lengths outside the range
      $40\,000 \pm 100$ are classified as non-conforming find
      the proportion of non-conforming components in a
      batch with lengths which are normally distributed
      with mean 40 000 and standard deviation 50. The
      units are thousandths of a mm. Use your operating
      characteristic to find the probability of accepting
      this batch.
    (ii) Find the probability of rejecting a batch with mean
      40 030 and standard deviation 60.
    (iii) Find from your operating characteristic the
      proportion non-conforming in a batch which would
      have a probability of 0.9 of being accepted by the
      sampling scheme.

(iv) It is required to have a probability of 0.9 of accepting a batch with mean 40 000 and standard deviation 50. This is to be achieved by defining components outside the range $40\,000 \pm k$ as non-conforming. Using your result in **(iii)** find k.

7 An electronic component is defective if its length (in 0.001 mm) is outside the range 11 975 to 12 025.

(a) An acceptance sampling scheme consists of taking a sample of 50 from each batch and accepting the batch if the sample contains two or fewer defective components. If the sample contains three or more defective components the batch is rejected.
Find, from tables, the probability of accepting batches containing 2%, 5%, 10% and 15% defective components and draw the operating characteristic.

(b) The customer regards the plan in **(a)** as having far too high a risk of accepting batches containing too many defective components. This customer regards 1 in a 1000 defective components as a bad batch.

(i) If lengths of components are normally distributed with mean 12 000 and standard deviation 6.4, what proportion are defective?

(ii) It is decided to define components outside the range $12\,000 \pm k$ as non-conforming. Find the value of k, to two significant figures, which will give 4% non-conforming components for the distribution in **(b)(i)**.

(iii) If the distribution of lengths in a batch is normal with mean 12 006 and standard deviation 6.4, find the proportion defective and the proportion non-conforming.

(iv) If the plan in **(a)** is applied to non-conforming instead of defective components find from your operating characteristic the probability of accepting the batch in **(b)(iii)**.

(c) Discuss, briefly, whether or not the plan in **(b)(iii)** is likely to satisfy the customer.

5.4 Selecting acceptance sampling plans

The operating characteristic summarises the implications of using a particular acceptance sampling plan. However it does not tell us which acceptance sampling plan to use. In practice this question is usually answered by following the advice of British Standard 6001, but it is possible to derive an appropriate plan if the sample size and an acceptable level of risk is specified.

For example, a plan might be required where a sample of size 50 is taken and where there is a probability of at least 0.95 of accepting a batch containing 1% non-conforming items.

Here $n = 50$ is specified and the value of r remains to be determined. For batches containing 1% non-conforming ($p = 0.01$) the probability of finding x or fewer non-conforming items can be found from binomial tables and is shown below.

x	$P(x$ or fewer$)$
0	0.605
1	0.911
2	0.986
3	0.998
4	1.000

The most severe plan possible is $n = 50$, $r = 1$. In this case the batch will only be accepted if the sample contains zero non-conforming items. The probability of this is 0.605 which is lower than the required 0.95.

The next most severe plan is $n = 50$, $r = 2$. In this case the batch will be accepted if the sample contains zero or one non-conforming items. The probability of this is 0.911 which is still lower than the required 0.95.

The next plan is $n = 50$, $r = 3$. In this case the batch will be accepted if the sample contains two or fewer non-conforming items. The probability of this is 0.986 which satisfies the requirement of a probability of 0.95 and so this plan is chosen.

Note plans with $r > 3$ would also meet the requirement. However, as well as ensuring a high probability of accepting good batches (in this case those containing 1% or fewer non-conforming) we wish to have as high a chance as possible of rejecting bad batches. Hence, in this case, the lowest value of r which meets the condition is chosen.

Alternatively the probability of rejecting a bad batch might be specified. For example, a plan might be required where a sample of size 50 is taken and where there is a probability of at least 0.8 of rejecting a batch containing 6% non-conforming items.

Again $n = 50$ is specified and the value of r remains to be determined. For batches containing 6% non-conforming items ($p = 0.06$) the probability of finding x or fewer non-conforming items can be found from binomial tables and is shown below. The probability of **not** finding x or fewer non-conforming items ($1 - P(x$ or fewer$)$) is also shown.

x	$P(x$ or fewer$)$	$1 - P(x$ or fewer$)$
0	0.045	0.955
1	0.190	0.810
2	0.416	0.584
3	0.647	0.353

The most severe plan possible is $n = 50$, $r = 1$. In this case the batch will only be accepted if the sample contains zero non-conforming items. The probability of the batch being rejected is 0.955. This satisfies the requirement of a probability of at least 0.8. However there may be a less severe plan which satisfies the requirement for rejecting bad batches (in this case those containing 6% or more non-conforming items) but gives a higher probability of accepting good batches.

The next most severe plan is $n = 50$, $r = 2$. In this case the batch will be accepted if the sample contains zero or one non-conforming items. The probability of the batch being rejected is 0.810 which again satisfies the requirement.

The next plan is $n = 50$, $r = 3$. In this case the batch will be accepted if the sample contains two or fewer non-conforming items. The probability of the batch being rejected by this plan is 0.584 which does not satisfy the requirement. Clearly any plans with $r > 3$ will not satisfy the requirement.

In this case there are two possible plans which satisfy the requirement and $n = 50$, $r = 2$ is chosen as, of the two, this gives the best chance of accepting good batches.

Worked example 5.3

(a) A manufacturer requires a plan with a probability of not more than 0.05 of rejecting a batch containing 3% non-conforming. If the sample size is 25, what should be the criterion for rejecting the batch if the risk is to be just met?

This implies a batch containing 3% non-conforming is regarded as satisfactory.

(b) It is decided to increase the number of items inspected to 50. What should be the criterion for accepting a batch if the risk of accepting a batch containing 15% non-conforming is to be as near as possible to 10%?

(c) Plot the operating characteristic for both plans on the same axes.

(d) Does the plan chosen in (b) satisfy the risk specified in (a)?

(e) Discuss the factors to be considered when deciding which of the two plans to use.

Solution

(a) For a batch containing 3% non-conforming the probability of r or fewer non-conforming items in a sample of 25 is found from the binomial distribution $n = 25$, $p = 0.03$ and is given below.

r	$P(r$ or fewer$)$
0	0.467
1	0.828
2	0.962
3	0.994

The manufacturer requires a plan with a probability of not more than 0.05 of rejecting a batch containing 3% non-conforming. That is, a probability of at least 0.95 of accepting the batch. The table shows that the probability of the sample containing two or fewer is 0.962, thus $n = 25$, $r = 3$ will just meet this requirement. (Note accepting if two or fewer are found implies rejecting if three or more are found.)

> Any value of r greater than three would also satisfy the condition. We choose the smallest value of r which satisfies the condition as this gives the highest probability of rejecting bad batches.

(b) Binomial distribution $n = 50$, $p = 0.15$.

r	$P(r$ or fewer$)$
0	0.000
1	0.003
2	0.014
3	0.046
4	0.112
5	0.219

A risk of about 10% or 0.10 of accepting a batch containing 15% non-conforming is given by accepting batches if four or fewer non-conforming items are found. (As can be seen from the table above, the probability of finding four or fewer is 0.112.) This gives the plan $n = 50$, $r = 5$.

(c)

proportion non-conforming	$P($accept$)$ $n = 25, r = 3$	$P($accept$)$ $n = 50, r = 5$
0.00	1.000	1.000
0.02	0.987	0.997
0.04	0.923	0.951
0.07	0.747	0.729
0.10	0.537	0.431
0.15	0.254	0.112
0.20	0.098	0.018

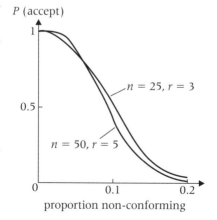

(d) From the operating characteristic for $n = 50$, $r = 5$, it can be seen that the probability of accepting a batch containing 3% or 0.03 non-conforming is about 0.98. Thus the probability of rejecting it is about 0.02 which is well below the 0.05 specified in **(a)**. Hence it does meet the risk.

(e) The plan requiring a sample of 50 will require more testing to be carried out and so will be more expensive. As can be seen from the operating characteristics, it discriminates better between good and bad batches, giving a higher probability of accepting good (small proportion non-conforming) batches and a higher probability of rejecting bad (large proportion non-conforming) batches.

The cost of the extra sampling should be balanced against the cost of making wrong decisions, i.e. the waste involved in rejecting a good batch and the problems and frustrations caused by accepting a bad batch.

EXERCISE 5B

1 Samples of size 50 are to be taken from large batches of pre-packed sandwiches. Sandwiches with insufficient filling or other deficiencies are classified as non-conforming. The batch will be rejected if too many non-conforming sandwiches are found in the sample. Find a suitable criterion for rejecting the batch if the risk of accepting a batch containing 10% non-conforming is is not to exceed 10%.

2 An acceptance sampling plan is to use a sample of size 40. Find an appropriate criterion for rejecting the batch in each of the following cases:

   (a) the risk of rejecting a batch containing 1% non-conforming sandwiches should not exceed 0.10,

   (b) the probability of accepting a batch containing 2% non-conforming sandwiches should be at least 0.99,

   (c) the risk of accepting a batch containing 15% non-conforming sandwiches should not exceed 5%,

   (d) the probability of rejecting a batch containing 10% non-conforming sandwiches should be at least 0.9.

3 **(a)** A manufacturer will accept a risk of not more than 10% of a batch of items containing 2% non-conforming being rejected. If a decision is to be made by examining a sample of 50 items, find the appropriate decision procedure.

   (b) Draw the operating characteristic for the above plan and indicate on the graph the ideal shape of the operating characteristics if batches containing up to 5% non-conforming are acceptable.

   (c) Would the plan found in **(a)** satisfy a customer who specified a risk of not more than 5% of a batch containing 11% non-conforming being accepted?

4 An acceptance sampling plan is to be based on a sample of size 25.

    (a) Find the appropriate acceptance criterion if the risk of accepting a batch containing 20% non-conforming items is not to exceed 10%.

    (b) Find the probability of rejecting a batch containing 1% non-conforming items using the plan found in **(a)**.

    (c) If a risk of 3% of rejecting a batch containing 1% non-conforming is acceptable find the appropriate acceptance criterion.

    (d) Find the probability of accepting a batch containing 20% non-conforming using the plan found in **(c)**.

5 (a) A random sample of 20 from a large batch of components is to be tested, and by counting the number non-conforming, a decision is to be made as to whether the batch should be accepted or rejected by the customer. If a risk of not more than 2% of a batch containing 1% non-conforming being rejected is acceptable, find an appropriate criterion for rejecting batches. Plot on graph paper, the operating characteristic for this plan.

    (b) If the sample size is increased to 50 but the acceptable risk of rejecting a batch containing 1% non-conforming is unchanged, plot the operating characteristic of this new scheme on the same axes.

    (c) Compare the risk of accepting a batch containing 9% non-conforming components for the two plans.

    (d) Sketch, on the same axes, the ideal shape of the operating characteristic if a batch containing up to 4% non-conforming is acceptable to the customer.

6 An acceptance sampling scheme consists of a sample of n burgers being taken from a batch. Burgers containing less than 1% meat are classified as non-conforming. The batch is rejected if r or more non-conforming burgers are found in the sample, otherwise it is accepted.

    (a) If $n = 30$ and $r = 2$ find from tables, the probability of accepting a batch containing 1%, 2%, 4%, 7%, 10%, 15% and 20% non-conforming burgers. Draw the operating characteristic.

    (b) Find from your operating characteristic the percentage non-conforming in a batch which has a probability of:
        (i) 0.9 of being accepted,
        (ii) 0.98 of being rejected.

A plan is required which satisfies two conditions.

Condition 1: A probability of at least 0.9 of accepting a batch containing 2% non-conforming.

Condition 2: A probability of at least 0.98 of rejecting a batch containing 15% non-conforming.

(c) If $n = 30$ find

    (i) the smallest value of r which will satisfy Condition 1,

    (ii) the largest value of r which will satisfy Condition 2.

    (iii) Explain why there is no plan with $n = 30$ which will satisfy both conditions.

(d) By finding a suitable value of r show that if $n = 50$ there is a plan which satisfies both conditions.

5.5 Double sampling plans

It is likely that a very good batch or a very bad batch will be detected with a relatively small sample but for an intermediate batch it is desirable to take a larger sample before deciding whether to accept or reject. Double sampling is an attempt to achieve this.

The following is an example of a double sampling plan.

Take a sample of size 30. Accept the batch if zero or one non-conforming items are found and reject the batch if three or more non-conforming items are found. If exactly two non-conforming items are found take a further sample of size 30. Accept the batch if a total of four or fewer (out of 60) non-conforming items are found, otherwise reject the batch.

This plan is denoted

$$n = 30; a = 1, r = 3$$
$$n = 30; a = 4, r = 5.$$

For double sampling it is necessary to specify both the acceptance number, a, and the rejection number, r.

Note that the acceptance and rejection numbers refer to all items that have been inspected, not just to the most recent sample. There is no theoretical reason why the first and second sample need be of the same size, but in practice this is virtually always the case.

 In double sampling, the number of non-conforming items in the first sample will determine whether a decision is made immediately or whether it is delayed until a second sample has been inspected.

Worked example 5.4 ────────────

A firm is to introduce an acceptance sampling scheme. Three alternative plans are considered.

Plan A: Take a sample of 50 and accept the batch if no non-conforming items are found, otherwise reject.

Plan B: Take a sample of 50 and accept the batch if two or fewer non-conforming items are found.

Plan C: Take a sample of 40 and accept the batch if no non-conforming items are found. Reject the batch if two or more are found. If one is found, then take a further sample of size 40. If a total of two or fewer (out of 80) is found, accept the batch, otherwise reject.

> This plan can be denoted
> $n = 40$; $a = 0$, $r = 2$
> $n = 40$; $a = 2$, $r = 3$.

(a) Find the probability of acceptance for each of the plans A, B and C if batches are submitted containing:
    (i) 1% non-conforming,
    (ii) 10% non-conforming.

(b) Without further calculation, sketch on the same axes the operating characteristic for plans A, B and C.

(c) Show that, for batches containing 1% non-conforming, the average number of items inspected when using plan C is similar to the number inspected when using plans A or B.

Solution

(a) **Plan A**: $n = 50$, accept if no non-conforming items are found.

$$p = 0.01 \quad P(0) = 0.605$$
$$p = 0.10 \quad P(0) = 0.005$$

Plan B: $n = 50$, accept if 0, 1 or 2 non-conforming items are found.

$$p = 0.01 \quad P(2 \text{ or fewer}) = 0.986$$
$$p = 0.10 \quad P(2 \text{ or fewer}) = 0.112$$

Plan C: The batch will be accepted if no non-conforming items are found in the first sample (in which case no second sample will be taken). It will also be accepted if one non-conforming item is found in the first sample and none or one found in the second sample. The possible ways of accepting the batch are shown below.

First sample	Second sample
0	
1	0
1	1

There are no other ways of accepting the batch – if two or more are found in the first sample the batch is immediately rejected and if one is found in the first sample and two or more in the second (giving a total of three or more) the batch is rejected.

The samples are of equal size and the batch is large so the probability of acceptance may be expressed as

$P(0) + P(1) \times P(1 \text{ or fewer})$

$\quad\quad p = 0.01 \quad P(0) = 0.6690 \quad P(1 \text{ or fewer}) = 0.9393$

$\quad\quad P(1) = 0.9393 - 0.6690 = 0.2703$

$P(\text{accept}) = 0.6690 + 0.2703 \times 0.9393 = 0.923$

$\quad\quad p = 0.10 \quad P(0) = 0.0148 \quad P(1 \text{ or fewer}) = 0.0805$

$\quad\quad P(1) = 0.0805 - 0.0148 = 0.0657$

$P(\text{accept}) = 0.0148 + 0.0657 \times 0.0805 = 0.020$

> We can assume that the probabilities are the same in both samples and can be found from the binomial distribution with $n = 40$.

(b) *P* (accept)

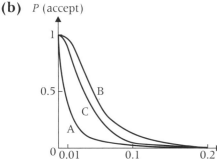

proportion non-conforming

(c) For Plan C, if the first sample contains zero or two or more non-conforming items, a decision as to whether to accept or reject the batch is made immediately. A second sample is only taken if the first sample contains exactly one non-conforming item. The expected number of items inspected is

$\quad\quad 40 + 40 \times P(1).$

For batches containing 1% non-conforming the expected number of items inspected is

$\quad\quad 40 + 40 \times 0.270 = 50.8.$

> This is the average number of items inspected if the plan is operated a large number of times.

Thus the average number inspected is similar to the 50 inspected in the single sample plans.

Note that this calculation only applies when $p = 0.01$. For other values of p you would have to make a further calculation. However it can be stated that if a single and a double sampling plan have similar operating characteristics (not the case here), the double sampling plan will, on average, require less items to be inspected than the single sampling plan. This will be true for any value of p. The disadvantage of double sampling plans is that they are more complex to operate than single sampling plans.

Worked example 5.5

The following acceptance sampling plans have similar operating characteristics.

Plan 1: Take a sample of size 80 and reject the batch if six or more non-conforming items are found.

Plan 2: Take a sample of size 50 and accept the batch if two or fewer non-conforming items are found. Reject the batch if five or more non-conforming items are found. If three or four non-conforming items are found take a further sample of size 50 and reject the batch if a total of seven or more non-conforming items (out of 100) are found, otherwise accept.

> This plan can be denoted
> $n = 50$; $a = 2$, $r = 5$
> $n = 50$; $a = 6$, $r = 7$.

(a) Verify that both plans have similar probabilities of accepting batches containing 4% non-conforming items. You are given that for the binomial

$$n = 80 \quad p = 0.04 \quad P(5 \text{ or fewer}) = 0.899.$$

(b) The cost of the sampling inspection is made up of the cost of obtaining the sample plus the cost of carrying out the inspection. A firm estimates that for a sample of size n the cost, in pence, of obtaining the sample is $(800 + 8n)$ pence and the cost of inspection is $48n$ pence. For batches containing 4% non-conforming items, compare the expected cost of the following three inspection procedures:

(i)   Use Plan 1.

(ii) Use Plan 2, obtaining the second sample of 50 only if required to do so by the plan;

(iii) Use Plan 2, but obtain a sample of 100. Inspect the first 50, but only inspect the second 50 if required to do so by the plan.

Solution

(a) For Plan 1, $n = 80$, $p = 0.04$; accept if five or fewer found. From given information $P(5 \text{ or fewer}) = 0.899$.

For Plan 2, the batch can be accepted in the following ways:

First sample	Second sample
0	
1	
2	
3	0
3	1
3	2
3	3
4	0
4	1
4	2

$P(\text{accept}) = P(0) + P(1) + P(2) + P(3)P(0) + P(3)P(1) +$
$P(3)P(2) + P(3)P(3) + P(4)P(0) + P(4)P(1) + P(4)P(2)$
$= P(2 \text{ or fewer}) + P(3)P(3 \text{ or fewer}) + P(4)P(2 \text{ or fewer})$

Both samples are of size 50 and if the batch is assumed to be large the probabilities may be found from tables of the binomial $n = 50$, $p = 0.04$
$= 0.6767 + (0.8609 - 0.6767)0.8609 + (0.9510 - 0.8609)0.6767$
$= 0.896$.
This probability is similar to the 0.899 obtained for Plan 1.

(b) **(i)** The cost for Plan 1 is $[800 + (8 \times 80)] + (48 \times 80) = £52.80$.

(ii) In this case the second sample of 50 will be obtained only if the first sample contains three or four defective items. The probability of this occurring is
$P(4 \text{ or fewer}) - P(2 \text{ or fewer})$
$= 0.9510 - 0.6767 = 0.2743$

The expected cost is the cost of obtaining and testing the first sample plus $0.2743 \times$ (the cost of obtaining and testing the second sample)
$= 800 + (8 \times 50) + (48 \times 50) + 0.2743[(800 + (8 \times 50) + (48 \times 50)]$
$= £45.87$

(iii) In this case the expected cost is the cost of obtaining a sample of 100 and testing 50 of these plus $0.2743 \times$ (the cost of testing a further 50)
$= 800 + (8 \times 100) + (48 \times 50) + (0.2743 \times 48 \times 50)$
$= £46.58$

> These are long run average costs and do not apply to individual samples.

Hence the expected cost of the double sampling plan is less than that of the single sampling plan. This does not depend on whether two separate samples of 50 are taken as required, or whether a single sample of 100 is taken. The calculation, of course, applies only to the case where batches containing 4% non-conforming items are submitted. However, the conclusion is probably true for all other possible batches. The double sampling plan is, however, more complex to operate.

EXERCISE 5C

1 (a) An acceptance sampling scheme consists of taking a sample of size 20 and accepting the batch if no non-conforming items are found. If two or more non-conforming items are found the batch is rejected. If one non-conforming item is found a further sample of 20 is taken and the batch is accepted if a total of two or fewer (out of 40) non-conforming items are found. Otherwise it is rejected. This plan is denoted

$n = 20; a = 0, r = 2$
$n = 20; a = 2, r = 3$.

Find the probability of accepting a batch containing 4% non-conforming items.

(b) Find the probability of accepting a batch containing 3% non-conforming items for the plan

$$n = 40; a = 0, r = 3$$
$$n = 40; a = 3, r = 4.$$

(c) Find the probability of accepting a batch containing 5% non-conforming item for the plan

$$n = 30; a = 0, r = 3$$
$$n = 30; a = 3, r = 4.$$

2 (a) Draw the operating characteristic for the plan

$$n = 13; a = 1, r = 4$$
$$n = 13; a = 4, r = 5.$$

(b) Verify that the plan in **(a)** has a similar probability of accepting a batch containing 4% non-conforming items as the single sampling plan $n = 20; a = 3, r = 4$.

(c) Give one advantage and one disadvantage of double sampling plans compared to single sampling plans.

3 (a) Large batches of wrappers for sliced loaves are to be checked by examining a random sample of 50. If the customer will accept a risk of not more than 5% of a batch containing 10% non-conforming wrappers being accepted, what should the criterion be for rejecting the batch?

(b) A double sampling plan is specified by

$$n = 20; a = 0, r = 2$$
$$n = 20; a = 2, r = 3.$$

(i) What is the probability of a batch containing 10% non-conforming wrappers being accepted?
(ii) What is the average number of items inspected when batches containing 10% non-conforming wrappers are submitted?

4 When checking large batches of goods the following acceptance sampling plans have similar operating characteristics.

Plan 1: Take a sample of size 50 and accept the batch if three or fewer non-conforming items are found, otherwise reject it.

Plan 2: Take a sample of size 30, accept the batch if zero or one non-conforming items are found and reject the batch if three or more are found. If exactly two are found, take a further sample of size 30. Accept the batch if a total of four or fewer (out of 60) are found, otherwise reject it.

(a) Verify that the two plans have similar probabilities of accepting a batch containing 5% non-conforming items.

(b) For the second plan evaluate the probability of accepting a batch containing 0, 0.02, 0.05, 0.10 and 0.15 non-conforming items. Use your results to:
   (i) draw an operating characteristic,
   (ii) sketch a graph of the expected number of items inspected against the proportion non-conforming in the batch.

(c) What factors should be considered when deciding which of the two plans is to be used?

5 A producer of fuses for cars has received complaints from a major customer regarding the quality of the fuses. As a temporary measure and to retain the customer, the producer is obliged to introduce a batch sampling inspection scheme. The customer demands that batches containing 10% non-conforming fuses must have at most a 5% chance of being accepted by any scheme, whereas the producer suggests that batches containing only 1% non-conforming fuses should have at least a 98% chance of being accepted.

(a) Using Poisson approximations, show that both of these requirements are satisfied if a random sample of 80 fuses is selected from a batch and the batch is only accepted if the sample contains three or fewer non-conforming fuses.

As an alternative, the following double sampling scheme is proposed.

Select a random sample of 50 fuses from a batch. If the sample contains one or fewer non-conforming fuses, accept the batch; if it contains four or more non-conforming fuses, reject the batch; otherwise select a second random sample of 50 fuses from the batch. Accept the batch if the total number of non-conforming fuses in the two samples is three or fewer, otherwise reject the batch.

(b) Using appropriate binomial distributions, determine whether or not this proposed scheme meets both the requirements.

For a sample of size n, the cost of sampling is £$(20 + 0.5n)$. This cost applies to all samples including the second sample in a double sampling scheme.

(c) Show that, for batches containing 5% non-conforming fuses, the above double sampling scheme is, on average, more costly than the single sampling scheme described in **(a)**.

6 An acceptance sampling scheme consists of taking a sample of 30 from incoming batches of components and accepting the batch if the sample contains one or fewer non-conforming components. If the sample contains two or more non-conforming components the batch is rejected.

(a) Find from tables the probability of accepting batches containing 1%, 2%, 3%, 5%, 7%, 10% and 15% non-conforming components. Draw the operating characteristic.

An alternative plan consists of taking a sample of 40 and accepting the batch if zero or one non-conforming components are found and rejecting the batch if three or more non-conforming components are found. If two non-conforming components are found a further sample of 40 is taken. The batch is then accepted if a total of three or fewer non-conforming components (out of 80) is found, otherwise it is rejected.

(b) Complete the following table by calculating the probability of accepting a batch containing 10% non-conforming components using this alternative plan.

Percentage non-conforming in batch	0	1	2	3	5	7	10	15
Probability of acceptance	1.000	0.989	0.927	0.807	0.510	0.273		0.0125

Draw the operating characteristic for this plan on the same axes as you have used in **(a)**.

(c) From your graph estimate:
   (i) the percentage non-conforming for which both plans have the same probability of acceptance;
   (ii) the percentage non-conforming which has a probability of 0.1 of being accepted by
       (A) the single sampling plan,
       (B) the double sampling plan.

(d) Compare the two plans.

5.6 Acceptance sampling by variable

Acceptance sampling can be carried out by measuring a variable rather than classifying an item as conforming or non-conforming. Variables such as thickness, strength or weight might be measured. A typical plan would be to take a sample of size n and reject the batch if the mean measurement, $\bar{x}$, is less than k. This would be appropriate for, say, the strength of a batch of climbing ropes where a large value is desirable. If the variable was, say, percentage of impurity in raw material, where a small value was desirable, the plan would be of the form – take a sample of size n and reject the batch if the mean measurement, $\bar{x}$, is greater than k. There will be other cases, such as the width of car doors being delivered to an assembly line where the batch will be rejected if $\bar{x}$ does not lie between k_1 and k_2.

Usually it is easier and quicker to classify an item as conforming or non-conforming than to make an exact measurement. However, the information gained from an exact measurement is greater and so smaller sample sizes are required. A decision as to whether to use attributes or variables will depend on the particular circumstances of each case.

A component for use in the manufacture of office machinery will fail to function if the temperature becomes too high. A company receiving batches of these components operates the following acceptance sampling scheme – test a sample of size 16 and reject the batch if the mean failure temperature is less than 95.0°C.

The operating characteristic is a graph of probability of acceptance against mean failure temperature and, as with acceptance sampling by attributes, summarises the implications of the plan.

> For acceptance sampling by variables the operating characteristic is a graph of probability of acceptance against batch mean.

It is reasonable to assume normal distribution since we are concerned with the mean of a reasonably large sample. If, for example, a batch with mean failure temperature 95.6°C is submitted it will be accepted if the sample mean exceeds 95.0°C.

$$z = \frac{95 - 95.6}{\frac{2.4}{\sqrt{16}}} = -1.00$$

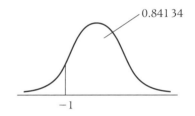

The probability of the batch being accepted is 0.841.

The operating characteristic can be constructed by carrying out a similar calculation for batches with different means (assuming the standard deviation remains at 2.4°C). The calculations can be put in a table as shown below. (Be careful to use the correct tail of the normal distribution, this will depend on the sign of z and will change when this changes.)

In this case
$k = 95$, $\sigma = 2.4$, $n = 16$.

μ	$\dfrac{k - \mu}{\dfrac{\sigma}{\sqrt{n}}}$	$P(\text{accept})$
93.2	3.0	0.001
93.8	2.0	0.023
94.4	1.0	0.159
94.7	0.5	0.309
95.0	0.0	0.500
95.3	−0.5	0.691
95.6	−1.0	0.841
96.2	−2.0	0.977
96.8	−3.0	0.999

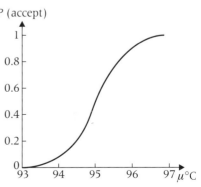

Note that the shape of the operating characteristic is a reflection in a vertical line of the typical shape for an attributes scheme. This is because, in this case, the good batches have large mean values whereas for attributes good batches have small proportions of non-conforming items.

An operating characteristic for percentage impurity, where a good batch has a low mean, would have shape shown opposite.

In other cases, such as the diameter of screw caps for bottles of vinegar, the mean of a good batch must be neither too big nor too small and the shape of the operating characteristic would be as shown opposite.

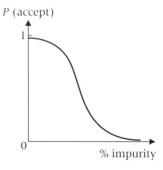

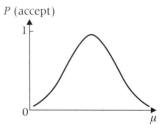

Worked example 5.6

(a) Before cement is delivered to a civil engineering site, a number of small bricks are made from it. Five are chosen at random and tested for compressive strength (measured in $GN\,m^{-2}$). This is known to be normally distributed with standard deviation 5.5. The batch of cement is accepted for delivery if the mean compressive strength of the five bricks is greater than 51. Draw the operating characteristic for this plan.

(b) It is decided to redesign the plan. The customer requires that the probability of accepting a batch with a mean strength of 47 or less should be less than 0.1. The manufacturer requires that the probability of rejecting a batch with a mean strength of 52.5 or more should be less than 0.05. By consulting your operating characteristic state which, if either, of these criteria are satisfied by the current plan.

(c) If n is the sample size and k is the compressive strength which must be exceeded by the sample mean for the batch to be accepted, find:
   (i) the smallest value of k which would meet the customer's requirements if $n = 6$,
   (ii) the minimum value of n to satisfy the manufacturer's requirements if k remains at 51.

(d) If k is changed to 49.4, find the minimum value of n to satisfy the customer's requirements. Verify that using this value of n the manufacturer's requirements will also be met.

(e) What factors should be considered when deciding whether to use acceptance sampling by variable or by attribute?

Solution

(a) The operating characteristic is a graph of probability of acceptance against mean strength of bricks from the batch of cement. First, suitable values of this mean strength must be chosen so that the probability of acceptance can be calculated and the graph drawn. The standard deviation is 5.5. Since samples of size five are being taken, the standard deviation of the sample mean is $5.5 / \sqrt{5} = 2.46$. For most purposes a graph which extends between two and three standard errors either side of k will be adequate. In this case, say, 44 to 58. Steps of two will give eight points and this will usually be adequate. If a more detailed graph is required, further points can be interpolated and the range can be extended.

μ	$\dfrac{51 - \mu}{\dfrac{5.5}{\sqrt{5}}}$	P(**accept**)
44	2.846	0.002
46	2.033	0.021
48	1.220	0.111
50	0.407	0.342
52	−0.407	0.658
54	−1.220	0.889
56	−2.033	0.979
58	−2.846	0.998

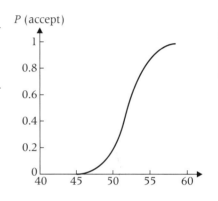

Note that interpolation was used in reading from tables of the normal distribution. However sufficiently accurate results can be obtained without interpolation.

(b) From the graph the probability of accepting a batch with a mean strength of 47 is approximately 0.05. This is less than 0.1 and so satisfies the customer's requirement.

The probability of accepting a batch with a mean strength of 52.5 is approximately 0.73. Hence the probability of rejecting it is approximately 0.27. This is much larger than 0.05 and so does not meet the manufacturer's requirement.

(c) (i) To satisfy the customer's requirement

$$z = \frac{k - 47}{\dfrac{5.5}{\sqrt{6}}} > 1.2816$$

$$k - 47 > 1.2816 \times 5.5 / \sqrt{6}$$

$$k > 47 + 2.878$$

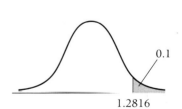

Smallest value of k is 49.9.

(ii) To satisfy the manufacturer's requirement

$$z = \frac{51 - 52.5}{\frac{5.5}{\sqrt{n}}} < -1.6449$$

$$-0.2727\sqrt{n} < -1.6449$$

$$\sqrt{n} > 6.032$$

$$n > 36.4$$

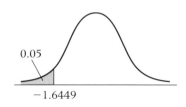

The minimum value of n to satisfy the manufacturer's requirement is 37.

(d) To satisfy the customer's requirement

$$z = \frac{49.4 - 47.0}{\frac{5.5}{\sqrt{n}}} > 1.2816$$

$$0.4364\sqrt{n} > 1.2816$$

$$\sqrt{n} > 2.936$$

$$n > 8.62$$

The minimum value of n to satisfy the customer's requirement is 9.

If mean strength is 52.5 and $n = 9$

$$z = \frac{49.4 - 52.5}{\frac{5.5}{\sqrt{9}}} = -1.691$$

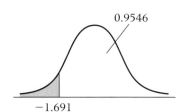

The probability of accepting the batch is 0.955. The probability of rejecting is $1 - 0.955 = 0.045$. This is less than 0.05 and so satisfies the manufacturer's requirement.

(e) It is usually easier and quicker to classify an item as conforming or non-conforming than to measure a variable. Variables plans are also more difficult for someone without statistical knowledge to operate – the value of the standard deviation must be known or estimated and the sample mean must be calculated. The advantage of a variables plan is that as variables are more informative than attributes a smaller sample size is required. When deciding between attributes and variables it is necessary to consider whether or not the cost and other advantages of taking a smaller sample outweigh the extra difficulties of using a variables plan.

EXERCISE 5D

1 An acceptance sampling plan consists of weighing a sample of six loaves of bread and accepting the batch if the sample mean is greater than 900 g. Draw the operating characteristic if the standard deviation is known from past experience to be 12 g.

2 An acceptance sampling plan consists of measuring the percentage of fat in a sample of eight pre-packaged portions of boiled ham. The batch is rejected if the mean proportion exceeds 42%. If the standard deviation is estimated to be 3%, draw the operating characteristic.

3 An acceptance sampling scheme consists of weighing n items and rejecting the batch if the mean weight is less than k. The weights of the items are known to be normally distributed with standard deviation 8 g.

(a) If $n = 8$ and $k = 150$ g, find the probability of rejecting a batch with mean weight 152 g.

(b) If $n = 10$ and $k = 160$ g find the probability of accepting a batch with mean weight 156 g.

(c) If $n = 12$ and $k = 203$ g, would the probability of rejecting a batch with mean weight 200 g exceed 0.9?

(d) If $n = 12$, find the smallest value of k which would give a probability of at least 0.9 of rejecting a batch with mean weight 200 g.

(e) If $n = 20$, find the largest value of k which would give a probability of at most 0.2 of rejecting a batch with mean weight 210 g.

(f) If $k = 203$ g, find the smallest value of n which would give a probability of at least 0.95 of rejecting a batch with mean weight 199 g.

(g) If $k = 210$ g, find the smallest value of n which would give a probability of at most 0.08 of rejecting a batch with mean weight 216 g.

4 The quality of a certain chemical is measured by the time it takes to react. (The shorter the time, the better the quality.) This time is known to be normally distributed with a standard deviation of 8 s. Nine samples are taken from each batch and the batch accepted if the mean reaction time is less than 33.5 s.

(a) Draw the operating characteristic for this plan.

(b) The manufacturer requires a plan which has a probability of rejection of less than 0.05 if the mean reaction time of the batch is 30 s. The customer requires a plan that has a probability of acceptance of less than 0.10 if the mean reaction time of the batch is 35 s. Use your operating characteristic to find which, if either, of these conditions this plan will meet.

(c) If the criterion for acceptance remains unchanged, find the smallest sample size that would enable the plan to satisfy the customer's requirement.

(d) If the criterion for acceptance is for the sample to be accepted if the mean is less than 32.8 s, find the smallest sample size that would enable the plan to satisfy the manufacturer's requirement. Verify that this plan would also satisfy the customer's requirement.

5 Before 25 kg bags of lawn sand are delivered to garden centres by a manufacturer, bags are chosen at random from large batches and the contents of each bag weighed. These weights are known to be normally distributed with a standard deviation of 0.5 kg.

It is proposed that a batch will be accepted if the mean weight of the contents of a random sample of four bags exceeds 24.8 kg.

(a) Copy and complete the following table and hence draw the operating characteristic curve for this proposed sampling plan.

Mean weight of contents of a bag	24.2	24.4	24.6	24.8	25.0	25.2	25.4
Probability of batch accepted				0.500		0.945	

The manufacturer and garden centres decide that the above proposal meets neither of their requirements, so a redesigned plan is needed.

The manufacturer requires that the probability of accepting a batch of bags with mean contents of 25 kg should be at least 0.95. Garden centres require that the probability of accepting a batch of bags with mean contents of 24.6 kg should be at most 0.01.

(b) Determine the minimum sample size and the weight which must be exceeded by the sample mean for a batch to be accepted.

(c) Discuss the advantages and disadvantages of using a variables plan compared to a plan based on attributes.

6 The weights of loaves produced by a large bakery are known to be normally distributed with a standard deviation of 12 g. A catering organisation buys a large number of loaves from the bakery. The following acceptance sampling plan is used – Take a random sample of size 10 and reject the batch if the mean weight is less than 1000 g.

(a) Draw the operating characteristic for this plan.

The catering organisation will accept a risk of 5% of a batch with a mean weight of 995 g or less being accepted. The bakery requires the risk of a batch with a mean weight of 1003 g or more being rejected to be not more than 2%.

(b) Use your operating characteristic to check whether the plan satisfies these requirements.

(c) Find an acceptance sampling plan which satisfies both these conditions. (You should state the minimum sample size and the weight which should be exceeded by the sample mean for a batch to be accepted.)

7 A wholesaler packs sugar into bags of nominal weight 1000 g with an automatic machine. It is known from previous experience that the weights of bags are normally distributed with standard deviation 5 g.

A retailer, who is considering the purchase of large batches of these bags does not want bags to be noticeably underweight and states that an acceptable sampling scheme must be such that if the mean weight per bag is 1000 g, the probability of the batch being accepted must be no more than 0.10.

The wholesaler, who wishes to avoid repacking the bags, states that if the mean weight per bag is 1005 g, the probability of rejection must be no more than 0.05.

(a) Design a sampling and decision procedure to satisfy both the wholesaler and retailer.

(b) Plot the operating characteristic for this sampling scheme.

(c) If batches of bags with a mean weight per bag of 1004 g are acceptable:
   (i) find from your operating characteristic the probability of rejecting such a batch,
   (ii) draw on your graph the ideal shape of the operating characteristic.

Key point summary

1 Acceptance sampling may be applied to large batches *p 105* of similar items. It is the process of deciding whether or not the batch is acceptable by testing a small sample of the items.

2 The operating characteristic for an acceptance *p 106* sampling by attributes plan is a graph of probability of acceptance against proportion non-conforming in the batch.

3 The probabilities may be found from the binomial   *p 106*
distribution provided the sample is random and the
sample size is small compared to the batch.

4 In double sampling, the number of non-conforming   *p 119*
items in the first sample will determine whether a
decision is made immediately or whether it is delayed
until a second sample has been inspected.

5 For acceptance sampling by variables the operating   *p 127*
characteristic is a graph of probability of acceptance
against batch mean.

Test yourself	What to review
1 For the plan $n = 40$, $r = 4$, find the probability of rejecting a batch containing 8% non-conforming.	*Section 5.3*
2 How, if at all, does the plan $n = 40$, $a = 3$, differ from the plan in question 1?	*Section 5.3*
3 The diagram opposite shows three operating characteristics, A, B and C. One is based on a sample of 20, another on a sample of 60 and the other shows the ideal shape. Identify which plan is which.	*Section 5.3*
4 Give one reason why a double sampling plan might be preferred to a single sampling plan and one reason why a single sampling plan might be preferred to a double sampling plan.	*Section 5.5*
5 A sampling plan consists of taking a sample of size 25, accepting the batch if zero non-conforming items are found and rejecting the batch if three or more non-conforming items are found. If one or two non-conforming items are found a further sample of 25 is taken and the batch accepted if a total of three or fewer non-conforming items are found. Otherwise the batch is rejected. Express the plan in symbols.	*Section 5.5*
6 Find the probability of accepting a batch containing 6% non-conforming items for the plan in question 5.	*Section 5.5*

Test yourself (*continued*)	What to review

7 An acceptance sampling plan consists of measuring a sample of five items and rejecting the batch if the mean length is less than 10.5 cm. If the standard deviation of lengths is 0.3 cm will the plan meet the following requirements?

Section 5.6

   (a) A probability of at least 0.9 of rejecting a batch with mean length 10.2 cm.

   (b) A probability of at least 0.95 of accepting a batch of mean length 10.9 cm.

8 Give one reason why a variables plan might be preferred to an attributes plan and one reason why an attributes plan might be preferred to a variables plan.

Section 5.6

Test yourself ANSWERS

1 0.399.

2 No difference.

3 A ideal, B $n = 60$, C $n = 20$.

4 A double sampling plan will require less sampling, on average, than a single sampling plan with a similar operating characteristic. A single sampling plan is simpler.

5 $n = 25$, $a = 0$ $r = 3$
$n = 25$, $a = 3$, $r = 4$.

6 0.633.

7 **(a)** Probability of rejecting $= 0.987$ – condition met;
(b) Probability of accepting $= 0.999$ – condition met.

8 A variables plan requires a smaller sample. An attributes plan is easier to apply.

Exam style practice paper

Time allowed 1 hour 15 minutes

Answer **all** questions

1 An ice cream manufacturer wishes to compare three different recipes P, Q and R. Subjects are to be asked to taste the ice cream and give it a mark out of 50. Two experimental designs are suggested.

	Design 1			Design 2	
P	**Q**	**R**	**P**	**Q**	**R**
S_1	S_5	S_9	S_1	S_2	S_4
S_2	S_6	S_{10}	S_2	S_3	S_1
S_3	S_7	S_{11}	S_3	S_1	S_3
S_4	S_8	S_{12}	S_4	S_4	S_2

In **Design 1** twelve subjects are randomly allocated, four to each recipe. In **Design 2** only four subjects are used (the order they appear in each column is unimportant).

(a) Write down the name given to:
   (i) Design 1,
   (ii) Design 2. (2 marks)

(b) Explain why **Design 2** is to be preferred to **Design 1**. (2 marks)

2 An instrument panel is being designed to control a complex industrial operation. It will be necessary for the operator to use both hands independently to operate the panel. To assist the designers, it was decided to time a number of operators, each carrying out the same task, using a simulated instrument panel, once with the left hand and once with the right hand.

The times, in seconds, were as follows:

Operator	A	B	C	D	E	F	G	H
Left hand, x	49	82	103	34	37	35	44	74
Right hand, y	34	47	59	29	27	26	65	47

One of the design aims is that the mean additional time required to operate the panel with the left hand instead of the right hand should not exceed 10 s.

(a) Use a paired *t*-test and the 5% significance level to investigate the claim that this aim has not been met.

(9 marks)

(b) Further investigation established that operator G was left-handed, all the other operators being right-handed. How would the analysis have differed if the aim had referred to the dominant and non-dominant hands rather than the left and right hands. (2 marks)

3 (a) An acceptance sampling plan is required to give a risk of not more than 8% of a batch of items containing 2% non-conforming being rejected. A decision is to be made by examining a sample of 50 items. Find the appropriate decision procedure. (3 marks)

(b) Find the probability of accepting batches containing 3%, 5%, 10% and 15% non-conforming items for the plan you found in **(a)**. Hence draw the operating characteristic. Indicate on your graph the ideal shape of the operating characteristic if batches containing up to 5% non-conforming are acceptable. (5 marks)

(c) Would the plan you found in **(a)** satisfy a customer who specified a risk of not more than 5% of a batch containing 11% non-conforming being accepted? Justify your answer. (2 marks)

4 A manufacturer of drinking glasses inspects samples of 60 at regular intervals and counts the number with visual blemishes. During a period when production was satisfactory the results for ten samples were as follows:

Sample	1	2	3	4	5	6	7	8	9	10
Number with blemishes	6	7	6	9	10	9	13	12	14	15

(a) Calculate, approximate, upper and lower, warning and action limits for a control chart for the proportion with blemishes. **You are not required to draw the chart**.

(5 marks)

(b) Evaluate the proportion with blemishes in each of the samples and comment. (3 marks)

(c) If charts using the limits you have calculated in **(a)** were used, state, giving a reason, what action would be indicated if the number with blemishes in the next sample was:

(I) 18, **(II)** 25, **(iii)** 1. (6 marks)

(d) Give **two** advantages and **one** disadvantage of using control charts for proportion non-conforming compared to setting up control charts for mean and range. Your answer need not be restricted to the context above. (3 marks)

5 A commuter in a large city can travel to work by car, bicycle or bus. She believes that the time she leaves home and also the day of the week may affect her average journey time. She records the following times, in minutes, from going out of her front door until reaching her desk at work.

Time of leaving	Method of transport		
	Car	Bicycle	Bus
8.00 a.m.	45(M)	28(W)	51(F)
8.30 a.m.	27(W)	31(F)	46(M)
9.00 a.m.	33(F)	29(M)	40(W)

(M), (W) or (F) indicate the journey was undertaken on Monday, Wednesday or Friday, respectively.

(a) Carry out an analysis of variance and investigate, at the 5% significance level, whether there are differences in the mean journey times for method of transport, time of leaving and day of the week. (12 marks)

(b) Interpret the results of your analysis as they apply to method of transport. (2 marks)

(c) In order to analyse the data it was necessary to assume there were no interactions. Explain the meaning of interactions in the context of this question. (2 marks)

(d) Explain why it was useful to include day of the week in the experimental design even though the commuter must travel on all weekdays and so cannot affect her average journey time by selecting particular days for her journeys. (2 marks)

Appendix

Table 1 Cumulative binomial distribution function

The tabulated value is $P(X \leqslant x)$, where R has a binomial distribution with parameters n and p.

x	0.01	0.02	0.03	0.04	0.05	0.06	0.07	0.08	0.09	0.10	0.15	0.20	0.25	0.30	0.35	0.40	0.45	0.50	x
n = 8 0	0.9227	0.8508	0.7837	0.7214	0.6634	0.6096	0.5596	0.5132	0.4703	0.4305	0.2725	0.1678	0.1001	0.0576	0.0319	0.0168	0.0084	0.0039	0
1	0.9973	0.9897	0.9777	0.9619	0.9428	0.9208	0.8965	0.8702	0.8423	0.8131	0.6572	0.5033	0.3671	0.2553	0.1691	0.1064	0.0632	0.0352	1
2	0.9999	0.9996	0.9987	0.9969	0.9942	0.9904	0.9853	0.9789	0.9711	0.9619	0.8948	0.7969	0.6785	0.5518	0.4278	0.3154	0.2201	0.1445	2
3	1.000	1.000	0.9999	0.9998	0.9996	0.9993	0.9987	0.9978	0.9966	0.9950	0.9786	0.9437	0.8862	0.8059	0.7064	0.5941	0.4770	0.3633	3
4			1.000	1.000	1.000	1.000	0.9999	0.9999	0.9997	0.9996	0.9971	0.9896	0.9727	0.9420	0.8939	0.8263	0.7396	0.6367	4
5							1.000	1.000	1.000	1.000	0.9998	0.9988	0.9958	0.9887	0.9747	0.9502	0.9115	0.8555	5
6											1.000	0.9999	0.9996	0.9987	0.9964	0.9915	0.9819	0.9648	6
7												1.000	1.000	0.9999	0.9998	0.9993	0.9983	0.9961	7
8														1.000	1.000	1.000	1.000	1.000	8
n = 12 0	0.8864	0.7847	0.6938	0.6127	0.5404	0.4759	0.4186	0.3677	0.3225	0.2824	0.1422	0.0687	0.0317	0.0138	0.0057	0.0022	0.0008	0.0002	0
1	0.9938	0.9769	0.9514	0.9191	0.8816	0.8405	0.7967	0.7513	0.7052	0.6590	0.4435	0.2749	0.1584	0.0850	0.0424	0.0196	0.0083	0.0032	1
2	0.9998	0.9985	0.9952	0.9893	0.9804	0.9684	0.9532	0.9348	0.9134	0.8891	0.7358	0.5583	0.3907	0.2528	0.1513	0.0834	0.0421	0.0193	2
3	1.000	0.9999	0.9997	0.9990	0.9978	0.9957	0.9925	0.9880	0.9820	0.9744	0.9078	0.7946	0.6488	0.4925	0.3467	0.2253	0.1345	0.0730	3
4		1.000	1.000	0.9999	0.9998	0.9996	0.9991	0.9984	0.9973	0.9957	0.9761	0.9274	0.8424	0.7237	0.5833	0.4382	0.3044	0.1938	4
5				1.000	1.000	1.000	0.9999	0.9998	0.9997	0.9995	0.994	0.9806	0.9456	0.8822	0.7873	0.6652	0.5269	0.3872	5
6							1.000	1.000	1.000	0.9999	0.9993	0.9961	0.9857	0.9614	0.9154	0.8418	0.7393	0.6128	6
7										1.000	0.999	0.994	0.9972	0.9905	0.9745	0.9427	0.8883	0.8062	7
8											1.000	0.9999	0.9996	0.9983	0.9944	0.9847	0.9644	0.9270	8
9												1.000	1.000	0.9998	0.9992	0.9972	0.9921	0.9807	9
10													1.000	0.9999	0.9997	0.9989	0.9968	10
11															1.000	1.000	0.9999	0.9998	11
12																	1.000	1.000	12
n = 15 0	0.8601	0.7386	0.6333	0.5421	0.4633	0.3953	0.3367	0.2863	0.2430	0.2059	0.0874	0.0352	0.0134	0.0047	0.0016	0.0005	0.0001	0.0000	0
1	0.9904	0.9647	0.9270	0.8809	0.8290	0.7738	0.7168	0.6597	0.6035	0.5490	0.3186	0.1671	0.0802	0.0353	0.0142	0.0052	0.0017	0.0005	1
2	0.9996	0.9970	0.9906	0.9797	0.9638	0.9429	0.9171	0.8870	0.8531	0.8159	0.6042	0.3980	0.3980	0.2361	0.1268	0.0271	0.0107	0.0037	2
3	1.000	0.9998	0.9992	0.9976	0.9945	0.9896	0.9825	0.9727	0.9601	0.9444	0.8227	0.6482	0.4613	0.2969	0.1727	0.0905	0.0424	0.0176	3
4		1.000	0.9999	0.9998	0.9994	0.9986	0.9972	0.9950	0.9918	0.9873	0.9383	0.8358	0.6865	0.5155	0.3519	0.2173	0.1204	0.0592	4
5			1.000	1.000	0.9999	0.9999	0.9997	0.9993	0.9987	0.9978	0.9832	0.9389	0.8516	0.7216	0.5643	0.4032	0.2608	0.1509	5
6					1.000	1.000	1.000	0.9999	0.9998	0.9997	0.9964	0.9819	0.9434	0.8689	0.7548	0.6098	0.4522	0.3036	6
7								1.000	1.000	1.000	0.9994	0.9958	0.9827	0.9500	0.8868	0.7869	0.6535	0.5000	7
8											0.9999	0.9992	0.9958	0.9848	0.9578	0.9050	0.8182	0.6964	8
9											1.000	0.9999	0.9992	0.9963	0.9876	0.9662	0.9231	0.8491	9
10												1.000	0.9999	0.9993	0.9972	0.9907	0.9745	0.9408	10
11													1.000	0.9999	0.9995	0.9981	0.9937	0.9824	11
12														1.000	0.9999	0.9997	0.9989	0.9963	12
13															1.000	1.000	0.9999	0.9995	13
14																	1.000	1.000	14

Table 1 Cumulative binomial distribution function (continued)

x	0.01	0.02	0.03	0.04	0.05	0.06	0.07	0.08	0.09	0.10	0.15	0.20	0.25	0.30	0.35	0.40	0.45	0.50	x
n = 20 0	0.8179	0.6676	0.5438	0.4420	0.3585	0.2901	0.2342	0.1887	0.1516	0.1216	0.0388	0.0115	0.0032	0.0008	0.0002	0.0000	0.0000	0.0000	0
1	0.9831	0.9401	0.8802	0.8103	0.7358	0.6605	0.5869	0.5169	0.4516	0.3917	0.1756	0.0692	0.0243	0.0076	0.0021	0.0005	0.0001	0.0000	1
2	0.9990	0.9929	0.9790	0.9561	0.9245	0.8850	0.8390	0.7879	0.7334	0.6769	0.4049	0.2061	0.0913	0.0355	0.0121	0.0036	0.0009	0.0002	2
3	1.000	0.9994	0.9973	0.9926	0.9841	0.9710	0.9529	0.9294	0.9007	0.8670	0.6477	0.4114	0.2252	0.1071	0.0444	0.0160	0.0049	0.0013	3
4		1.000	0.9997	0.9990	0.9974	0.9944	0.9893	0.9817	0.9710	0.9568	0.8298	0.6296	0.4148	0.2375	0.1182	0.0510	0.0189	0.0059	4
5			1.000	0.9999	0.9997	0.9991	0.9981	0.9962	0.9932	0.9887	0.9327	0.8042	0.6172	0.4164	0.2454	0.1256	0.0553	0.0207	5
6				1.000	1.000	0.9999	0.9997	0.9994	0.9987	0.9976	0.9781	0.9133	0.7858	0.6080	0.4166	0.2500	0.1299	0.0577	6
7						1.000	1.000	0.9999	0.9998	0.9996	0.9941	0.9679	0.8982	0.7723	0.6010	0.4159	0.2520	0.1316	7
8								1.000	1.000	0.9999	0.9987	0.9900	0.9591	0.8867	0.7624	0.5956	0.4143	0.2517	8
9										1.000	0.9998	0.9974	0.9861	0.9520	0.8782	0.7553	0.5914	0.4119	9
10											1.000	0.9994	0.9961	0.9829	0.9468	0.8725	0.7507	0.5881	10
11												0.9999	0.9991	0.9949	0.9804	0.9435	0.8692	0.7483	11
12												1.000	0.9998	0.9987	0.9940	0.9790	0.9420	0.8684	12
13													1.000	0.9997	0.9985	0.9935	0.9786	0.9423	13
14														1.000	0.9997	0.9984	0.9936	0.9793	14
15															1.000	0.9997	0.9985	0.9941	15
16																1.000	0.9997	0.9987	16
17																	1.000	0.9998	17
18																		1.000	18
n = 25 0	0.7778	0.6035	0.4670	0.3604	0.2774	0.2129	0.1630	0.1244	0.0946	0.0718	0.0172	0.0038	0.0008	0.0001	0.0000	0.0000	0.0000	0.0000	0
1	0.9742	0.9114	0.8280	0.7358	0.6424	0.5527	0.4696	0.3947	0.3286	0.2712	0.0931	0.0274	0.0070	0.0016	0.0003	0.0001	0.0000	0.0000	1
2	0.9980	0.9868	0.9620	0.9235	0.8729	0.8129	0.7466	0.6768	0.6063	0.5371	0.2537	0.0982	0.0321	0.0090	0.0021	0.0004	0.0001	0.0000	2
3	0.9999	0.9986	0.9938	0.9835	0.9659	0.9402	0.9064	0.8649	0.8169	0.7636	0.4711	0.2340	0.0962	0.0332	0.0097	0.0024	0.0005	0.0001	3
4	1.000	0.9999	0.9992	0.9972	0.9928	0.9850	0.9726	0.9549	0.9314	0.9020	0.6821	0.4207	0.2137	0.0905	0.0320	0.0095	0.0023	0.0005	4
5		1.000	0.9999	0.9996	0.9988	0.9969	0.9935	0.9877	0.9790	0.9666	0.8385	0.6167	0.3783	0.1935	0.0826	0.0294	0.0086	0.0020	5
6			1.000	1.000	0.9998	0.9995	0.9987	0.9972	0.9946	0.9905	0.9305	0.7800	0.5611	0.3407	0.1734	0.0736	0.0258	0.0073	6
7					1.000	0.9999	0.9998	0.9995	0.9989	0.9977	0.9745	0.8909	0.7265	0.5118	0.3061	0.1536	0.0639	0.0216	7
8						1.000	1.000	0.9999	0.9998	0.9995	0.9920	0.9532	0.8506	0.6769	0.4668	0.2735	0.1340	0.0539	8
9								1.000	1.000	0.9999	0.9979	0.9827	0.9287	0.8106	0.6303	0.4246	0.2424	0.1148	9
10										1.000	0.9995	0.9944	0.9703	0.9022	0.7712	0.5858	0.3843	0.2122	10
11											0.9999	0.9985	0.9893	0.9558	0.8476	0.7323	0.5426	0.3450	11
12											1.000	0.9996	0.9966	0.9825	0.9396	0.8462	0.6937	0.5000	12
13												0.9999	0.9991	0.9940	0.9745	0.9222	0.8173	0.6550	13
14												1.000	0.9998	0.9982	0.9907	0.9656	0.9040	0.7878	14
15													1.000	0.9995	0.9971	0.9868	0.9560	0.8852	15
16														0.9999	0.9992	0.9957	0.9826	0.9461	16
17														1.000	0.9998	0.9988	0.9942	0.9784	17
18															1.000	0.9997	0.9984	0.9927	18
19																0.9999	0.9996	0.9980	19
20																1.000	0.9999	0.9995	20
21																	1.000	0.9999	21
22																		1.000	22
n = 30 0	0.7397	0.5455	0.4010	0.2939	0.2146	0.1563	0.1134	0.0820	0.0591	0.0424	0.0076	0.0012	0.0002	0.0000	0.0000	0.0000	0.0000	0.0000	0
1	0.9639	0.8795	0.7731	0.6612	0.5535	0.4555	0.3694	0.2958	0.2343	0.1837	0.0480	0.0105	0.0020	0.0003	0.0000	0.0000	0.0000	0.0000	1
2	0.9967	0.9783	0.9399	0.8831	0.8122	0.7324	0.6487	0.5654	0.4855	0.4114	0.1514	0.0442	0.0106	0.0021	0.0003	0.0000	0.0000	0.0000	2
3	0.9998	0.9971	0.9881	0.9694	0.9392	0.8974	0.8450	0.7842	0.7175	0.6474	0.3217	0.1227	0.0374	0.0093	0.0019	0.0003	0.0000	0.0000	3
4	1.000	0.9997	0.9982	0.9937	0.9844	0.9685	0.9447	0.9126	0.8723	0.8245	0.5245	0.2552	0.0979	0.0302	0.0075	0.0015	0.0002	0.0000	4
5		1.000	0.9998	0.9989	0.9967	0.9921	0.9838	0.9707	0.9519	0.9268	0.7106	0.4275	0.2026	0.0766	0.0233	0.0057	0.0011	0.0002	5
6			1.000	0.9999	0.9994	0.9983	0.9960	0.9918	0.9848	0.9742	0.8474	0.6070	0.3481	0.1595	0.0586	0.0172	0.0040	0.0007	6
7				1.000	0.9999	0.9997	0.9992	0.9980	0.9959	0.9922	0.9302	0.7608	0.5143	0.2814	0.1238	0.0435	0.0121	0.0026	7
8					1.000	1.000	0.9999	0.9996	0.9990	0.9980	0.9722	0.8713	0.6736	0.4315	0.2247	0.0940	0.0312	0.0081	8
9							1.000	0.9999	0.9998	0.9995	0.9903	0.9389	0.8034	0.5888	0.3575	0.1763	0.0694	0.0214	9
10								1.000	1.000	0.9999	0.9971	0.9744	0.8943	0.7304	0.5078	0.2915	0.1350	0.0494	10
11										1.000	0.9992	0.9905	0.9493	0.8407	0.6548	0.4311	0.2327	0.1002	11
12											0.9998	0.9969	0.9784	0.9155	0.7802	0.5785	0.3592	0.1808	12
13											1.000	0.9991	0.9918	0.9599	0.8737	0.7145	0.5025	0.2923	13
14												0.9998	0.9973	0.9831	0.9348	0.8246	0.6448	0.4278	14
15												0.9999	0.9992	0.9936	0.9699	0.9029	0.7691	0.5722	15
16												1.000	0.9998	0.9979	0.9876	0.9519	0.8644	0.7077	16
17													0.9999	0.9994	0.9955	0.9788	0.9286	0.8192	17
18													1.000	0.9998	0.9986	0.9917	0.9666	0.8998	18
19														1.000	0.9996	0.9971	0.9682	0.9506	19
20															0.9999	0.9991	0.9950	0.9786	20
21															1.000	0.9998	0.9984	0.9919	21
22																1.000	0.9996	0.9974	22
23																	0.9999	0.9993	23
24																	1.000	0.9998	24
25																		1.000	25

Table 1 Cumulative binomial distribution function (continued)

n = 40

x	0.01	0.02	0.03	0.04	0.05	0.06	0.07	0.08	0.09	0.10	0.15	0.20	0.25	0.30	0.35	0.40	0.45	0.50	x
0	0.6690	0.4457	0.2957	0.1954	0.1285	0.0842	0.0549	0.0356	0.0230	0.0148	0.0015	0.0002	0.0000	0.0000	0.0000	0.0000	0.0000	0.0000	0
1	0.9393	0.8095	0.6615	0.5210	0.3991	0.2990	0.2201	0.1594	0.1140	0.0805	0.0121	0.0015	0.0001	0.0000	0.0000	0.0000	0.0000	0.0000	1
2	0.9925	0.9543	0.8822	0.7855	0.6767	0.5665	0.4625	0.3694	0.2894	0.2228	0.0486	0.0079	0.0010	0.0001	0.0000	0.0000	0.0000	0.0000	2
3	0.9993	0.9918	0.9686	0.9252	0.8619	0.7827	0.6937	0.6007	0.5092	0.4231	0.1302	0.0285	0.0047	0.0006	0.0001	0.0000	0.0000	0.0000	3
4	1.000	0.9988	0.9933	0.9790	0.9520	0.9104	0.8546	0.7868	0.7103	0.6290	0.2633	0.0759	0.0160	0.0026	0.0003	0.0000	0.0000	0.0000	4
5		0.9999	0.9988	0.9951	0.9861	0.9691	0.9419	0.9033	0.8535	0.7937	0.4325	0.1613	0.0433	0.0086	0.0013	0.0001	0.0000	0.0000	5
6		1.000	0.9998	0.9990	0.9966	0.9909	0.9801	0.9624	0.9361	0.9005	0.6067	0.2859	0.0962	0.0238	0.0044	0.0006	0.0001	0.0000	6
7			1.000	0.9998	0.9993	0.9977	0.9942	0.9873	0.9758	0.9581	0.7559	0.4371	0.1820	0.0553	0.0124	0.0021	0.0002	0.0000	7
8				1.000	0.9999	0.9995	0.9985	0.9963	0.9919	0.9845	0.8646	0.5931	0.2998	0.1110	0.0303	0.0061	0.0009	0.0001	8
9					1.000	1.000	0.9997	0.9990	0.9976	0.9949	0.9328	0.7318	0.4395	0.1959	0.0644	0.0156	0.0027	0.0003	9
10						1.000	0.9999	0.9998	0.9994	0.9985	0.9701	0.8392	0.5839	0.3087	0.1215	0.0352	0.0074	0.0011	10
11							1.000	1.000	0.9999	0.9996	0.9880	0.9125	0.7151	0.4406	0.2053	0.0709	0.0709	0.0032	11
12									1.000	0.9999	0.9957	0.9568	0.8209	0.5772	0.3143	0.1285	0.0386	0.0083	12
13										1.000	0.9986	0.9806	0.8968	0.7032	0.4408	0.2112	0.0751	0.0192	13
14											0.9996	0.9921	0.9456	0.8074	0.5721	0.3174	0.1326	0.0403	14
15											0.9999	0.9971	0.9738	0.8849	0.6946	0.4402	0.2142	0.0769	15
16											1.000	0.9990	0.9884	0.9367	0.7978	0.5681	0.3185	0.1341	16
17												0.9997	0.9953	0.9680	0.8761	0.6885	0.4391	0.2148	17
18												0.9999	0.9983	0.9852	0.9301	0.7911	0.5651	0.3179	18
19												1.000	0.9994	0.9937	0.9637	0.8702	0.6844	0.4373	19
20													0.9998	0.9976	0.9827	0.9256	0.7870	0.5627	20
21													1.000	0.9991	0.9925	0.9608	0.8669	0.6821	21
22														0.9997	0.9970	0.9811	0.9233	0.7852	22
23														0.9999	0.9989	0.9917	0.9595	0.8659	23
24														1.000	0.9996	0.9966	0.9804	0.9231	24
25															0.9999	0.9988	0.9914	0.9597	25
26															1.000	0.9996	0.9966	0.9808	26
27																0.9999	0.9988	0.9917	27
28																1.000	0.9996	0.9968	28
29																	0.9999	0.9989	29
30																	1.000	0.9997	30
31																		0.9999	31
32																		1.000	32

n = 50

x	0.01	0.02	0.03	0.04	0.05	0.06	0.07	0.08	0.09	0.10	0.15	0.20	0.25	0.30	0.35	0.40	0.45	0.50	x
0	0.6050	0.3642	0.2181	0.1299	0.0769	0.0453	0.0266	0.0155	0.0090	0.0052	0.0003	0.0000	0.0000	0.0000	0.0000	0.0000	0.0000	0.0000	0
1	0.9106	0.7358	0.5553	0.4005	0.2794	0.1900	0.1265	0.0827	0.0532	0.0338	0.0029	0.0002	0.0000	0.0000	0.0000	0.0000	0.0000	0.0000	1
2	0.9862	0.9216	0.8108	0.6767	0.5405	0.4162	0.3108	0.2260	0.1605	0.1117	0.0142	0.0013	0.0001	0.0000	0.0000	0.0000	0.0000	0.0000	2
3	0.9984	0.9822	0.9372	0.8609	0.7604	0.6473	0.5327	0.4253	0.3303	0.2503	0.0460	0.0057	0.0005	0.0000	0.0000	0.0000	0.0000	0.0000	3
4	0.9999	0.9968	0.9832	0.9510	0.8964	0.8206	0.7290	0.6290	0.5277	0.4312	0.1121	0.0185	0.0021	0.0002	0.0000	0.0000	0.0000	0.0000	4
5	1.000	0.9995	0.9963	0.9856	0.9622	0.9224	0.8650	0.7919	0.7072	0.6161	0.2194	0.0480	0.0070	0.0007	0.0001	0.0000	0.0000	0.0000	5
6		0.9999	0.9993	0.9964	0.9882	0.9711	0.9417	0.8981	0.8404	0.7702	0.3613	0.1034	0.0194	0.0025	0.0002	0.0000	0.0000	0.0000	6
7		1.000	0.9999	0.9992	0.9968	0.9906	0.9780	0.9562	0.9232	0.8779	0.5188	0.1904	0.0453	0.0073	0.0008	0.0001	0.0000	0.0000	7
8			1.000	0.9999	0.9992	0.9973	0.9927	0.9833	0.9672	0.9421	0.6681	0.3073	0.0916	0.0183	0.0025	0.0002	0.0000	0.0000	8
9				1.000	0.9998	0.9993	0.9978	0.9944	0.9875	0.9755	0.7911	0.4437	0.1637	0.0402	0.0067	0.0008	0.0001	0.0000	9
10					1.000	0.9998	0.9994	0.9983	0.9957	0.9906	0.8801	0.5836	0.2622	0.0789	0.0160	0.0022	0.0002	0.0000	10
11						1.000	0.9999	0.9995	0.9987	0.9968	0.9372	0.7107	0.3816	0.1390	0.0342	0.0057	0.0006	0.0000	11
12							1.000	0.9999	0.9996	0.9990	0.9699	0.8139	0.5110	0.2229	0.0661	0.0133	0.0018	0.0002	12
13								1.000	0.9999	0.9997	0.9868	0.8894	0.6370	0.3279	0.1163	0.0280	0.0045	0.0005	13
14									1.000	0.9999	0.9947	0.9393	0.7481	0.4468	0.1878	0.0540	0.0104	0.0013	14
15										1.000	0.9981	0.9692	0.8369	0.5692	0.2801	0.0955	0.0220	0.0033	15
16											0.9983	0.9856	0.9017	0.6839	0.3889	0.1561	0.0427	0.0077	16
17											0.9998	0.9937	0.9449	0.7822	0.5060	0.2369	0.0765	0.0164	17
18											0.9999	0.9975	0.9713	0.8594	0.6216	0.3356	0.1273	0.0325	18
19											1.000	0.9991	0.9861	0.9152	0.7264	0.4465	0.1297	0.0595	19
20												0.9997	0.9937	0.9522	0.8139	0.5610	0.2862	0.1013	20
21												0.9999	0.9974	0.9749	0.8813	0.6701	0.3900	0.1611	21
22												1.000	0.9990	0.9877	0.9290	0.7660	0.5019	0.2399	22
23													0.9996	0.9944	0.9604	0.8438	0.6134	0.3359	23
24													0.9999	0.9976	0.9793	0.9022	0.7160	0.4439	24
25													1.000	0.9991	0.9900	0.9427	0.8034	0.5561	25
26														0.9997	0.9955	0.9686	0.8721	0.6641	26
27														0.9999	0.9981	0.9840	0.9220	0.7601	27
28														1.000	0.9993	0.9924	0.9556	0.8389	28
29															0.9997	0.9966	0.9765	0.8987	29
30															0.9999	0.9986	0.9884	0.9405	30
31															1.000	0.9995	0.9947	0.9675	31
32																0.9998	0.9978	0.9836	32
33																0.9999	0.9991	0.9923	33
34																1.000	0.9997	0.9967	34
35																	0.9999	0.9987	35
36																	1.000	0.9995	36
37																		0.9998	37
38																		1.000	38

Table 3 Normal distribution function

The tabulated value is $\Phi(z) = P(Z \leqslant z)$,
where Z is the standardised normal random variable, N(0, 1).

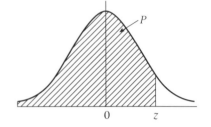

z	0.00	0.01	0.02	0.03	0.04	0.05	0.06	0.07	0.08	0.09
0.0	0.50000	0.50399	0.50798	0.51197	0.51595	0.51994	0.52392	0.52790	0.53188	0.53586
0.1	0.53983	0.54380	0.54776	0.55172	0.55567	0.55962	0.56356	0.56749	0.57142	0.57535
0.2	0.57926	0.58317	0.58706	0.59095	0.59483	0.59871	0.60257	0.60642	0.61026	0.61409
0.3	0.61791	0.62172	0.62552	0.62930	0.63307	0.63683	0.64058	0.64431	0.64803	0.65173
0.4	0.65542	0.65910	0.66276	0.66640	0.67003	0.67364	0.67724	0.68082	0.68439	0.68793
0.5	0.69146	0.69497	0.69847	0.70194	0.70540	0.70884	0.71226	0.71566	0.71904	0.72240
0.6	0.72575	0.72907	0.73237	0.73565	0.73891	0.74215	0.74537	0.74857	0.75175	0.75490
0.7	0.75804	0.76115	0.76424	0.76730	0.77035	0.77337	0.77637	0.77935	0.78230	0.78524
0.8	0.78814	0.79103	0.79389	0.79673	0.79955	0.80234	0.80511	0.80785	0.81057	0.81327
0.9	0.81594	0.81859	0.82121	0.82381	0.82639	0.82894	0.83147	0.83398	0.83646	0.83891
1.0	0.84134	0.84375	0.84614	0.84849	0.85083	0.85314	0.85543	0.85769	0.85993	0.86214
1.1	0.86433	0.86650	0.86864	0.87076	0.87286	0.87493	0.87698	0.87900	0.88100	0.88298
1.2	0.88493	0.88686	0.88877	0.89065	0.89251	0.89435	0.89617	0.89796	0.89973	0.90147
1.3	0.90320	0.90490	0.90658	0.90824	0.90988	0.91149	0.91309	0.91466	0.91621	0.91774
1.4	0.91924	0.92073	0.92220	0.92364	0.92507	0.92647	0.92785	0.92922	0.93056	0.93189
1.5	0.93319	0.93448	0.93574	0.93699	0.93822	0.93943	0.94062	0.94179	0.94295	0.94408
1.6	0.94520	0.94630	0.94738	0.94845	0.94950	0.95053	0.95154	0.95254	0.95352	0.95449
1.7	0.95543	0.95637	0.95728	0.95818	0.95907	0.95994	0.96080	0.96164	0.96246	0.96327
1.8	0.96407	0.96485	0.96562	0.96638	0.96712	0.96784	0.96856	0.96926	0.96995	0.97062
1.9	0.97128	0.97193	0.97257	0.97320	0.97381	0.97441	0.97500	0.97558	0.76615	0.97670
2.0	0.97725	0.97778	0.97831	0.97882	0.97932	0.97982	0.98030	0.98077	0.98124	0.98169
2.1	0.98214	0.98257	0.98300	0.98341	0.98382	0.98422	0.98461	0.98500	0.98537	0.98574
2.2	0.98610	0.98645	0.98679	0.98679	0.98713	0.98745	0.98778	0.98809	0.98840	0.98899
2.3	0.98928	0.98956	0.89883	0.99010	0.99036	0.99061	0.99086	0.99111	0.99134	0.99158
2.4	0.99180	0.99202	0.99224	0.99245	0.99266	0.99286	0.99305	0.99324	0.99343	0.99361
2.5	0.99379	0.99396	0.99413	0.99430	0.99446	0.99461	0.99477	0.99442	0.99506	0.99520
2.6	0.99534	0.99547	0.99560	0.99573	0.99585	0.99598	0.99609	0.99621	0.99632	0.99643
2.7	0.99653	0.99664	0.99674	0.99693	0.99693	0.99702	0.99711	0.99720	0.99728	0.99736
2.8	0.99744	0.99752	0.99760	0.99767	0.99774	0.99781	0.99788	0.99795	0.99801	0.99807
2.9	0.99813	0.99819	0.99825	0.99831	0.99836	0.99841	0.99846	0.99851	0.99856	0.99861
3.0	0.99865	0.99689	0.99874	0.99878	0.99882	0.99886	0.99889	0.99893	0.99896	0.99900
3.1	0.99903	0.99906	0.99910	0.99913	0.99916	0.99918	0.99921	0.99924	0.99926	0.99929
3.2	0.99931	0.99934	0.99936	0.99938	0.99940	0.99942	0.99944	0.99946	0.99948	0.99950
3.3	0.99952	0.99953	0.99955	0.99957	0.99958	0.99960	0.99961	0.99962	0.99964	0.99965
3.4	0.99966	0.99968	0.99969	0.99970	0.99971	0.99972	0.99973	0.99974	0.99975	0.99976
3.5	0.99977	0.99978	0.99978	0.99979	0.99980	0.99981	0.99981	0.99982	0.99983	0.99983
3.6	0.99984	0.99985	0.99985	0.99986	0.99986	0.99987	0.99987	0.99988	0.99988	0.99989
3.7	0.99989	0.99990	0.99990	0.99990	0.99991	0.99991	0.99992	0.99992	0.99992	0.99992
3.8	0.99993	0.99993	0.99993	0.99994	0.99994	0.99994	0.99994	0.99995	0.99995	0.99995
3.9	0.99995	0.99995	0.99996	0.99996	0.99996	0.99996	0.99996	0.99996	0.99997	0.99997

Table 4 Percentage points of the normal distribution

The table gives the values of z satisfying $P(Z \leqslant z) = p$,
where Z is the standardised normal random variable, $N(0, 1)$.

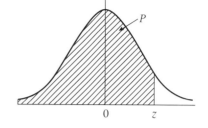

p	0.00	0.01	0.02	0.03	0.04	0.05	0.06	0.07	0.08	0.09
0.50	0.000	0.025	0.050	0.075	0.100	0.126	0.151	0.176	0.202	0.228
0.60	0.253	0.279	0.305	0.332	0.358	0.385	0.412	0.440	0.468	0.496
0.70	0.524	0.553	0.583	0.613	0.643	0.674	0.706	0.739	0.772	0.806
0.80	0.842	0.878	0.915	0.954	0.994	1.036	1.080	1.126	1.175	1.227
0.90	1.282	1.341	1.405	1.476	1.555					

p	0.000	0.001	0.002	0.003	0.004	0.005	0.006	0.007	0.008	0.009
0.95	1.645	1.655	1.665	1.675	1.685	1.695	1.706	1.717	1.728	1.739
0.96	1.751	1.762	1.774	1.787	1.799	1.812	1.825	1.838	1.852	1.866
0.97	1.881	1.896	1.911	1.927	1.943	1.960	1.977	1.995	2.014	2.034
0.98	2.054	2.075	2.097	2.120	2.144	2.170	2.197	2.226	2.257	2.290
0.99	2.326	2.366	2.409	2.457	2.512	2.576	2.652	2.748	2.878	3.090

Table 5 Percentage points of Students *t*-distribution

The table gives the values of *x* satisfying $P(X \leqslant x) = p$,
where *X* is a random variable having the Student's *t*-distribution
with *v*-degrees of freedom.

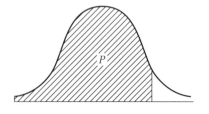

p	0.9	0.95	0.975	0.99	0.995
v					
1	3.078	6.314	12.706	31.821	63.657
2	1.886	2.920	4.303	6.965	9.925
3	1.638	2.353	3.182	4.541	5.841
4	1.533	2.132	2.776	3.747	4.604
5	1.476	2.015	2.571	3.365	4.032
6	1.440	1.943	2.447	3.143	3.707
7	1.415	1.895	2.365	2.998	3.499
8	1.397	1.860	2.306	2.896	3.355
9	1.383	1.833	2.262	2.821	3.250
10	1.372	1.812	2.228	2.764	3.169
11	1.363	1.796	2.201	2.718	3.106
12	1.356	1.782	2.179	2.681	3.055
13	1.350	1.771	2.160	2.650	3.012
14	1.345	1.761	2.145	2.624	2.977
15	1.341	1.753	2.131	2.602	2.947
16	1.337	1.746	2.121	2.583	2.921
17	1.333	1.740	2.110	2.567	2.898
18	1.330	1.734	2.101	2.552	2.878
19	1.328	1.729	2.093	2.539	2.861
20	1.325	1.725	2.086	2.528	2.845
21	1.323	1.721	2.080	2.518	2.831
22	1.321	1.717	2.074	2.508	2.819
23	1.319	1.714	2.069	2.500	2.807
24	1.318	1.711	2.064	2.492	2.797
25	1.316	1.708	2.060	2.485	2.787
26	1.315	1.706	2.056	2.479	2.779
27	1.314	1.703	2.052	2.473	2.771
28	1.313	1.701	2.048	2.467	2.763

p	0.9	0.95	0.975	0.99	0.995
v					
29	1.311	1.699	2.045	2.462	2.756
30	1.310	1.697	2.042	2.457	2.750
31	1.309	1.696	2.040	2.453	2.744
32	1.309	1.694	2.037	2.449	2.738
33	1.308	1.692	2.035	2.445	2.733
34	1.307	1.691	2.032	2.441	2.728
35	1.306	1.690	2.030	2.438	2.724
36	1.306	1.688	2.028	2.434	2.719
37	1.305	1.687	2.026	2.431	2.715
38	1.304	1.686	2.024	2.429	2.712
39	1.304	1.685	2.023	2.426	2.708
40	1.303	1.684	2.021	2.423	2.704
45	1.301	1.679	2.014	2.412	2.690
50	1.299	1.676	2.009	2.403	2.678
55	1.297	1.673	2.004	2.396	2.668
60	1.296	1.671	2.000	2.390	2.660
65	1.295	1.669	1.997	2.385	2.654
70	1.294	1.667	1.994	2.381	2.648
75	1.293	1.665	1.992	2.377	2.643
80	1.292	1.664	1.990	2.374	2.639
85	1.292	1.663	1.998	2.371	2.635
90	1.291	1.662	1.987	2.368	2.632
95	1.291	1.661	1.985	2.366	2.629
100	1.290	1.660	1.984	2.364	2.626
125	1.288	1.657	1.979	2.357	2.616
150	1.287	1.655	1.976	2.351	2.609
200	1.286	1.653	1.972	2.345	2.601
∞	1.282	1.645	1.960	2.326	2.576

Table 7 Percentage points of the *F*-distribution

The tables give the values of *x* satisfying $P(X \leqslant x) = p$,
where *X* is a random variable having the *F*-distribution
with v_1 degrees of freedom in the numerator and
v_2 degrees of freedom in the denominator.

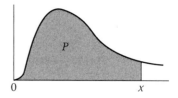

F-Distribution ($p = 0.995$)
Use for one-tail tests at significance level 0.5% or two-tail tests at significance level 1%.

v_1	1	2	3	4	5	6	7	8	9	10	11	12	15	20	25	30	40	50	100	∞	v_1
v_2																					v_2
1	16211	20000	21615	22500	23056	23437	23715	23925	24091	24224	24334	24426	24630	24836	24960	25044	25148	25211	25337	25464	1
2	198.5	199.0	199.2	199.2	199.3	199.3	199.4	199.4	199.4	199.4	199.4	199.4	199.4	199.4	199.5	199.5	199.5	199.5	199.5	199.5	2
3	55.55	49.80	47.47	46.19	45.39	44.84	44.43	44.13	43.88	43.69	43.52	43.39	43.08	42.78	42.59	42.47	42.31	42.21	42.02	41.83	3
4	31.33	26.28	24.26	23.15	22.46	21.97	21.62	21.35	21.14	20.97	20.82	20.70	20.44	20.17	20.00	19.89	19.75	19.67	19.50	19.32	4
5	22.78	18.31	16.53	15.56	14.94	14.51	14.20	13.96	13.77	13.62	13.49	13.38	13.15	12.90	12.76	12.66	12.53	12.45	12.30	12.14	5
6	18.635	14.544	12.917	12.028	11.464	11.073	10.786	10.566	10.391	10.250	10.133	10.034	9.814	9.589	9.451	9.358	9.241	9.170	9.026	8.879	6
7	16.236	12.404	10.882	10.050	9.522	9.155	8.885	8.678	8.514	8.380	8.270	8.176	7.968	7.754	7.623	7.534	7.422	7.354	7.217	7.076	7
8	14.688	11.042	9.596	8.805	8.302	7.952	7.694	7.496	7.339	7.211	7.104	7.015	6.814	6.608	6.482	6.396	6.288	6.222	6.088	5.951	8
9	13.614	10.107	8.717	7.956	7.471	7.134	6.885	6.693	6.541	6.417	6.314	6.227	6.032	5.832	5.708	5.625	5.519	5.454	5.322	5.188	9
10	12.826	9.427	8.081	7.343	6.872	6.545	6.302	6.116	5.968	5.847	5.746	5.661	5.471	5.274	5.153	5.071	4.966	4.902	4.772	4.639	10
11	12.226	8.912	7.600	6.881	6.422	6.102	5.865	5.682	5.537	5.418	5.320	5.236	5.049	4.855	4.736	4.654	4.551	4.488	4.359	4.226	11
12	11.754	8.510	7.226	6.521	6.071	5.757	5.525	5.345	5.202	5.085	4.988	4.906	4.721	4.530	4.412	4.331	4.228	4.165	4.037	3.904	12
13	11.374	8.186	6.926	6.233	5.791	6.482	5.253	5.076	4.935	4.820	4.724	4.643	4.460	4.270	4.153	4.073	3.970	3.908	3.780	3.647	13
14	11.060	7.922	6.680	5.998	5.562	5.257	5.031	4.857	4.717	4.603	4.508	4.428	4.247	4.059	3.942	3.862	3.760	3.697	3.569	3.436	14
15	10.798	7.701	6.476	5.803	5.372	5.071	4.847	4.674	4.536	4.424	4.329	4.250	4.070	3.883	3.766	3.687	3.585	3.523	3.394	3.260	15
20	9.944	6.986	5.818	5.174	4.762	4.472	4.257	4.090	3.956	3.847	3.756	3.678	3.502	3.318	3.203	3.123	3.022	2.959	2.828	2.690	20
25	9.475	6.598	5.462	4.835	4.433	4.150	3.939	3.776	3.645	3.537	3.447	3.370	3.196	3.013	2.898	2.819	2.716	2.652	2.519	2.377	25
30	9.180	6.355	5.239	4.623	4.228	3.949	3.742	3.580	3.450	3.344	3.255	3.179	3.006	2.823	2.708	2.628	2.524	2.459	2.323	2.176	30
40	8.828	6.066	4.976	4.374	3.986	3.713	3.509	3.350	3.222	3.117	3.028	2.953	2.781	2.598	2.482	2.401	2.296	2.230	2.088	1.932	40
50	8.626	5.902	4.826	4.232	3.849	3.579	3.376	3.219	3.092	2.988	2.900	2.825	2.653	2.470	2.353	2.272	2.164	2.097	1.951	1.786	50
100	8.241	5.589	4.542	3.963	3.589	3.325	3.127	2.972	2.847	2.744	2.657	2.583	2.411	2.227	2.108	2.024	1.912	1.840	1.681	1.485	100
∞	7.879	5.298	4.279	3.715	3.350	3.091	2.897	2.744	2.621	2.519	2.432	2.358	2.187	2.000	1.877	1.789	1.669	1.590	1.402	1.001	∞

F-Distribution ($p = 0.99$)
Use for one-tail tests at significance level 1% or two-tail tests at significance level 2%.

v_1	1	2	3	4	5	6	7	8	9	10	11	12	15	20	25	30	40	50	100	∞	v_1
v_2																					v_2
1	4052	5000	5403	5625	5764	5859	5928	5981	6022	6056	6083	6106	6157	6209	6240	6261	6287	6303	6334	6366	1
2	98.50	99.00	99.17	99.25	99.30	99.33	99.36	99.37	99.39	99.40	99.41	99.42	99.43	99.45	99.46	99.47	99.47	99.48	99.49	99.50	2
3	34.12	30.82	29.46	28.71	28.24	27.91	27.67	27.49	27.35	27.23	27.13	27.05	26.87	26.69	26.58	26.50	26.41	26.35	26.24	26.13	3
4	21.20	18.00	16.69	15.98	15.52	15.21	14.98	14.80	14.66	14.55	14.45	14.37	14.20	14.02	13.91	13.84	13.75	13.69	13.58	13.46	4
5	16.26	13.27	12.06	11.39	10.97	10.67	10.46	10.29	10.16	10.05	9.96	9.89	9.72	9.55	9.45	9.38	9.29	9.24	9.13	9.02	5
6	13.745	10.925	9.780	9.148	8.746	8.466	8.260	8.102	7.976	7.874	7.790	7.718	7.559	7.396	7.296	7.229	7.143	7.091	6.987	6.880	6
7	12.246	9.547	8.451	7.847	7.460	7.191	6.993	6.840	6.719	6.620	6.538	6.469	6.314	6.155	6.058	5.992	5.908	5.858	5.755	5.650	7
8	11.259	8.649	7.591	7.006	6.632	6.371	6.178	6.029	5.911	5.814	5.734	5.667	5.515	5.359	5.263	5.198	5.116	5.065	4.963	4.859	8
9	10.561	8.022	6.992	6.422	6.057	5.802	5.613	5.467	5.351	5.257	5.178	5.111	4.962	4.808	4.713	4.649	4.567	4.517	4.415	4.311	9
10	10.044	7.559	6.552	5.994	5.636	5.386	5.200	5.057	4.942	4.849	4.772	4.706	4.558	4.405	4.311	4.247	4.165	4.115	4.014	3.909	10
11	9.646	7.206	6.217	5.668	5.316	5.069	4.886	4.744	4.632	4.539	4.462	4.397	4.251	4.099	4.005	3.941	3.860	3.810	3.708	3.602	11
12	9.330	6.927	5.953	5.412	5.064	4.821	4.640	4.499	4.388	4.296	4.220	4.155	4.010	3.858	3.765	3.701	3.619	3.569	3.467	3.361	12
13	9.074	6.701	5.739	5.2095	4.862	4.620	4.441	4.302	4.191	4.100	4.025	3.960	3.815	3.665	3.571	3.507	3.425	3.375	3.272	3.165	13
14	8.862	6.515	5.564	5.035	4.695	4.456	4.278	4.140	4.030	3.939	3.864	3.800	3.656	3.505	3.412	3.348	3.266	3.215	3.112	3.004	14
15	8.683	6.359	5.417	4.893	4.556	4.318	4.142	4.004	3.895	3.805	3.730	3.668	3.522	3.372	3.278	3.214	3.132	3.081	2.977	2.868	15
20	8.096	5.849	4.938	4.431	4.103	3.871	3.699	3.564	3.457	3.368	3.294	3.231	3.088	2.938	2.843	2.778	2.695	2.643	2.535	2.421	20
25	7.770	5.568	4.675	4.177	3.855	3.627	3.457	3.324	3.217	3.129	3.056	2.993	2.850	2.699	2.604	2.538	2.453	2.400	2.289	2.169	25
30	7.562	5.390	4.510	4.018	3.699	3.473	3.304	3.173	3.067	2.979	2.906	2.843	2.700	2.549	2.453	2.386	2.299	2.245	2.131	2.006	30
40	7.314	5.179	4.313	3.828	3.514	3.291	3.124	2.993	2.888	2.801	2.727	2.665	2.522	2.369	2.271	2.203	2.114	2.058	1.938	1.805	40
50	7.171	5.057	4.199	3.720	3.408	3.186	3.020	2.890	2.785	2.698	2.625	2.562	2.419	2.265	2.167	2.098	2.007	1.949	1.825	1.683	50
100	6.895	4.824	3.984	3.513	3.208	2.988	2.823	2.694	2.590	2.503	2.430	2.368	2.223	2.067	1.965	1.893	1.797	1.735	1.598	1.427	100
∞	6.635	4.605	3.782	3.319	3.017	2.802	2.639	2.511	2.407	2.321	2.248	2.185	2.039	1.878	1.773	1.696	1.592	1.523	1.358	1.000	∞

Table 7 Percentage points of the *F*-distribution (continued)

F-Distribution ($p = 0.975$)
Use for one-tail tests at significance level 2.5% or two-tail tests at significance level 5%.

v_1	1	2	3	4	5	6	7	8	9	10	11	12	15	20	25	30	40	50	100	∞	v_1
v_2																					**v_2**
1	647.8	799.5	864.2	899.6	921.8	937.1	948.2	956.7	963.3	968.6	973.0	976.7	984.9	993.1	998.1	1001.4	1005.6	1008.1	1013.2	1018.3	**1**
2	38.51	39.00	39.17	39.25	39.30	39.33	39.36	39.37	39.39	39.40	39.41	39.41	39.43	39.45	39.46	39.46	39.47	39.48	39.49	39.50	**2**
3	17.44	16.04	15.44	15.10	14.88	14.73	14.62	14.54	14.47	14.42	14.37	14.34	14.25	14.17	14.12	14.08	14.04	14.01	13.96	13.90	**3**
4	12.22	10.65	998	9.60	9.36	9.20	9.07	8.98	8.90	8.84	8.79	8.75	8.66	8.56	8.50	8.46	8.41	8.38	8.32	8.26	**4**
5	10.01	8.43	7.76	7.39	7.15	6.98	6.85	6.76	6.68	6.62	6.57	6.52	6.43	6.33	6.27	6.23	6.18	6.14	6.08	6.02	**5**
6	8.813	7.260	6.599	6.227	5.988	5.820	5.695	5.600	5.523	5.461	5.410	5.366	5.269	5.168	5.107	5.065	5.012	4.980	4.915	4.849	**6**
7	8.073	6.542	5.890	5.523	5.285	5.119	4.995	4.899	4.823	4.761	4.709	4.666	4.568	4.467	4.405	4.362	4.309	4.276	4.210	4.142	**7**
8	7.571	6.059	5.416	5.053	4.817	4.652	4.529	4.433	4.357	4.295	4.243	4.200	4.101	3.999	3.937	3.894	3.840	3.807	3.739	3.670	**8**
9	7.209	5.715	5.078	4.718	4.484	4.320	4.197	4.102	4.026	3.964	3.912	3.868	3.769	3.667	3.604	3.560	3.505	3.472	3.403	3.333	**9**
10	6.937	5.456	4.826	4.468	4.236	4.072	3.950	3.855	3.779	3.717	3.665	3.621	3.522	3.419	3.355	3.311	3.255	3.221	3.152	3.080	**10**
11	6.724	5.256	4.630	4.275	4.044	3.881	3.759	3.664	3.588	3.526	3.474	3.430	3.330	3.226	3.162	3.118	3.061	3.027	2.956	2.883	**11**
12	6.554	5.096	4.474	4.121	3.891	3.728	3.607	3.512	3.436	3.374	3.321	3.277	3.177	3.073	3.008	2.963	2.906	2.871	2.800	2.725	**12**
13	6.414	4.965	4.347	3.996	3.767	3.604	3.483	3.388	3.312	3.250	3.197	3.153	3.053	2.948	2.882	2.837	2.780	2.744	2.671	2.595	**13**
14	6.298	4.857	4.242	3.892	3.663	3.501	3.380	3.285	3.209	3.147	3.095	3/050	2.949	2.844	2.778	2.732	2.674	2.638	2.565	2.487	**14**
15	6.200	4.765	4.153	3.804	3.576	3.415	3.293	3.199	3.123	3.060	3.008	2.963	2.862	2.756	2.689	2.644	2.585	2.549	2.474	2.395	**15**
20	5.871	4.461	3.859	3.515	3.289	3.128	3.007	2.913	2.837	2.774	2.721	2.676	2.573	2.464	2.396	2.349	2.287	2.249	2.170	2.085	**20**
25	5.686	4.291	3.694	3.353	3.129	2.969	2.848	2.753	2.677	2.613	2.560	2.515	2.411	2.300	2.230	2.182	2.118	2.079	1.996	1.906	**25**
30	5.568	4.182	3.589	3.250	3.026	2.867	2.746	2.651	2.575	2.511	2.458	2.412	2.307	2.195	2.124	2.074	2.009	1.969	1.882	1.787	**30**
40	5.424	4.051	3.463	3.126	2.904	2.744	2.624	2.529	2.452	2.388	2.334	2.288	2.182	2.068	1.994	1.943	1.875	1.832	1.741	1.637	**40**
50	5.340	3.975	3.390	3.054	2.833	2.674	2.553	2.458	2.381	2.317	2.263	2.216	2.109	1.993	1.919	1.866	1.796	1.752	1.656	1.545	**50**
100	5.179	3.828	3.250	2.917	2.696	2.537	2.417	2.321	2.244	2.179	2.125	2.077	1.968	1.849	1.770	1.715	1.640	1.592	1.483	1.347	**100**
∞	5.024	3.689	3.116	2.786	2.567	2.408	2.288	2.192	2.114	2.048	1.993	1.945	1.833	1.708	1.626	1.566	1.484	1.428	1.296	1.000	**∞**

F-Distribution ($p = 0.95$)
Use for one-tail tests at significance level 5% or two-tail tests at significance level 10%.

v_1	1	2	3	4	5	6	7	8	9	10	11	12	15	20	25	30	40	50	100	∞	v_1
v_2																					**v_2**
1	161.4	199.5	215.7	224.6	230.2	234.0	236.8	238.9	240.5	241.9	243.0	243.9	245.9	248.0	249.3	250.1	251.1	251.8	253.0	254.3	**1**
2	18.51	19.00	19.16	19.25	19.30	19.33	19.35	19.37	19.38	19.40	19.40	19.41	19.43	19.45	19.46	19.46	19.47	19.48	19.49	19.50	**2**
3	10.13	9.55	9.28	9.12	9.01	8.94	8.89	8.85	8.81	8.79	8.76	8.74	8.70	8.66	8.63	8.62	8.59	8.58	8.55	8.53	**3**
4	7.71	6.94	6.59	6.39	6.26	6.16	6.09	6.04	6.00	5.96	5.94	5.91	5.86	5.80	5.77	5.75	5.72	5.70	5.66	5.63	**4**
5	6.61	5.79	5.41	5.19	5.05	4.95	4.88	4.82	4.77	4.74	4.70	4.68	4.62	4.56	4.52	4.50	4.46	4.44	4.41	4.36	**5**
6	5.987	5.143	4.757	4.534	4.387	4.284	4.207	4.147	4.099	4.060	4.027	4.000	3.938	3.874	3.835	3.808	3.774	3.754	3.712	3.669	**6**
7	5.591	4.737	4.347	4.120	3.972	3.866	3.787	3.726	3.677	3.637	3.603	3.575	3.511	3.445	3.404	3.376	3.340	3.319	3.275	3.230	**7**
8	5.318	4.459	4.066	3.838	3.688	3.581	3.500	3.438	3.388	3.347	3.313	3.284	3.218	3.150	3.108	3.079	3.043	3.020	2.975	2.928	**8**
9	5.117	4.256	3.863	3.633	3.482	3.374	3.293	3.230	3.179	3.137	3.102	3.073	3.006	2.936	2.893	2.864	2.826	2.803	2.756	2.707	**9**
10	4.965	4.103	3.708	3.478	3.326	3.217	3.135	3.072	3.020	2.978	2.943	2.913	2.845	2.774	2.730	2.700	2.661	2.637	2.588	2.538	**10**
11	4.844	3.982	3.587	3.357	3.204	3.095	3.012	2.948	2.896	2.854	2.818	2.788	2.719	2.646	2.601	2.570	2.531	2.507	2.457	2.404	**11**
12	4.747	3.885	3.490	3.259	3.106	2.996	2.913	2.849	2.796	2.753	2.717	2.687	2.617	2.544	2.498	2.466	2.426	2.401	2.350	2.296	**12**
13	4.667	3.806	3.411	3.179	3.025	2.915	2.832	2.767	2.714	2.671	2.635	2.604	2.533	2.459	2.412	2.380	2.339	2.314	2.261	2.206	**13**
14	4.600	3.739	3.344	3.112	2.958	2.848	2.764	2.699	2.646	2.602	2.565	2.534	2.463	2.388	2.341	2.308	2.266	2.241	2.187	2.131	**14**
15	4.543	3.682	3.287	3.056	2.901	2.790	2.707	2.641	2.588	2.544	2.507	2.475	2.403	2.328	2.280	2.247	2.204	2.178	2.123	2.066	**15**
20	4.351	3.493	3.098	2.866	2.711	2.599	2.514	2.447	2.393	2.348	2.310	2.278	2.203	2.124	2.074	2.039	1.994	1.966	1.907	1.843	**20**
25	4.242	3.385	2.991	2.759	2.603	2.490	2.405	2.337	2.282	2.236	2.198	2.165	2.089	2.007	1.955	1.919	1.872	1.842	1.779	1.711	**25**
30	4.171	3.316	2.992	2.690	2.534	2.421	2.334	2.266	2.211	2.165	1.126	2.092	2.015	1.932	1.878	1.841	1.792	1.761	1.695	1.622	**30**
40	4.085	3.232	2.839	2.606	2.449	2.336	2.249	2.180	2.124	2.077	2.038	2.003	1.924	1.839	1.783	1.744	1.693	1.660	1.589	1.509	**40**
50	4.034	3.183	2.790	2.557	2.400	2.286	2.199	2.130	2.073	2.026	1.986	1.952	1.871	1.784	1.727	1.687	1.634	1.599	1.525	1.438	**50**
100	3.936	3.087	2.696	2.463	2.305	2.191	2.103	2.032	1.975	1.927	1.886	1.850	1.768	1.676	1.616	1.573	1.515	1.477	1.392	1.283	**100**
∞	3.841	2.996	2.605	2.372	2.214	2.099	2.010	1.938	1.880	1.831	1.789	1.752	1.666	1.571	1.506	1.459	1.394	1.350	1.243	1.000	**∞**

Table 10 Critical values of the Wilcoxon signed rank statistic

The table gives the lower tail critical values of the statistic T.

The upper tail critical values are given by $\frac{1}{2}n(n+1) - T$.

T is the sum of the ranks of observations with the same sign.
Since T is discrete, exact significance levels cannot usually be obtained.
The critical values tabulated are those with significance levels closest to the stated value.
The critical region includes the tabulated value.

| One-tail | 10% | 5% | 2.5% | 1% | 0.5% |
Two-tail	20%	10%	5%	2%	1%
n					
3	0				
4	1	0			
5	2	1	0		
6	4	2	1	0	
7	6	4	2	0	0
8	8	6	4	2	0
9	11	8	6	3	2
10	14	11	8	5	3
11	18	14	11	7	5
12	22	17	14	10	7
13	26	21	17	13	10
14	31	26	21	16	13
15	37	30	25	20	16
16	42	36	30	24	19
17	49	41	35	28	23
18	55	47	40	33	28
19	62	54	46	38	32
20	70	60	52	43	37

Table 11 Critical values of the Mann–Whitney statistic

The table gives the lower tail critical values of the statistic U.
The upper tail critical values are given by $mn - U$.

$$U = T - \frac{n(n+1)}{2} \text{ where } T \text{ is the sum of the ranks of the sample of size } n.$$

Since U is discrete, exact significance levels cannot usually be obtained.
The critical values tabulated are those with significance levels closest to the stated value.
The critical region includes the tabulated value.

One-tail 5%   Two-tail 10%

n	m	2	3	4	5	6	7	8	9	10	11	12
2			0	0	0	0	1	1	1	2	2	2
3		0	0	1	1	2	3	3	4	5	5	6
4		0	1	2	3	4	5	6	7	8	9	10
5		0	1	3	4	5	7	8	10	11	12	14
6		0	2	4	5	7	9	11	12	14	16	18
7		1	3	5	7	9	11	13	15	18	20	22
8		1	3	6	8	11	13	16	18	21	24	26
9		1	4	7	10	12	15	18	21	24	27	30
10		2	5	8	11	14	18	21	24	28	31	34
11		2	5	9	12	16	20	24	27	31	35	39
12		2	6	10	14	18	22	26	30	34	39	43

One-tail 2.5%   Two-tail 5%

n	m	2	3	4	5	6	7	8	9	10	11	12
2					0	0	0	0	0	1	1	1
3				0	0	1	2	2	3	3	4	4
4			0	1	2	2	3	4	5	6	7	8
5		0	0	2	3	4	5	6	7	9	10	11
6		0	1	2	4	5	7	8	10	12	13	15
7		0	2	3	5	7	9	11	13	15	17	18
8		0	2	4	6	8	11	13	15	18	20	22
9		0	3	5	7	10	13	15	18	21	23	26
10		1	3	6	9	12	15	18	21	24	27	30
11		1	4	7	10	13	17	20	23	27	30	34
12		1	4	8	11	15	18	22	26	30	34	38

Table 12 Control charts for variability

The range charts, multiply σ by the appropriate value of D.
For standard deviation charts, multiply σ by the appropriate value of E.
To obtain an estimate of σ, multiply the mean range by the appropriate value of b.
Normal distribution is assumed.

Sample size	$D_{0.999}$	$D_{0.975}$	$D_{0.025}$	$D_{0.001}$	$E_{0.999}$	$E_{0.975}$	$E_{0.025}$	$E_{0.001}$	b
2			3.170	4.654			2.24	3.29	0.8862
3	0.060	0.303	3.682	5.063	0.03	0.16	1.92	2.63	0.5908
4	0.199	0.595	3.984	5.309	0.09	0.27	1.76	2.33	0.4857
5	0.367	0.850	4.197	5.484	0.15	0.35	1.67	2.15	0.4299
6	0.535	1.066	4.361	5.619	0.20	0.41	1.60	2.03	0.3946
7	0.691	1.251	4.494	5.730	0.25	0.45	1.55	1.93	0.3698
8	0.835	1.410	4.605	5.823	0.29	0.49	1.51	1.86	0.3512
10	1.085	1.674	4.784	5.973	0.36	0.55	1.45	1.76	0.3249
12	1.293	1.884	4.925	6.096	0.41	0.59	1.41	1.69	0.3069

Answers

EXERCISE 1A

1 (a) The group prescribed the new drug;

(b) In blind trials patients do not know whether their treatment contains the drug or not. Hence results are not affected by patients' expectations.

2 Blind trials ensure the patient does not know whether the treatment administered contains the drug or not. Therefore progress is not affected by patients' expectations. In double blind trials, the medical staff dealing with the patients involved in the trial, as well as those patients themselves, do not know whether the treatment contains the drug or not. Therefore the attitude of medical staff to the patient is not influenced by a knowledge of whether that patient is receiving the drug. The effect of the new drug can be more fairly assessed in a double blind trial.

3 (a) Repeated observations under apparently identical conditions. If a trial consists of measuring the distance ridden on a tyre produced by the new process, before sustaining a puncture, replicates would consist of repeating the trial.

(b) Experimental error is the effect of factors other than the production process on the results of the trial, e.g. weight of cyclist, terrain on which bicycle ridden, style of riding, etc.

(c) Experimental error will be reduced by testing tyres produced by new and standard process in same conditions, e.g. use same cyclist, bicycle model, type of journey.

4 A number of factors, in addition to the route, will affect the journey time, e.g. the driver, the road and weather conditions and the load carried. This can be dealt with by replication – that is timing the journey for each route several times so that an estimate of the magnitude of the experimental error can be made.

Alternatively it may be feasible to use paired comparisons where each driver follows each route under, as far as possible, the same conditions and with the same load.

Where a choice has to be made, such as which route should be driven first, this should be made by a random process.

5 (a) Students self-selected whether to study at their own pace or not.

They are not randomly selected and therefore may all be, for example, less able, less well-motivated students. This large factor means that the effect of teaching method cannot be measured fairly.

(b) Students should be randomly assigned to each method.

6 (a) Neither the twins nor the medical staff involved in the trial know whether or not the new treatment or the placebo is involved;

(b) A non-active treatment (containing no drug);

(c) ts $= 1\frac{1}{2}$ $\mathbf{H_0}$: No difference in treatments, $\mathbf{H_1}$: new treatment better
cv $= 6$ $1\frac{1}{2} < 6$, evidence to reject $\mathbf{H_0}$. Suggests new treatment results in higher percentage improvement.

7 (a) ts $= 3.19$ $\qquad$ $\mathbf{H_0}$: $\mu = 190$
cv $= 1.96$ $\quad$ $3.19 > 1.96$ $\quad$ $\mathbf{H_1}$: $\mu \neq 190$
Evidence to reject $\mathbf{H_0}$.
Suggests mean take home pay not £190 (greater);

(b) (i) No effect. Large sample so CLT means $\bar{x}$ normally distributed.

(ii) Conclusion affected – doubt cast. If sample not random, it may include all higher paid workers so cannot be representative of all manual workers.

8 (a) ts $= 4$ $\qquad$ $\mathbf{H_0}$: No difference in takings
cv $= 2$ $\quad$ $4 > 2$ $\quad$ Accept $\mathbf{H_0}$. $\quad$ $\mathbf{H_1}$: Takings increased with new supplier
No evidence to suggest any difference;

(b) No conclusion should be drawn from a single trial as replication, repeated trials, are necessary. Individual trials, takings, will vary due to experimental error – other factors such as day of week, or weather. The statistician has designed a paired trial with each day of each week allocated to New or Old supplier. This will eliminate experimental error due to week/day of week and enable a true comparison of takings.

9 (a) Any difference due to age/strength/fitness of people involved is minimised as the same person is measured after each type of exercise;

(b) Each person is allocated randomly to upper body or leg exercise on day 1 or day 2. Any experimental error due to the effect of doing an exercise first or second should be minimised.

(c) The time on each exercise is limited and consistent.

(d) The paired comparison.

10 (a) (i) Completely randomised design,
(ii) randomised block design.

(b) (i) One-factor analysis of variance,
(ii) two-factor analysis of variance.

(c) (i) In design 3 the same subjects mark each soap powder thus reducing experimental error compared to design 1 where different subjects mark each soap powder,
(ii) In design 2, although each subject marks three soap powders, all soap powders are marked by a different set of subjects and so design 3 is preferred.

2 Analysis of paired comparisons

EXERCISE 2A

1 $t = -1.50$, cv ± 2.228 accept no difference.

2 $t = -3.12$, cv $- 1.812$ conclude sales have increased.

3 $t = 3.28$, cv 1.833 conclude Crackshot more accurate.

4 Assume students can be regarded as a random sample and differences normally distributed.
$t = -1.20$, cv ± 2.201 accept mean difference is five words.

5 $t = -2.54$, cv $- 1.812$ conclude satellite sensors give higher readings.

6 $t = 2.97$, cv ± 2.365 conclude difference (A higher).

7 Assume differences normally distributed.
$t = 0.87$, cv ± 2.365 accept no difference.

8 $t = 2.68$, cv 1.833 conclude time of useful consciousness reduced.

9 $t = 2.38$, cv 1.796 claim substantiated.

10 (a) $t = 1.88$, cv ± 2.365 accept no difference;

(b) Samples not independent.

11 (a) (i) $t = 3.28$, cv ± 2.776 conclude difference (4th round scores lower);

(ii) Assume differences are normally distributed. As the differences must be natural numbers and are small in magnitude the resulting discrete distribution may not approximate well to a normal distribution which is continuous;

(b) 5+ Probability of all signs same if $\mathbf{H_0}$ true is 0.0625. Accept no difference.
No point in carrying out this test as it is impossible to reject the hypothesis even if, as in this case, all signs are the same;

(c) ts 0, cv 0 conclude difference (4th round scores lower); no reason to doubt distribution of differences is symmetrical;

(d) Wilcoxon's signed-rank test seems most appropriate as assumption of symmetrical distribution of differences is plausible and it is possible to accept or reject $\mathbf{H_0}$.

12 (a) 6+ 2− P(6 or more +) = 0.1445 accept no difference;

(b) (i) Much longer than any other,

(ii) Sign test still valid, joint using new process known to have lasted longer;

(iii) No. Cannot rank differences for joint 4;

(c) cv = 1.943 conclude joints using new process last longer;

(d) t-test has more chance of detecting a difference if one exists. In this case it detected a difference and sign test did not, even though there was one less observation for the t-test. (It is possible but unlikely that the t-test has wrongly detected a difference).

13 (a) (i) 5+ P(5+ or 5−) = 0.0625 accept no difference in median clotting times,

(ii) $t = 3.32$ cv ± 3.182 conclude difference (slower after);

(b) (i) sign test valid but pointless as not possible to reject null hypothesis at 5% significance level, even if all five signs the same. The t-test requires differences to be normally distributed. With only four differences there is little evidence either way but the assumption is plausible. Even with only four differences it is possible to establish a significant difference.

(ii) It would not be possible to use Wilcoxon's signed-rank test on all five differences as the rank of the difference for person 4 cannot be determined.

3 Analysis of variance (ANOVA)

EXERCISE 3A

1 $F = 4.48$, cv 3.25 conclude difference between mean healing times.

2 $F = 25.9$, cv 3.885 conclude difference between mean lifetimes.

3 $F = 2.01$, cv 3.885 accept no difference between brands.
Assume normal distribution with common variance of times for each brand. Outlier of 424 for brand C casts doubt on assumption of normal distribution and also suggests variance for C probably larger than for other brands.

4 $F = 2.46$, cv $= 3.885$ accept no difference between mean oven temperatures.
Estimates of μ, α_1, α_2 and α_3 are 485, 6, -2 and -4, respectively. Estimates of ε_{ij} are

3	6	-10	5	-4
6	11	-4	-5	-8
8	2	6	-9	-7

Assumption of normal distribution with common variance appears plausible.

5 $F = 12.8$, cv $= 5.035$ conclude difference between hospitals.

6 $F = 4.01$, cv $= 2.98$ conclude difference between diets.
Was death of pigs related to diets? If so, these diets should be avoided. Could pigs which died be regarded as a random sample? Were they showing unusually high or unusually low weight gains at the time when they died?

EXERCISE 3B

1 $F = 4.18$, cv 5.14 accept no difference between assessors.

2 Assume normal distribution with common variance and no interaction.
$F(\text{copper}) = 178$ $F(\text{temperature}) = 19.1$ cv(both) $= 3.863$ conclude difference due to copper content and due to temperatures.

3 Blocking factor is Sites. Useful because it substantially reduces SS_E ($F = 11.0$) and thus makes it easier to establish a difference between genotypes if such a difference exists. $F = 83.3$, cv $= 8.649$ conclude difference between genotypes.

4 Assume normal distribution with common variance and no interaction. $F = 35.2$, cv $= 3.49$ conclude difference between solutions. Using Days as a blocking factor makes a very large reduction in SS_E ($F = 122$) and thus makes it easier to establish a difference between solutions if such a difference exists.

5 F(occupation) = 6.34, cv = 5.143 conclude difference between occupations.

F(training) = 1.21, cv = 4.757 accept no difference between training methods.

Age and gender will have contributed to the experimental error and hence to SS_E. However as they have not been included in the experimental design it would be difficult to take account of them in the analysis, particularly given the small amount of data.

6 F(arrangement) = 10.1, cv = 4.459 conclude difference between arrangements.

F(technician) = 2.08, cv = 3.838 accept no difference between technicians.

C has the highest mean time and A the lowest, hence there is evidence that reaction times would be reduced if C was replaced by A.

It would be useful to know whether the likely saving of just over a second on average is of importance in dealing with the emergency. Are there any other features of the designs – clarity in non-emergency situations, cost, comfort of operator, etc. which might suggest B or C should be used despite A giving the quickest reaction to an emergency.

EXERCISE 3C

1 (a) e.g.

A	C	B	D	F	E
B	D	C	E	A	F
C	E	D	F	B	A
D	F	E	A	C	B
E	A	F	B	D	C
F	B	A	C	E	D

(b) (i) 12, **(ii)** 20, **(iii)** 30.

2 F(rows) = 6, F(columns) = 10.5, F(letters) = 2.5, cv = 9.780 accept no difference between rows or between letters, conclude difference between columns.

3 (a) F(paint) = 19.0, F(drying) = 7.00, F(quality) = 4.00, cv = 19.00 conclude difference between paints (although could be affected by rounding error in critical value), accept no difference between drying times or between qualities;

(b) Assumes normal distribution with common variance and no interactions (the latter is given in (**a**)).

4 (a) F(nozzle) = 7.05, cv = 9.780 accept no difference between nozzles (although there would be at 5%);

(b) Temperature effective as blocking factor ($F = 33.85$). Operator reasonably effective but less so than Temperature ($F = 5.05$).

5 (a) $F = 2.90$, cv = 3.259 accept no difference between agents;

(b) Rubber effective ($F = 11.7$), machines reduces SS_E but not by a significant amount ($F = 2.49$).

MIXED EXERCISE

1 F(people) = 9.39, cv = 3.490 conclude difference between people

F(work) = 6.90, cv = 3.259 conclude difference between kinds of work A and C had more words per minute, on average, than B or D, thus difference between people may have been due to them using different types of typewriter.

2 $F = 5.24$, cv $= 3.982$ conclude difference between methods of storage. Method 3: 4.90–6.50.

3 F(cloth) $= 0.44$ accept no difference between cloths
F(strength) $= 9.01$, cv $= 3.838$ conclude difference between strengths
Maximum index appears to be in region of 15% strength. Might conduct further trials with strengths around 15%. Say 13%, 14%, 15%, 16%, 17% to obtain a more precise estimate of strength to give maximum index.

4 (a) $F = 0.64$, cv $= 4.256$ accept no difference between tenderisers;

(b) F(tenderiser) $= 7.55$, cv $= 6.94$ conclude difference between tenderisers
F(time) $= 16.4$, cv $= 6.94$ conclude difference between times;

(c) In **(b)**, the experimental error had been reduced by cooking at the same temperature and by including times as a blocking factor. This gave more chance than in **(a)** of detecting a difference between tenderisers if such a difference exists.

5 (b) F(rows) $= 2.75$, F(columns) $= 3.925$, F(letters) $= 4.825$, cv $= 2.711$ conclude differences between rows, between columns and between letters.

6 (a) $F = 68.2$, cv $= 4.431$ conclude difference between paints;

(b) Arrange paints in order of mean drying times to provide information on which paints dry quickest. Possibly, further analysis could be undertaken to investigate whether the differences between particular paints are significant.

7 (a) $F = 0.55$, cv $= 4.256$ accept no difference between methods of transport;

(b) By including time of day as a blocking factor and carrying out a two-way analysis of variance, the experimental error could be reduced thus giving more chance of detecting a difference if one exists;

(c) e.g. weather, comfort, convenience.

8 (a) $F = 4.51$, cv $= 3.57$ conclude difference between springs;

(b) F(speed) $= 69.1$, cv $= 18.51$ conclude difference between speeds;
F(spring) $= 3.86$, cv $= 19.00$ accept no difference between springs;

(c) Experiment in **(b)** has reduced experimental error by using the same truck and using speed as a blocking factor. This will give more chance of detecting a difference if one exists. However, this is counterbalanced by the fact that there is much less data in **(b)** and so a much higher F-ratio is required to establish significance. A further improvement would be to use the same driver and surface conditions for all trials.

9 (a) Assume normal distribution with common variance
$F = 9.81$, cv $= 3.885$ conclude difference between journey times;

(b) Mon 31, Wed / Fri 25;

(c) $t = 4.40$, cv $= 1.782$ conclude journey time longer on Mondays.

10 (b) F(driver) $= 12.9$, cv $= 4.757$ conclude difference between drivers;

(c) a: -0.100, b: 0.475, c: -0.400, d: 0.025;

(d) Journey ($F = 1.92$) and bus ($F = 0.53$) contribute little to the experimental error.

11 Randomised block; $F = 5.76$, cv $= 5.143$ conclude difference between salts; Assumed no interaction.

12 **(a)** $F(\text{design}) = 8.89$, cv $= 5.143$ conclude difference between designs
$F(\text{employee}) = 50.3$, cv $= 4.757$ conclude difference between employees;

(b) Effect of design and order confounded, i.e., if employees improved with practice this would be confused with the effect of designs. Would be better for the order to be chosen at random or as far as possible balanced (not possible to achieve perfect balance as there are six possible orders and only three designs).

(c) A multiplicative model may be more realistic as a fast worker is more likely to take, say, 20% less than average time rather than, say, 20 minutes less than average time. The lengthier the task the more time a fast worker is likely to save.

13 **(a)** $F = 15.2$, cv $= 3.885$ conclude difference between methods of transport;

(b) O: 16.0, C: 27.6, R: 28.6. It appears that open wagons give poor keeping qualities but there is little to choose between covered and refrigerated lorries. In view of the cost of refrigerated lorries, covered lorries are likely to be the best option.

(c) Could have collected data from farms with the same breed of cattle and used distance as a blocking factor, thus reducing experimental error. (Other answers are possible.)

14 **(a)** $F(\text{depth}) = 18.5$, cv $= 8.649$ conclude difference between depths;

(b) Yes $(F = 45.4)$.

15 **(a)** $F = 4.56$, cv $= 3.25$ conclude difference between teaching techniques;

(b) $t = 3.45$, cv $= \pm 2.121$ conclude difference between techniques (higher scores using A).

16 **(a)** $F = 6.99$, cv $= 5.412$ conclude difference between formulations;

(b) *Nuisance factors* of little importance, $F(\text{batch}) = 0.47$, $F(\text{operator}) = 0.75$.

4 Statistical process control

Note that because the limits are usually close together it is often important to give more than 3 s.f. In some cases where the lower limits are very small it is appropriate to give less than 3 s.f.

EXERCISE 4A

1 **(a)** warning limits   4.971 and 5.029
action limits   4.954 and 5.046;

(b) **(i)** $\bar{x} = 4.99$ no action,
(ii) $\bar{x} = 4.935$ action,
(iii) $\bar{x} = 5.04$ take another sample immediately,
(iv) $\bar{x} = 4.9775$ no action,
(v) $\bar{x} = 4.965$ take another sample immediately.

2 **(a)** warning limits   698.25 and 701.75
action limits   697.24 and 702.76;

(b) **(i)** $\bar{x} = 699.74$ no action,
(ii) $\bar{x} = 697.54$ take another sample immediately,
(iii) $\bar{x} = 704.36$ action.

3 (a) warning   14.372 and 14.628
action   14.298 and 14.702;

(b) (i) $\bar{x} = 14.61$ take another sample immediately,
(ii) $\bar{x} = 14.557$ take another sample immediately,
(iii) $\bar{x} = 14.255$ take action.

EXERCISE 4B

1 (a) warning limits   698.25 and 701.75
action limits   697.24 and 702.76;

(b) warning limits   0.70 and 3.34
action limits   0.30 and 4.30;

(c) (i) $\bar{x} = 699.74$ $s = 3.33$ no action (just),
(ii) $\bar{x} = 697.54$ $s = 2.08$ take another sample immediately,
(iii) $\bar{x} = 704.36$ $s = 2.99$ take action (mean).

2 (a) means   warning limits   12.85 and 20.55
action limits   10.63 and 22.77
s.d.   warning limits   0.544 and 6.528
action limits   0.102 and 8.942;

(b) (i) $\bar{x} = 18.8$ $s = 1.706$ no action,
(ii) $\bar{x} = 23.9$ $s = 1.815$ take action (mean),
(iii) $\bar{x} = 12.83$ $s = 7.050$ take another sample immediately,
(iv) $\bar{x} = 21.7$ $s = 2.088$ take another sample immediately,
(v) $\bar{x} = 9.87$ $s = 2.108$ take action (mean).

3 (a) (i) warning limits   14.372 and 14.628
action limits   14.298 and 14.702,
(ii) warning limits   0.0656 and 0.256
action limits   0.0320 and 0.325;

(b) (i) $\bar{x} = 14.615$ $s = 0.160$ no action,
(ii) $\bar{x} = 14.528$ $s = 0.317$ take another sample immediately,
(iii) $\bar{x} = 14.207$ $s = 0.182$ take action (mean),
(iv) $\bar{x} = 14.447$ $s = 0.390$ take action (variability),
(v) $\bar{x} = 14.560$ $s = 0.058$ take another sample to check for
improvement,
(vi) $\bar{x} = 14.255$ $s = 0.123$ take action (mean).

4 (a) (i) warning   118.69 and 121.32
action   117.93 and 122.07,
(ii) warning   1.275 and 6.295
action   0.550 and 8.226;

(b) $\bar{x} = 122.0$ range $= 9$ take action (variability and possible mean)
$\bar{x} = 122.8$ range $= 7$ take action (mean and possible variability).

EXERCISE 4C

1 2.456, 1.06.

2 3.62.

3 (a) (i) 2.31,
(ii) 2.26 both estimates similar;

(b) means warning   73.85 and 77.80
action   72.70 and 78.95
ranges warning   1.92 and 9.47
action   0.83 and 12.39;

(c) $\bar{x} = 77.2$ range $= 6$ no action.

4 (a) 16.98;

(b) warning   735.1 and 764.9;

action   726.5 and 773.5;

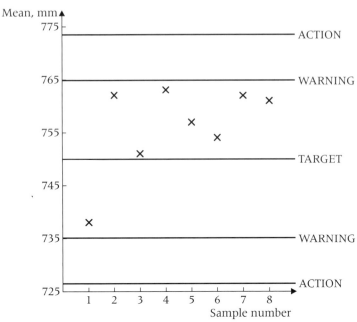

(c) 71.3, 93.1;

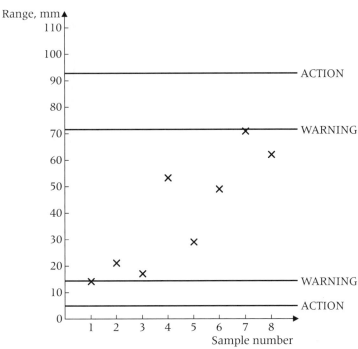

(d) Although all points are within the warning limits seven consecutive means are above target. There also seems to be a steady increase in variability. Even though the individual points do not indicate action, the overall pattern suggests that action may be advisable.

5 (a) (i) 0.0112,

(ii) 0.01075, both estimates similar;

(b) warning   4.989 and 5.011
action   4.983 and 5.016
all points within warning limits;

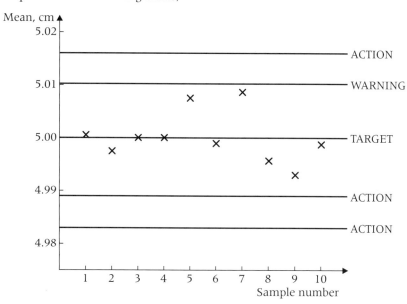

(c) warning   0.0029 and 0.0189
action   0.0010 and 0.0250
all points within warning limits, process under control.

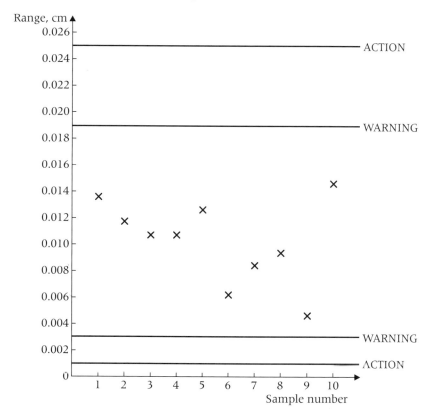

EXERCISE 4D

1 (a) Cannot consistently meet tolerances;

(b) Can just meet tolerances if mean exactly on target;

(c) Can meet tolerances comfortably.

2 (a) s.d. 17.6 (19.1 if estimated from mean range. If this is used control chart limits will be a little different)

means   warning   32.75 and 67.25

action   22.81 and 77.19

s.d.   warning   4.75 and 30.98

action   1.58 and 41.01;

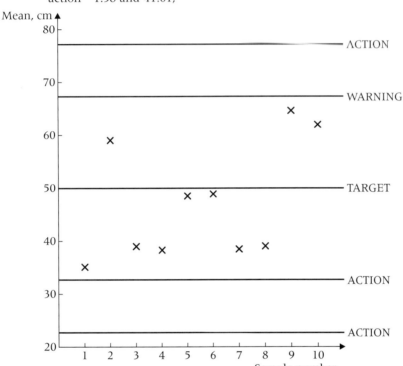

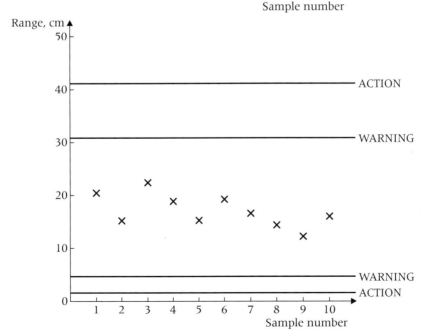

(b) (i) $\bar{x} = 59.0$ $s = 9.87$ no action,
     (ii) $\bar{x} = 52.0$ $s = 37.39$ take another sample immediately,
     (iii) $\bar{x} = 95.5$ $s = 9.33$ take action;

(c) Can meet tolerances;

(d) (i) 0.9065,
     (ii) 0.903. ★ 0.993

> If sd $= 19.1$ is used, the answers to **(b)** and **(c)** are unaffected, but **(d)** will be a little different.

3 (a) 4.924; (5.16 if estimated from mean range. If this value is used, the limits and C_p will be slightly different.)

   (b) (i) warning 205.68 and 214.32; action 203.20 and 216.80,
      (ii) warning 1.723 and 8.223; action 0.739 and 10.587;

   (c) Variability under control but one point on means chart outside action limits so action needed on means;

   (d) (i) $\bar{x} = 196.4$ $s = 4.84$ take action (means),
      (ii) $\bar{x} = 208.5$ $s = 3.91$ no action,
      (iii) $\bar{x} = 208.8$ $s = 12.15$ action (variability),
      (iv) $\bar{x} = 209.8$ $s = 3.174$ no action;

   (e) $C_p = 0.677 < 1$ specification cannot be consistently met.

4 (a) 2.268
     warning 98.01 and 101.99
     action 96.87 and 103.13;

   (b) warning 0.794 and 3.787
     action 0.340 and 4.876,
     Variability okay, all but one mean above target – action probably required on means even though no point outside warning limits;

   (c) $\bar{x} = 100.44$ $s = 2.144$ no action;

   (d) limits cannot be met consistently.

5 (a) 15.1;

   (b) 0.35;

   (c) warning 14.69 and 15.31
     action 14.52 and 15.48;

   (d) warning 0.1225 and 0.5845
     action 0.0525 and 0.7525;

   (e) Process under control;

   (f) 17.0, far too many unsatisfactory – would improve if mean reduced.

6 Can meet tolerances provided mean close to target.

EXERCISE 4E

1 warning 0.187 and 0.445
  action 0.113 and 0.520.

2 (a) warning 0.077 and 0.243
    action 0.029 and 0.291;

   (b) (i) 0.36 take action,
     (ii) 0.20 no action,
     (iii) 0.27 take another sample immediately,
     (iv) 0.04 take another sample to check for improvement.

3(a) warning 0.074 and 0.263
    action 0.019 and 0.318;

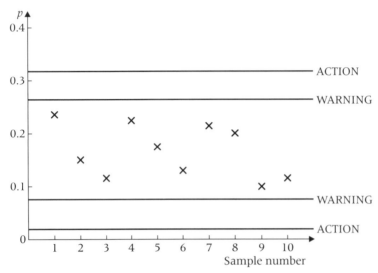

(b) (i) 0.30 take another sample immediately,
(ii) 0.40 take action,
(iii) 0.017 below lower action limit, check for mistakes – try to maintain improvement;

(c) Only one chart needed, easier to classify – break/doesn't break – than to measure breaking strain – larger samples needed.

4 (a) 65, 0.15;

(b) warning 0.063 and 0.237
action 0.013 and 0.287;

(c) Sample 6 between warning and action limits. As there are 12 samples and there is no sign of an upward trend one point outside warning limits is not a cause for concern. Production appears to be satisfactory.

5 (a) 0.164
warning 0.083 and 0.245
action 0.036 and 0.292;

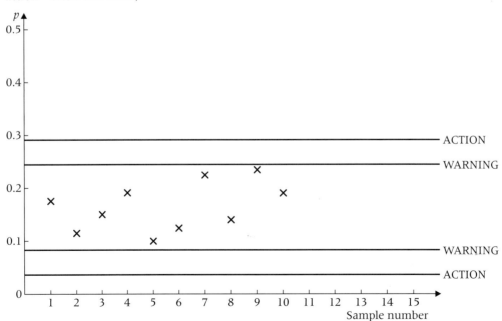

(b) (i) 0.275 take another sample,
(ii) 0.225 no action,
(iii) 0.3375 take action,
(iv) 0.025 below lower action limit, check for mistakes/try to maintain improvement;

(c) 0.69.

5 Acceptance sampling

EXERCISE 5A

1

p	0.02	0.04	0.06	0.08	0.10	0.20
P(Acc)	0.9114	0.7358	0.5527	0.3947	0.2712	0.0274

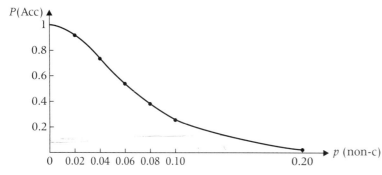

2

p	0.01	0.02	0.04	0.08	0.10	0.20	0.30
P(Acc)	0.9980	0.9929	0.9561	0.7879	0.6769	0.2061	0.0355

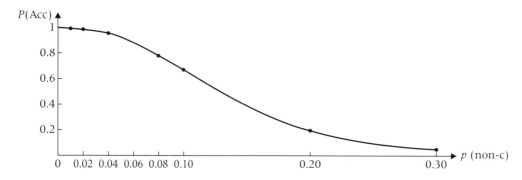

3 (a)

p	0.01	0.02	0.03	0.04	0.05	0.06	0.07	0.08	0.09	0.10	0.15	0.20
P(A)	0.99	0.92	0.81	0.68	0.54	0.42	0.31	0.23	0.16	0.11	0.01	0.00

(b)

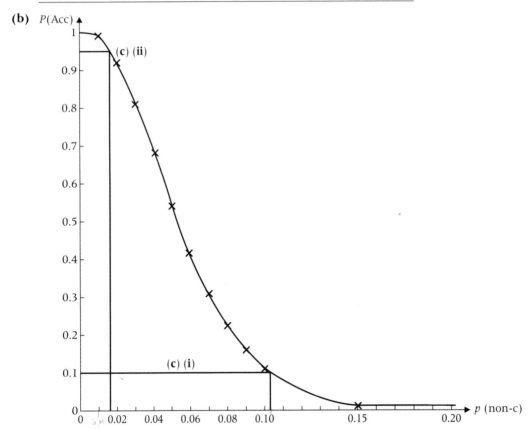

(c) (i) $p = 0.103$,   **(ii)** $p = 0.018$.

4 (a) (i)

(p)	0.01	0.02	0.04	0.07	0.10	0.15	0.20
P(Acc)	0.9980	0.9868	0.9235	0.7466	0.5371	0.2537	0.0982

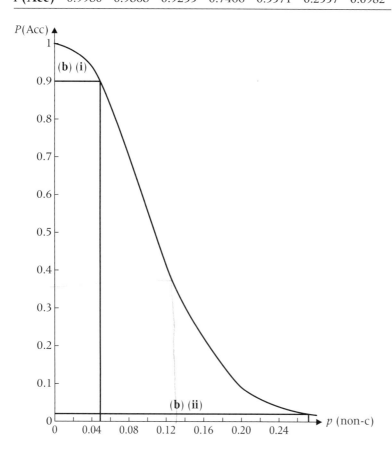

(ii)

p	0.01	0.02	0.04	0.07	0.10	0.15	0.20
P(Acc)	0.9993	0.9918	0.9252	0.6937	0.4231	0.1302	0.0285

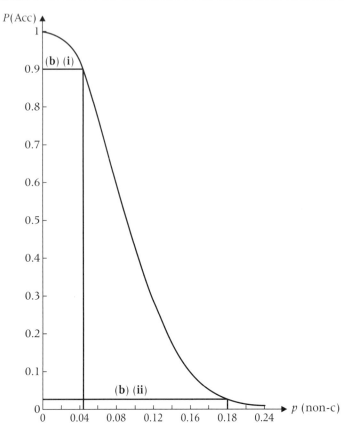

(b) (i) $n = 25$, $r = 2$, $p = 0.045$; $n = 40$, $r = 3$, $p = 0.044$;
(ii) $n = 25$, $r = 2$, $p = 0.270$; $n = 40$, $r = 3$, $p = 0.210$.

5 (a) n is fixed at 20 or 40, the probability that a bowl is defective should be constant for large production – defective bowls should occur independently;

(b)

p	0.00	0.01	0.02	0.03	0.04	0.05	0.06	0.07	0.08	0.09	0.10	0.15	0.20
Plan A	1.0	0.98	0.94	0.88	0.81	0.74	0.66	0.59	0.52	0.45	0.39	0.18	0.07
Plan B	1.0	1.0	0.99	0.97	0.93	0.86	0.78	0.69	0.60	0.51	0.42	0.13	0.03

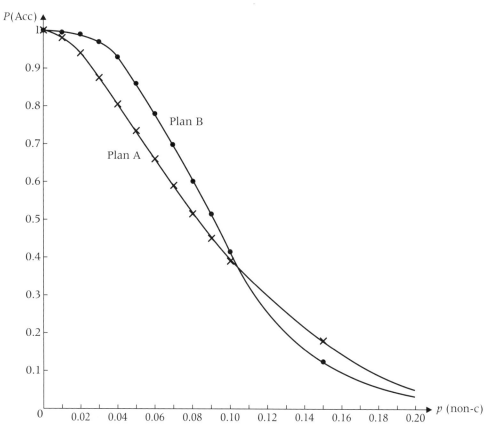

(d) Plan B – negligible extra cost of sampling 40 rather than 20
   – higher probability of accepting 'good' (very low p values) batches
   – probability of acceptance at 10% very close for both plans
   – lower probability of accepting 'bad' ($p > 0.10$) batches.

6 (a)

p	0.01	0.03	0.05	0.10	0.15	0.20
P(accept)	0.99	0.81	0.54	0.11	0.014	0.001

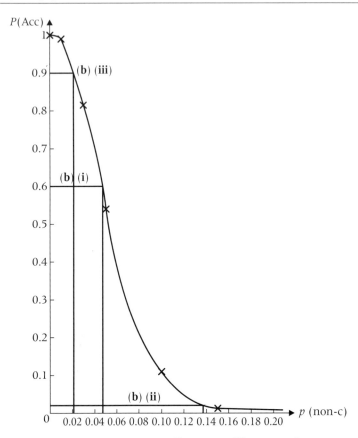

(b) **(i)** 0.0455, $P(\text{accept}) = 0.600$, **(ii)** 0.025, **(iii)** 0.022, **(iv)** 115.

7 (a)

p	0.02	0.05	0.10	0.15
P(accept)	0.92	0.54	0.11	0.014

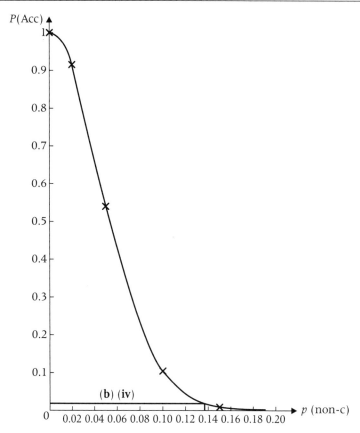

(b) (i) 0.0001,
   (ii) 13,
   (iii) proportion defective 0.0015
       proportion non-conforming 0.138,
   (iv) 0.025.
(c) There is a very small probability of accepting this batch which
   has a proportion defective only a little higher than 1 in 1000 –
   customer probably satisfied.

EXERCISE 5B

1 $r = 2$ Accept if fewer than two non-conforming. $P(0, 1) = 0.0338$.

2 (a) $r = 2$ Accept if fewer than two non-conforming.
   $P(0, 1) = 0.9393 > 0.9$;

   (b) $r = 4$ Accept if fewer than four non-conforming.
   $P(0, 1, 2, 3) = 0.9918 > 0.99$;

   (c) $r = 3$ Accept if fewer than three non-conforming.
   $P(0, 1, 2) = 0.0485 < 0.05$;

   (d) $r = 2$ Accept if fewer than two non-conforming.
   $P(0, 1) = 0.0805 < 0.10$.

3 (a) $r = 3$ Accept if fewer than three non-conforming.
   $P(0, 1, 2) = 0.9216 > 0.90$;

(b)

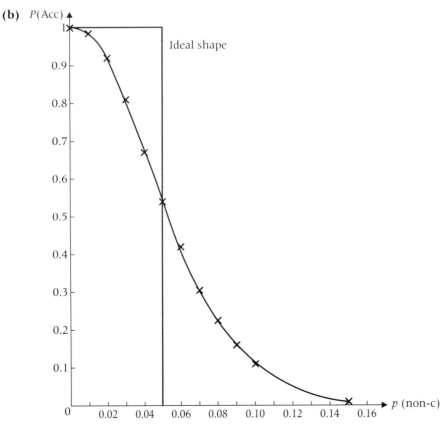

(c) No, $P(\text{Acc})$ for $p = 0.11 > 0.05$.

4 (a) $r = 3$ Accept if fewer than three non-conforming.
$P(0, 1, 2) = 0.0982 < 0.10$;

(b) $P(\text{reject}) = 1 - 0.998 = 0.002$;

(c) $r = 2$ Accept if fewer than two non-conforming.
$P(0, 1) = 0.9742 \approx 0.97$;

(d) $P(\text{Accept}) = 0.0274$.

5 (a) $r = 2$ Accept if fewer than two non-conforming.
$P(0, 1) = 0.9831 > 0.98$.

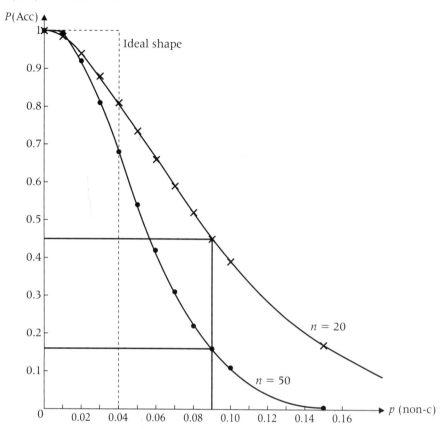

(b) $r = 3$ this time;

(c) $p = 0.09$ for $n = 20$ $P(\text{Acc}) = 0.4516$ much larger for **(a)**
for $n = 50$ $P(\text{Acc}) = 0.1605$;

(d) dashed line on graph.

6 (a)

p	0.01	0.02	0.04	0.07	0.10	0.15	0.20
P(Acc)	0.96	0.88	0.66	0.37	0.18	0.05	0.01

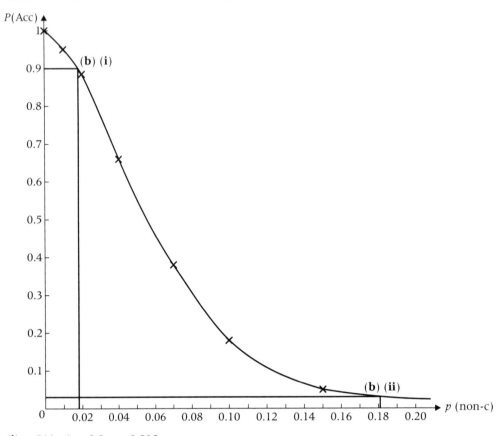

(b) (i) $P(\text{Acc}) = 0.9\ p = 0.018$
(ii) $P(\text{Acc}) = 0.02\ p = 0.18$

(c) (i) $r = 3$,
(ii) $r = 1$,
(iii) the smallest value which satisfies **(i)** is too large to satisfy **(ii)**.

(d) $r = 3$ satisfies both.

EXERCISE 5C

1 (a) 0.740;
  (b) 0.764;
  (c) 0.633.

2 (a)

p	0.01	0.05	0.10	0.15	0.20	0.50
P(Acc)	1.00	0.99	0.895	0.68	0.425	0.002

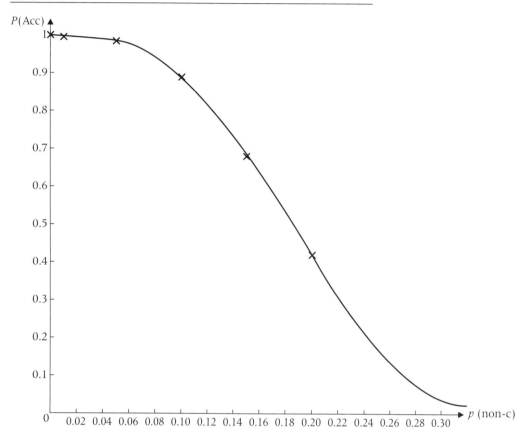

  (b) $P(0, 1, 2, 3) = 0.9926$ $n = 20$
      plan in (a) $P(\text{Acc}) = 0.9964$ similar;

  (c) Advantage – double means less items sampled on average
      Disadvantage – double is more complex to operate.

3 (a) Reject if two or more faulty $r = 2$;

  (b) (i) 0.227,
      (ii) 25.4.

4 (a) Plan 1: probability $= 0.7604$
      Plan 2: probability $= 0.7636$;

(b) (i)

p	0	0.02	0.05	0.10	0.15
P(Acc)	1	0.98	0.76	0.28	0.06

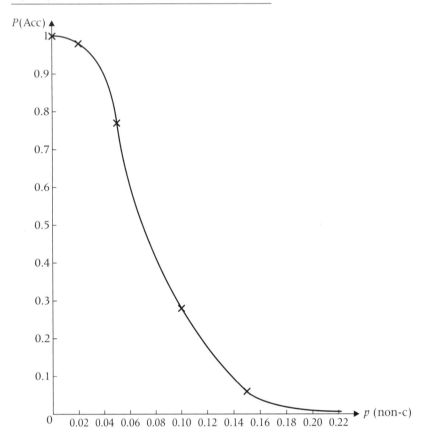

(ii)

p	0	0.02	0.05	0.10	0.15
Exp no	30	33.0	37.8	36.8	33.1

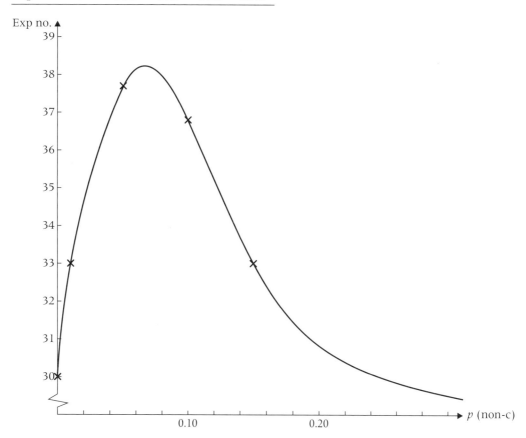

(c) Cost of inspecting (fewer inspected on average in Plan 2)
Difficulty of implementing Plan 2
Customer/manufacturer requirements.

5 (a) $p = 0.1$ $\lambda = 8$ $P(\leqslant 3) = 0.042 \leqslant 0.05$ satisfied
$p = 0.01$ $\lambda = 0.8$ $P(\leqslant 3) = 0.991 \geqslant 0.98$ satisfied;

(b) $p = 0.1$ $P(\leqslant 3) = 0.037 \leqslant 0.05$ satisfied
$p = 0.01$ $P(\leqslant 3) = 0.987 \geqslant 0.98$ satisfied;

(c) single scheme costs £60
double scheme expected to cost £66.65.

6 (a)

p	0.01	0.02	0.03	0.05	0.07	0.10	0.15
P(Acc)	0.96	0.88	0.77	0.55	0.37	0.18	0.05

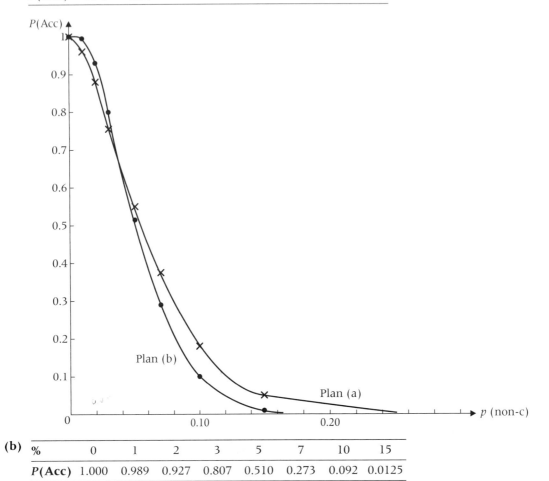

(b)

%	0	1	2	3	5	7	10	15
P(Acc)	1.000	0.989	0.927	0.807	0.510	0.273	0.092	0.0125

(c) (i) 4%, **(ii) (A)** 13%, **(B)** 9.5%;

(d) The plan in **(a)** has a lower chance of accepting a 'good' batch (low p) and a higher chance of accepting a 'bad' patch (higher p). The plan in **(b)** is better able to discriminate good/poor batches but may be more complicated/costly.

EXERCISE 5D

1

μ	910	908	906	904	902	900	898	896	894	892	890
P(Acc)	0.98	0.95	0.89	0.79	0.66	0.50	0.34	0.21	0.11	0.05	0.02

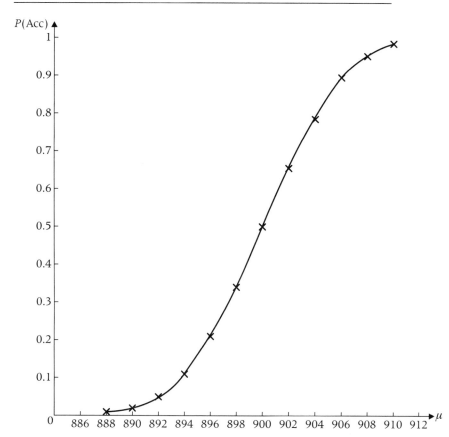

2

μ	44.5	44	43.5	43	42.5	42	41.5	41	40.5	40	39.5
P(Acc)	0.01	0.03	0.08	0.17	0.32	0.50	0.68	0.83	0.92	0.97	0.99

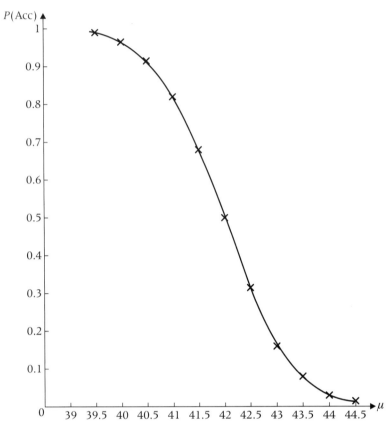

3 (a) 0.240;

(b) $1 - 0.943 = 0.057$;

(c) $0.903 > 0.9$, yes;

(d) 203;

(e) 208.5;

(f) 11;

(g) 4.

4 (a)

μ	29	30	31	32	33	33.5	34	35	36	37	38
P(Acc)	0.95	0.91	0.83	0.71	0.57	0.5	0.43	0.29	0.17	0.09	0.05

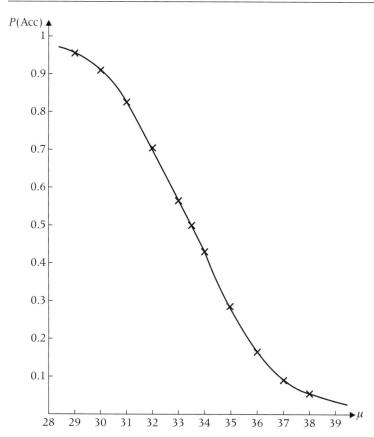

(b) $\mu = 30$ $P(\text{Acc}) = 0.91$ $P(\text{Rej}) = 0.09 > 0.05$ not met

$\mu = 35$ $P(\text{Acc}) = 0.29 > 0.10$ not met;

(c) $n = 47$;

(d) $n = 23$

customer $P(\text{Acc}) = 0.094 < 0.10$ met.

5 (a)

μ	24.2	24.4	24.6	24.8	25	25.2	25.4
P(Acc)	0.008	0.055	0.212	0.500	0.788	0.945	0.992

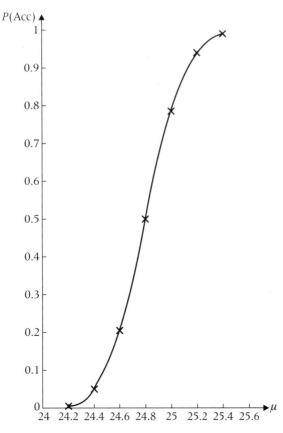

(b) $n = 25$
$k = 24.84$;

(c) Quicker, easier to judge by attributes – conforming/non-conforming.
Information gained from using exact measurements is more useful.
Depends on the nature of items involved and demands of customer/manufacturer.

6 (a)

μ	992	994	996	998	1000	1002	1004	1006	1008
P(Acc)	0.02	0.06	0.15	0.30	0.5	0.70	0.85	0.94	0.98

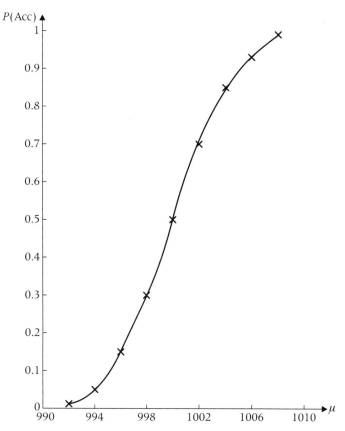

(b) $\mu = 995$ $P(\text{Acc}) = 0.09 > 0.05$ **not** satisfied
$\mu = 1003$ $P(\text{Acc}) = 0.78$ $P(\text{Rej}) = 0.22 > 0.02$ **not** satisfied;

(c) $n = 31$
$k = 998.55$ (Accept if $\bar{x} \leqslant k$).

7 (a) $n = 9$
$k = 1002.14$ (Accept if $\bar{x} \geqslant k$);

(b)

μ	998	999	1000	1001	1002	1003	1004	1005	1006
P(Acc)	0.01	0.03	0.10	0.25	0.47	0.70	0.87	0.96	0.99

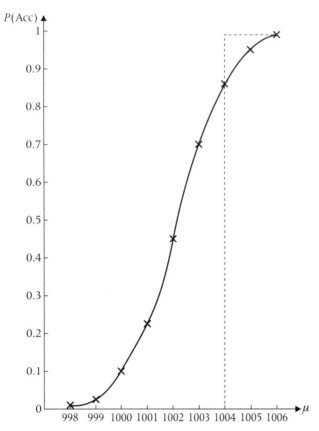

(c) **(i)** $P(\text{Acc}) = 0.87$ $P(\text{Rej}) = 0.13$;
(ii) see graph in **(b)**.

Exam style practice paper

1 (a) **(i)** Completely randomised design,
(ii) Randomised block design;

(b) By using the same subjects to taste all three recipes the experimental error is reduced.

2 (a) $t = 0.772$, cv 1.895 no significant evidence to show claim has not been met;

(b) Identical test except that the difference for G would have been 21 instead of −21.

3 (a) Reject the batch if 3 or more non-conforming items found in the sample of 50;

(b) 0.811, 0.541, 0.112, 0.014;

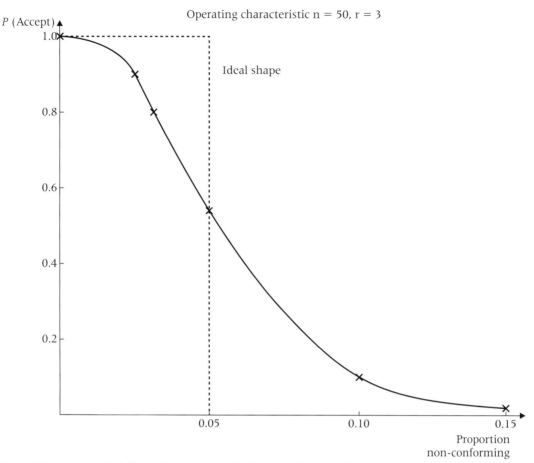

Operating characteristic n = 50, r = 3

Ideal shape

P (Accept)

Proportion non-conforming

(c) From the graph probability of accepting a batch containing 11% non-conforming is about 8%. It is clearly more than 5% and so would not satisfy the customer.

4 (a) warning limits   0.074 and 0.263
action limits   0.019 and 0.318;

(b) 0.100, 0.117, 0.100, 0.150, 0.167, 0.150, 0.217, 0.200, 0.233, 0.250
All points lie within warning limits but there is a definite upward trend. This casts some doubt on the suitability of the data for setting up control charts;

(c) (i) 0.300, between warning and action limits – take another sample immediately, if new sample outside warning limits take action,

(ii) 0.417, above upper action limit – take action to reduce proportion non-conforming,

(iii) 0.017, below lower action limit – no action, investigate and try to maintain improvement;

(d) Advantages – only one chart needed; easier to classify as conforming/non-conforming than to take a measurement. Disadvantage – larger sample needed for equivalent control.

5 (a)

Source	DF	SS	MS	F
Method	2	412.7	206.3	22.9
Time	2	98.7	49.3	5.5
Day	2	116.7	58.3	6.5
Error	2	18.0	9.0	
Total	8	646.0		

cv $F_{[2,2]} = 19.0$

Conclude difference between method of transport but no significant evidence of differences between time of leaving or day of the week;

(b)

	Car	Bicycle	Bus
Mean time	35.0	29.3	45.7

Analysis of variance showed a significant difference between method of transport so bicycle clearly faster than bus. It also appears to be faster than car but this difference (and the difference between car and bus) may not be significant.

(c) Assumes, for example, that if, apart from experimental error, bicycle is quickest when leaving at 8.00 a.m. on Wednesday, it will also be quickest (and by the same amount) when leaving at any of the times on any of the days;

(d) Day of week accounted for nearly 20% of total sum of squares. It has substantially reduced Error sum of squares, making it easier to detect differences between methods if they exist.

Index